*The Organized
Labor Movement
in Puerto Rico*

The Organized Labor Movement in Puerto Rico

Miles Galvin

Rutherford • Madison • Teaneck
Fairleigh Dickinson University Press

London: Associated University Presses

©1979 by Associated University Presses, Inc.

Associated University Presses, Inc.
Cranbury, New Jersey 08512

Associated University Presses
Magdalen House
136-148 Tooley Street
London SE1 2TT, England

Library of Congress Cataloging in Publication Data

Galvin, Miles E.
    The organized labor movement in Puerto Rico.

    Bibliography: p.
    Includes index.
    1. Trade-unions—Puerto Rico—History.   I. Title.
HD6592.G34   331.88'097295   77-74389
ISBN 0-8386-2009-4

PRINTED IN THE UNITED STATES OF AMERICA

To Peter Huegel and
César Andreu Iglesias

Contents

List of Tables

9

List of Abbreviations and Acronyms

AFL	American Federation of Labor
AFL-CIO	American Federation of Labor - Congress of Industrial Organizations
AID	Agency for International Development
ATLAS	Agrupación de Trabajadores Latinoamericanos (Latin American Workers Group - Peronist)
CAS	Comité de Acción Sindical (Trade Union Action Committee)
CGT	Confederación General de Trabajadores (General Confederatión of Labor)
CLAT	Confederación Latinoamericana de Trabajadores (Latin American Confederation of Labor)
CTAL	**Confederación de Trabajadores de America Latina** (Latin American Workers Confederation)
CUT	Central Unica de Trabajadores (Workers Central Organization)
CUTE	Confederación Unida de Trabajadores del Estado (United Confederation of Public Employees)
EDA	Economic Development Administration ("Fomento")
FLT	Federación Libre de los Trabajadores (Free Federation of Labor)
FTPR	Federación del Trabajo de Puerto Rico (Federation of Labor of Puerto Rico)
FUT	Frente Unido de Trabajadores (United Workers Front)
IBT	International Brotherhood of Teamsters
ICFTU	International Confederation of Free Trade Unions
MOU	Movimiento Obrero Unido (United Labor Movement)

MPI	Movimiento Pro-Independencia (Pro-Independence Movement)
NEA	National Education Association
NLRB	National Labor Relations Board
ORIT	Organización Regional Interamericana de Trabajadores (Interamerican Regional Organization of Workers)
PDP	Partido Popular Democrático (Popular Democratic Party)
PIP	**Partido Independentista Puertorriqueño (Puerto Rico Independence Party)**
PNP	Partido Nuevo Progresista (New Progressive Party)
PRLRA	Puerto Rico Labor Relations Act
PSP	Partido Socialista Puertorriqueño (Puerto Rico Socialist Party)
SIU	Seafarers International Union
UAW	United Automobile Workers
UGT	Unidad General de Trabajadores (General Workers Unit)
UNT	Unión Nacional de Trabajadores (National Workers' Union)
UTAMA	Unión de Trabajadores de la Autoridad Metropolitana de Autobuses (Union of Workers of the Metropolitan Transit Authority)
UTIER	Unión de Trabajadores de la Industria Electrica y del Riego (Union of Workers of the Water Resources Authority)
WFTU	World Federation of Trade Unions

Preface and Acknowledgments

This is an account of the development of the organized labor movement in Puerto Rico. It is a story that merits telling if for no other reason than that the many strands involved in the making of the Puerto Rican working class have previously not been drawn together into a single narrative. The investigation for the study has been conducted as objectively as possible, but with a bias on the side of the working class for which the author makes no apology.

Much of the research for this study was done while I was in residence as a member of the faculty of the Labor Relations Institute of the University of Puerto Rico from 1960 to 1966 and again from 1970 to 1974. Some of the writing was originally done in connection with my 1972 dissertation for the University of Wisconsin, "Collective Bargaining in the Public Sector in Puerto Rico." Portions of one chapter of this study appeared in my essay "The Early Development of the Organized Labor Movement in Puerto Rico," which was published by *Latin American Perspectives* 3, no. 3 (Summer 1976).

The sources include a great deal of personal observation, some participation in the events described, examination of some primary sources, and the weaving together of many secondary sources. The writings of Gordon K. Lewis, Angel G. Quintero Rivera, Gervasio L. García, Robert W. Anderson, Lloyd Reynolds, Peter Gregory, Félix Mejías, David F. Ross, and Kal Wagenheim were especially helpful, as was the autobiography of Santiago Iglesias Pantín.

So many individuals have been helpful to me in trying to understand labor relations in Puerto Rico—especially the worker/students and fellow faculty of the Labor Relations Institute of the University of Puerto Rico—that it would be impossible to mention all of them. A few have been so especially considerate, however, that it would be impossible not to mention them. Appreciation is expressed to Osiris Sánchez, Alfredo Nazario, María Rosario, Peter Huegel, Pedro Grant, Frank Zorilla, Luis Silva Recio, Luis Ernesto Ramos Yordán, José Ramón Morales, Evaristo Toledo, and Harold Lidin. Debts of gratitude are expressed here as memorials to the late Adelaide Romero de Barela and César Andreu Iglesias.

My colleagues at the Industrial Mission of Puerto Rico, Richard Gillett, Mario Roche, and José A. Cay, are remembered for their efforts in seeking alternatives for the working people of Puerto Rico. In like manner, my *compañeros* at the Puerto Rican Association of University Professors, Georg Fromm, Arcadio Díaz Quiñones, and Guillermo Bobonis, are fondly recalled.

Recognition is gratefully expressed to University of Wisconsin advisers Richard U. Miller, William Glade, and Everett Kassalow for patiently guiding me. Similar gratitude is expressed to Rutgers University colleagues Richard Dwyer and Simeon Larson for encouragingly prodding me, thereby keeping my nose to the grindstone through many months of rewriting, despite frequent discouragement. Graduate assistants Jesse Pou Rivera and Luis A. Aguayo Rodriguez were both extremely helpful at different stages of the research.

An expression of gratitude to my family for tolerating the manic behavior associated with prolonged periods of research and writing is made with profound sincerity to my wife Obdulia, my son Paul César, and to the memory of Dolores Martínez. My appreciation also to my mother, Mabel R. Galvin, and my brother, Bill Galvin, for helping in countless ways, but specifically for the drudgery of proofreading many drafts.

I also wish to thank the following publishers for permission to quote from published works:

The Brookings Institution, for permission to quote from *Porto Rico and Its Problems* by Victor S. Clark and associates, 1930.
Editorial Edil, for permission to quote from *The Long Uphill Path:*

A Historical Study of Puerto Rico's Program of Economic Development by David F. Ross, 1969.

Monthly Review Press, for permission to quote from *Puerto Rico, Freedom and Power in the Caribbean* by Gordon K. Lewis, Copyright © 1963 by Gordon K. Lewis. Reprinted by permission of Monthly Review Press.

North American Congress on Latin America, for permission to quote from "U.S. Unions in Puerto Rico" 10, no. 5 (May-June 1976).

Richard D. Irwin, Inc., for permission to quote from *Wages, Productivity, and Industrialization in Puerto Rico* by Lloyd G. Reynolds and Peter Gregory, with the assistance of Luz M. Torruellas, 1965.

Stanford University Press, for permission to quote from *Party Politics in Puerto Rico* by Robert W. Anderson, 1965.

The University of Chicago Press, for permission to quote from *Puerto Rico's Economic Future* by Harvey S. Perloff. Copyright 1950 by the University of Chicago. All rights reserved. Published 1950. Composed and printed by The William Byrd Press, Inc., Richmond, Virginia, U.S.A.

In addition, I would like to express my appreciation to the Office of the Commonwealth of Puerto Rico, New York, for granting me permission to reproduce photographs from its collection.

Introduction

This is an account of the development of the organized labor movement in Puerto Rico, a Caribbean island community dominated by and "freely associated" with the United States. It is a record of the birth pangs of a boisterous and typically socialist-syndicalist-anarchist movement of the early Latin American genre and its subsequent maturation into a domesticated Caribbean version of the North American style of "pure and simple" business unionism. It describes the formation of a movement that in its beginnings was bent ideologically on the revolutionary, radical transformation of a colonial society and traces that movement's evolution into the present pragmatic amalgam of occupational interest groups pressing for reformist concessions within the system. The principal historians of Latin American labor movements have tended to brush lightly over Puerto Rico perhaps because it is an awkwardly unique case that fits none of the stereotypes.[1]

The setting is the West Indies, a chain of partially submerged mountains running from the southern tip of Florida to the northernmost point of South America, the highest peaks of which have remained above water to form an erratic string of islands. Within the West Indies group the islands of Cuba, Jamaica, Hispaniola (the Domincan Republic and Haiti), and Puerto Rico constitute the Greater Antilles. To the north lies the Atlantic Ocean; to the south, the Caribbean Sea. Approximately 95 miles long and 35 miles wide, Puerto Rico measures 3,421 square miles, a land area smaller than that of the state of Connecticut. Into this compact area are jammed more than three million people, about 900 for each square mile[2]—a density more than ten times that of the United States as a whole

17

(Connecticut has about 350). Only a small portion of the land, the narrow coastal plain and the slopes of some of the mountains, which occupy most of the topography, is arable. Located in the tropical zone, the temperature usually ranges between seventy-three and seventy-nine degrees, and rain falls from as little as 30 inches annually in the semi-arid southwestern region to as much as 180 inches annually in the mountains of the northeast. The island is located squarely in the hurricane route and suffers sporadic disasters as a result.[3]

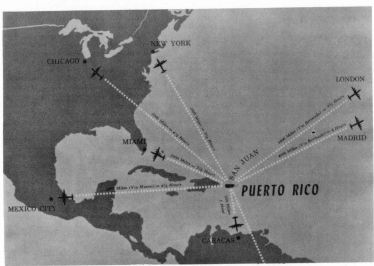

Puerto Rico, Caribbean island midway between two cultures. *Courtesy of the Commonwealth of Puerto Rico.*

The island and its thirty thousand indigenous inhabitants were encountered by Columbus in 1493 and remained under Spanish control until the Spanish American War of 1898.[4] San Juan Bautista, as the island was originally denominated,[5] was not immediately colonized because the *conquistadores* and later the first contingents of colonizers moved westward across the sea in search of additional, hopefully more lucrative territories. This initial neglect remained a distinguishing characteristic of Spain's dominion. As Robert Anderson has pointed out, Puerto Rico shared in very little of the grandeur of the Spanish Empire.

As a small, underpopulated, resource-poor island whose value to its imperial overseer was purely military, Puerto Rico displayed none of the great institutions that are normally associated with Spain's American Empire. Instead of the great ecclesiastical and civil hierarchies of the vice-royalties of Middle and South America, there was rule by generally pedestrian military governors. The religious orders barely touched Puerto Rico, and the Church itself played no significant role on the island. A university was not established until 1903, after the Spaniards had left. Neither the city, as a focus of intellectual or aristocratic activity, nor the encomienda, as the principal form of land ownership and exploitation, was important in Puerto Rico. Population was concentrated in the mountainous rural areas rather than in the urban seat of political and military power.[6]

Approximately ninety-five miles long and thirty-five miles wide, Puerto Rico has a land area smaller than Connecticut. *Courtesy of Commonwealth of Puerto Rico.*

Juan Ponce de León, the island's first colonizer and governor, arrived in Puerto Rico in 1508 and the adventurous spirit his memory recalls symbolically personifies early Spanish rule. The period was highlighted by the subjugation of the relatively pacific Taino Indians[7] and the establishment of rudimentary *encomiendas*,[8] the exploitation and rapid depletion of gold mines, the suppression of short-lived Indian revolts, the importation of

African slaves, and sporadic harassment by pirates. Disenchantment with agrarian colonization soon set in as the conquest continued further west. The population quickly declined to 426 Spaniards, 1,148 Indians, and 2,077 African slaves by 1530 when further emigration was banned.

Following a brief revival of mining in the hitherto unexploited mountainous interior, the island's inhabitants turned to the production of sugar, developing extensive plantations in the coastal lowlands and establishing the first grinding mill in 1523. The prosperity that this activity engendered was short-lived, for the island's sugar producers failed to match the advances in technology introduced in other West Indian islands such as Jamaica. Long before the end of the first century of colonization the economy had slumped into a state of static subsistence, with commerce limited to small-scale production of beef and tobacco.

The second and most of the third centuries of Spanish colonization saw Puerto Rico sinking deeper into the stagnation of a colonial backwater, the diminutive possession's main value to the imperial power being that of a military garrison and strategically situated harbor for stopping en route to and from the Old World. Only one census was taken in the seventeenth century, in 1673, and counted barely 365 free men plus their families and slaves residing in the capital city. The somnolence was interrupted only by illicit commerce with the French, Dutch, and British island possessions, to such a degree that smuggling eventually emerged as Puerto Rico's principal economic activity. The labor force, not yet a proletarian wage-earning class, was comprised in the main of subjugated natives and a relatively small number of African slaves. The first shopkeepers and artisans began to populate the towns.

The eighteenth century was marked by something of an arousal from the prior torpor principally as the result of the closing, by the resentful British, of the ports of Jamaica and Barbados to ships from the American Republic, which in 1776 had declared its independence. This development resulted in an expansion of trade with the mainland for Puerto Rico and other Spanish islands in the Caribbean. A new cash crop, coffee, was introduced and intensively cultivated. Spain undertook construction of further fortifications in San Juan during this period, relaxed commercial controls, and otherwise stimulated the economy. Labor was performed by slaves and sharecropping subsistence farmers.

Most of this early commercial activity was limited to the coastal settlements, however, and most of the island's inhabitants were little affected. The Spanish king in 1765 commissioned Field Marshall Alejandro O'Reilly to make a military, social, and economic survey of the island, Puerto Rico's first island-wide demographic accounting. His census reported a population of 44,883, including 5,037 slaves. An excerpt from the report reveals the standard of living then prevailing:

To form an idea of how these natives have lived and still live, it is enough to say that there are only two schools in the whole island. . . . In the towns (the capital included) there are few permanent inhabitants besides the curate; the others are always in the country, except Sundays and feast-days, when those living near to where there is a church come to hear mass. During these feast-days they occupy houses that look like hen-coops. They consist of a couple of rooms, most of them without doors or windows, and therefore open day and night. . . . There is little distinction among the people. The only difference between them consists in the possession of a little more or less property, and, perhaps, the rank of subaltern officer in the militia.[9]

Nonetheless, a culture was developing—a unique Puerto Rican culture. Field Marshall O'Reilly further reported to the king that "whites mixed with blacks and mulattos 'without any repugnance whatsoever.' "[10] The inhabitants were no longer Taínos, creoles, or Africans, but Puerto Ricans, and "a Spaniard would have found peculiarities in the character and types of people, in their customs, music, dances, and their form of leisure."[11]

A certain limited degree of change did begin to occur during the 1800s, the fourth and final century of Spanish rule. As Spain's political fortunes waxed and waned as the result of the gradual loss of her colonies in the New World, of the effect of the Napoleonic Wars, and of the rise and fall of constitutional regimes, Puerto Rico, by extension, also enjoyed occasional brief interludes of civil liberty and economic reform, only to relapse into subjugation and stagnation, often under military domination even more despotic than in previous centuries.

The characteristics of nineteenth-century Puerto Rico have often been described[12] and can be succinctly summarized: socially, its elite was a plutocracy mounted on a diseased and illiterate mass;

religiously, the elites were formally Catholic, the masses informally Catholic and spiritualistic; ethnically, the society was European, African, and Indian with resultant mixtures; intellectually, a parochial and insular backwater largely impervious to progressive ideology; structurally, a colony—the only one of Spain's American domains in which no sustained move for independence was ever made.

Several authorities maintain that Puerto Rico's immunity from revolt was not entirely the result of her size and topography, which taken together rendered an uprising of any sort extremely difficult, but instead was probably the result of the fact that as one Spanish dominion after another rebelled, Puerto Rico became increasingly a haven for immigrants and exiles who might otherwise have continued on to the continent: French from Louisiana; refugee planters from war-torn Haiti; creoles and Spaniards from Florida, Mexico, Central and South America—conservatives all.[13] Puerto Rico traditionally has harbored a disproportionately large number of inhabitants whose very reason for being there is to avoid upheaval. The presence of a very large and influential colony of exiles from Cuba since 1960 is the most recent manifestation of this reactionary political tendency.

Despite this, and despite the fact that no sustained movements were ever made to alter fundamentally Spanish colonial traditions, a labor force, in the modern sense, began to develop during the final decades of the Spanish regime. This new class has continued to evolve through a series of partial transformations, with each new phase superimposed on previous phases and with prior characteristics rarely being entirely erased for modernization proceeded without the total elimination of traditional society. A nucleus of working people who had become conscious of individual weakness and potential collective strength, that is to say, a labor *movement*, began to take shape and emerge as a social force.

The growth of the labor movement and the shaping of modern industrial relations in Puerto Rico can be divided chronologically, in very approximate fashion, into eight overlapping stages:

1.   The last few decades of the Spanish colonial regime, which ended in 1898 with the invasion by U.S. military forces followed by investors from the mainland, during which time efforts at implementing radical European ideology then penetrating the insular fastness were outlawed as criminal conspiracies.

2. The period of U.S. military occupation, 1898-1900, during which the embryonic labor movement struggled for legal recognition and during which a group of Puerto Rican artisans carried on what might be termed a "lonely hearts flirtation" with the Socialist Labor Party in the United States.

3. The initial years of U.S. civil, colonial rule, 1900-1903, during which freedom of association was grudgingly granted, but harassment of the labor movement continued through the elite-manipulated device of turning workers against workers in fraternal warfare.

4. An overlapping period, 1901-1904, in which the correspondence "courtship" with the mainland Socialists became face to face, the upshot being the jilting of the mainland Socialist Party by Puerto Rican labor and marriage with the American Federation of Labor (AFL) in an effort by insular labor to obtain metropolitan protection from rapacious local entrepreneurs.

5. The heroic period immediately prior to, during, and following World War I, in which the Puerto Rican labor movement, legally sanctioned, ideologically cohesive, and fraternally united, could turn to the task of confronting the employers, now principally mainland corporations in league with local elites, in encounter after bloody encounter, in tests of economic strength and resistance.

6. An electorally successful but organizationally disastrous period of ideological indecision and partisan political activity, before and during the depression years of the late 1920s and early 1930s, highlighted by the formation of a progressive-reactionary coalition smelling of corruption and contributing to the tarnishing of labor's militant image.

7. The period of the late 1930s and early 1940s highlighted by the demise of labor's conservative old guard, the rise to power of radically oriented labor idealogues together with the young liberals of the Popular Democratic Party (PDP), the subsequent purge of the radicals, and the consequent splitting asunder of the insular labor movement.

8. And, since World War II, urbanization and industrial diversification, with "Operation Bootstrap"—Puerto Rico's developmental program—the theme, and the influx into—in pursuit of runaway industries from the mainland—and rise to and fall from dominance in the insular labor movement of the "international"

unions from the U.S. mainland, and the upsurge of conflict in the public sector.

To the fleshing out of this chronological skeleton we now turn.

The Organized
Labor Movement
in Puerto Rico

1

Labor during the
Spanish Colonial Regime

It has long been accepted unquestioningly that labor as a movement began to take form in Puerto Rico only a year or two prior to the invasion by the United States in 1898. Inasmuch as modern industrial and labor relations cannot, by definition, exist in preindustrial societies and since the full impact of industrialization was not felt in Puerto Rico until after the massive invasion of capital from the United States on the heels of the military occupation, it has been natural to look for the origins of the labor movement near the date of the transfer of power from Spain to the United States. A closer historical look, however, reveals that the "industrialization" of the labor force, and its proletarianization, had commenced *prior* to the colonization by the United States. Recent analysis,[1] principally by Angel Quintero Rivera and Gervasio García Rodríguez, has also established that a significant number of remarkably militant labor organizations existed in Puerto Rico, some dating from at least fifty years before the demise of Spanish sovereignty.

It is important, therefore, that *industrialism* be defined and clarified, because the concepts involved are frequently used in misleading fashion when describing what allegedly occurred not only in Puerto Rico but also in most other "developing" countries.

In the literature describing the developmental process, it is common to encounter the statement that the societal transformation is from an agricultural to an industrial way of life.

27

This is not an especially accurate description of what occurs anywhere, and, in certain industrializing societies—as in Puerto Rico—serves to confuse the nature of the metamorphosis of the labor force.

An example of this conceptual confusion is provided by Charles Myers in his description of the development of modern industrial relations in India. "Industrialization," he explains, "requires not only the recruitment and training of an industrial labor force but also its commitment to an industrial, as opposed to an agricultural way of life."[2] The concept that agricultural and industrial ways of life are in opposition has some limited relevance in India, a country in which *agriculture* by and large continues to be synonomous with subsistence farming, and where *industrialization* has meant the development of urban manufacturing rather than rural "agribusiness," but it is essentially meaningless as a general distinction.

The confusion arises, in part, because of imprecise definition of two distinct phenomena: urbanism and industrialism. Urbanism, of course, is the characteristic way of life of city dwellers, results from the process of urbanization, and is independent of modes of production. *Urban* is the antonym of *rural*, but is not necessarily synonymous with industry. *Industrialism*, on the other hand, means the rational organization of the factors of production, *any* sort of production of goods or services—primary, secondary, or tertiary—in such a way (usually through the application of technology) that a surplus of income over outlay results. Industrialism grew out of, and is properly contrasted with, the status-oriented, noncalculating, traditional systems that preceded the industrial revolution.

The confusion is compounded by the tendency to think of all agricultural activities—no matter the scale, organization, or ends—as *farming*. This has probably come about because agriculture was originally of a subsistence rather than commercial nature, just as *manufacturing*—originally meaning "made by hand"—traditionally was handicraft in local barter markets rather than the rationalized, commercial production of the modern factory system. The confusion persists despite the obvious replacement in modern societies of most subsistence farming with agribusiness and the ready acceptance of such nomenclature as the *sugar industry*, the *cotton industry*, or the *wine grape industry*. If there are agricultural industries, as clearly there are, then a distinction between *agriculture* and *industry* has to be meaningless.

A more meaningful distinction is between production of an industrial character in modern society and production based on subsistence farming and/or artisanry in traditional society. The location of industrial activity—in a rural or urban environment—is irrelevant (as Carey McWilliams in his instructively entitled book, *Factories in our Fields*, pointed out many years ago).

It would, for example, clearly be misleading to categorize Belgian copper mining in Africa, or French rubber extraction in Indochina, or British cotton production in Egypt, or American banana cultivation in Central America as *nonindustrial activities* simply because the physical environment in which these resources are exploited is rural rather than urban. The United Fruit Company is no less an industrial organization than the General Motors Corporation.

The issue is not simply one of semantics. There are perhaps subtle, but nonetheless important political implications involved in the fact that we readily recognize that rural coal miners in Pennsylvania are engaged in an industrial activity, but are slow to recognize that rural grape pickers in California also are. The careless interchangeability of such concepts as *economic growth, economic development, modernization, urbanization,* and *industrialization*,[3] detracts from our capacity to understand the formation of industrial labor forces in developing societies. The oft-presented picture of a one-step developmental transition from a traditional to a modern way of life, with agriculture identified with traditional society and industrialism with modern society, is in most cases not only inaccurate but misleading, in that it blurs the industrial nature of the early stages of colonialism.

With regard to the development of the labor force in Puerto Rico it is especially important that these industrial realities be emphasized, inasmuch as the notion that the industrial age was ushered into Puerto Rico sometime after World War II under the hegemony of the Popular Democratic Party persists despite abundant testimony to the contrary by such authorities as Eugenio Fernández Méndez, Gordon Lewis, Angel Quintero Rivera, and Sidney Mintz, among others.

The authors of *Social Class and Social Change in Puerto Rico*, for example, describe Puerto Rico as having moved in the 1940s from being "a society largely dominated by agriculture to one in which industry plays an increasingly important role in the national economy."[4] No such shift took place, however, inasmuch as industrialized agriculture had been playing a dominant role in the economy of Puerto Rico for many decades prior to World War II.

Earl Parker Hanson, who is chief among those authors persistently referring to the Popular Democratic Party's administration as "revolutionary," points to 1940 as the year in which Puerto Rico "launched a remarkable program of industrialization to get employment and to diversify the economy."[5] That the economy was "diversified" after 1940, there can be no question. The idea that "industrialization" was "launched" by the Popular Democractic Party, however, obscures the intensely industrial nature of more than half a century of agro-industrial, colonial development in Puerto Rico prior to 1940.

The reality—and it is an important basis for understanding labor relationships in Puerto Rico—is that the industrialization of the Puerto Rican economy commenced during the closing decades of Spanish domination in the nineteenth century and was abruptly accelerated following the invasion by U.S. forces at the turn of the present century, although the political modernization of Puerto Rican society did not gain impetus until the late 1930s, nor economic diversification until after World War II.

Economic activity in Puerto Rico, throughout most of the Spanish colonial period, had been limited to commerce, small-scale manufacture for local consumption, and agriculture. Crops were produced both for subsistence[6] and for commerce in a semifeudal, semicommercial sharecropping system,[7] with some steam but mostly animal power, rudimentary tools, and an almost exclusive reliance on manual labor.

Nevertheless, the transition from traditional to modern society had already commenced in Puerto Rico during the nineteenth century, a period that Quintero Rivera aptly calls the "gateway to capitalism,"[8] when the economy was transformed into

> an active agrarian capitalism of sugar and coffee plantations. This plantation system of the Spanish West Indian world was in its epoch the revolutionary equivalent of the factory system which. . .transformed in a thousand ways European society.[9]

The impetus for the rationalization of agricultural production came, in part, from the establishment of trade relations with the United States in the second decade of the nineteenth century and the consequent commercial opportunities. An additional element, resulting from the dismemberment of the European powers' empires in the Western Hemisphere, was the arrival of large numbers of planters and their families from the newly liberated republics, accompanied by slaves, tools, and agricultural machinery. It was also at this time that the Spanish government not only provided these technologically more advanced newcomers with land, but also abolished many of the impediments to trade in agricultural products that had previously been imposed on Puerto Rico to favor Spanish producers.[10] By the mid-1800s the outlines of industrialism were clearly visible:

> The typical sugar plantation. . .was characterized by four distinctive aspects: first, the usual division of labor between the employing class and workers. . . .Second, the predominance of the technique of monocultivation. Third, the capitalist nature of the system, manifested in the value of the purchase and sale of slaves, land and equipment which made it essential that large amounts of wealth be available; and, finally, the relationship of the entire productive effort to the state of the export market which served to transform the plantation owner into an astute "businessman" accustomed to measuring success and to considering ideas in terms of the economic benefit which would derive.[11]

The transition can be traced by looking at the conversion of land from subsistence to commercial agricultural production during the nineteenth century (see Table 1). In 1830, a year at the beginning of the period when agriculture was becoming commercialized, a total of only 35,000 cuerdas (one *cuerda* equals 0.9712 acre) was devoted to the cultivation of the three cash crops, sugar cane, coffee, and tobacco. This was slightly more than two percent of total farm land. By 1896, just before the U.S. military invasion, the total for the three crops had reached 188,000 *cuerdas*, 9 percent of the total.[12] The amount of land devoted to growing sugar cane nearly tripled in the twenty-year period between 1834 and 1854.[13]

TABLE 1

ESTIMATES OF AMOUNTS OF LAND DEVOTED TO PRINCIPAL COMMERCIAL
AGRICULTURAL CROPS IN PUERTO RICO, 1830 - 1945
(In thousands of *cuerdas*;   1 *cuerda* = 0.9712 acre)

Commercial Crop	1830	1896	1909	1919	1929	1945
Sugar cane	15	62	145	239	251	302
Coffee	17	122	187	194	192	180
Tobacco	3	4	22	39	39	56
Total farm area	1,524	2,089	2,085	2,022	1,979	1,849
Percentage of total area devoted to three cash crops	2.3	9.0	17.0	23.3	24.4	29.1

SOURCE: Harvy S. Perloff, *Puerto Rico's Economic Future* (Chicago, Ill.: The University of Chicago Press, 1950), pp. 83-84.

It is important to keep in mind that only a small proportion of land in Puerto Rico is arable. Almost one-fouth of the island slopes forty-five degrees or more and only about twenty-five percent is approximately level. This limitation accounts for the fact that the total farm area has remained relatively constant over the past one hundred years and it also means that any land pressed into commercial production, as it increasingly came to be, was land converted from traditional, subsistence tillage. In 1830, for example, there were 635,000 *cuerdas* devoted to pasture land, and in 1945 there were still only 643,000 *cuerdas* so utilized. Even subsistence farming was gradually squeezed out and by 1898 "land in the coastal plain had become too valuable to permit planting part of it in garden crops for the benefit of the workers."[14]

By the 1870s the traditional, small-scale sugar mill or *trapiche*, had begun to give way to the modern, centralized sugar factory or *central* with enormous capital investments. The Puerto Rican economy and way of life were being industrialized in order to take advantage of lucrative opportunities to trade in agricultural products. The semi-feudal hacienda was being transformed into a commercial plantation. Capital was being accumulated and reinvested in increased productive capacity. The nascent industrialists in Puerto Rico were beginning to communicate with and adopt the ideology and methodology of capitalist society outside the island. Systems for providing credit to the planter class by the merchant class developed, and political parties representing the interests of each of these groups were formed. Specialization and resultant division of labor became more pronounced. Absentee ownership and administration by overseers increased. The production of sugar temporarily declined, but trade in and production of coffee increased. Leaf tobacco, which had traditionally been exported, was increasingly processed in Puerto Rico. By the final decade of the nineteenth century, several cigar factories, with all the characteristics of industrial establishments anywhere, had been established. A demographic shift from rural to urban areas had commenced and, simultaneously, as manufactured goods from outside the island became more readily available and attainable, artisanry declined. The service industries such as printing and construction made their appearance. What is also very important is that Puerto Rico had become a monetary society in which such elements as profit on investment, interest, rates of exchange, currency devaluation, and price inflation became matters of pressing concern to increasingly larger sectors of the population.

Land was concentrated in fewer hands throughout the nineteenth century. In 1833 approximately half the adult population owned land; by the end of the century, this proportion had been cut in half.[15] The population of Puerto Rico at the end of the Spanish colonial domination stood at about a million people, with nearly 60 percent engaged in the cultivation of sugar, coffee, and tobacco, another 20 percent in domestic service, and seven percent each in trade, transportation, and manufacturing.[16] It is also important to note that Puerto Rico, unlike many of the other Caribbean colonies, was never predominantly a slave economy. The proportion of slaves in the total population never exceeded about 12 percent and slavery was abolished altogether in 1873.

The beginnings of the disintegration of traditional society during the last half of the nineteenth century, as a result of the increasing industrialization of agriculture, gave rise to the proletarianization of the working class in Puerto Rico.[17] One of the crucial elements in this transformation was the introduction of the wage system and with it the buying and selling of human labor as a commodity in what comes to be known as a labor market. It was during this period that management of the sugar plantations established payment systems based on vouchers or *vales*, which could be exchanged for consumer goods only at company stores.[18] The employing class in Puerto Rico, motivated by a desire to stimulate labor mobility in response to fluctuating production demands, took the lead in seeking the repeal of the then existent legislation requiring laborers to carry regulatory passbooks, which had the effect of limiting laborers to a small number of employers in a confined locality. This was the same legisation that they had requested some years earlier at a time when the goal was that of creating a disciplined labor force and compelling workers to build the roads and bridges required for the infrastructure of a developing economy.[19]

Concerted activity by the working class during most of the Spanish colonial regime, although certainly present, had been limited and sporadic. The minuscule urban enterprises operating in largely local markets, the autonomy of the urban artisans and their guildlike organizations, and the semifeudal nature of agriculture—all heavily paternalistic and rigidly traditional—constituted a situation in which labor did not, until midway through the nineteenth century, as I have noted, become aware of its new condition as a factor of production to be marketed and exploited in the modern, cost-minimizing, competitive sense. A sense of injustice and an urge to collective action, when present, were focused on social and political inequities rather than on the employment relationship. Several strikes in 1894 and 1895, for example, protested monetary instability.

Conflict based on employment relationships was a new phenomenon. Regulations requiring laborers to carry a passbook had long made blacklisting and labor force control routine matters. Protective labor legislation was nonexistent, while a Spanish colonial version of the "conspiracy doctrine," which held it a crime to attempt collectively to raise the "price" of labor, was rigorously enforced.[20] The property-owning class had been thoroughly frightened by Marx and Engels's *Communist Manifesto* in 1848 and attempted to thwart class consciousness in any way possible.

Mutual benefit, cooperative associations of urban artisans had been permitted to function throughout the Spanish colonial regime, always with close governmental supervision and, officially, limited to the encouragement of industriousness and frugality. Despite these constraints, a structure and a tradition of occupational and class solidarity were taking form during the late nineteenth century. With or without the impending intervention by the United States, Puerto Rico could not have moved very far into the present century without the breakdown of traditional society. Just below the surface, elements desirous of change were stirring and needed only the slightest impetus to emerge.

The personal dimension of impetus for the disintegration of traditional labor relationships, and the consequent evolution of those relationships, was provided by an unlikely combination of European immigrants: an English cigar maker, Samuel Gompers, who came to the United States in 1863 and who was to become the guiding genius of the American Federation of Labor (AFL) from its founding in 1886 through his death in 1924, and a Spanish carpenter named Santiago Iglesias Pantín. When Iglesias disembarked in Puerto Rico in late 1896, two years before the U.S. invasion, the old society had begun to disintegrate, and, once Iglesias joined forces with Gompers, as we shall see, the consolidation of this transformation and, for labor, the direction it was to take, were virtually guaranteed.

Although it has long been conventionally accepted that Iglesias initiated the organization of labor in Puerto Rico,[21] recent research[22] has established that a number of workers' organizations were active considerably before the arrival of the "founder" in 1896. Strikes had taken place[23] and groups of urban handicraftsmen—printers, tinsmiths, carpenters, cigar makers, painters, shoemakers, and others—had become the clandestine recipients of anarcho-syndicalist and other radical ideas emanating from Europe long before the turn of the century.[24] Iglesias's role was more catalytic than fundamental, accelerating elements already in motion. The arrival of Iglesias and the advent of industrialization were coincidental and complementary.[25]

For some months after the arrival of Iglesias, the more militant artisans of San Juan, the capital city, concentrated on encouraging the political and social consciousness of the working class.[26] Study circles were formed, and, on May 1, 1897, the radical labor weekly *"Ensayo Obrero"* first saw the light of day.[27] On June 1, 1897, the groundwork was laid for the establishment of a regional federation of the workers' international movement[28] with which nuclei of venturesome craftsmen could loosely affiliate. One of the central objectives of the organizers was the abolition of fear and deference on the part of the working classes in their dealings with the controlling elites. In this respect Iglesias enjoyed a formidable, ethnic advantage. Not only was he neither Black, mulatto, mestizo, nor creole, as were most of the island's workers; he was a pure-blooded, bona fide *peninsular*. His Iberian origin served as both inspiration and protection, for workers and colonial authorities alike were impressed that the unorthodox Spaniard did not conspire covertly, but instead proceeded with what he audaciously maintained to be universal human rights imported from Europe whence culture derived. Iglesias took advantage of this element of uncertain admiration and tolerance in order to speak out and to encourage his fellow workers to express themselves freely, not to their employers (some of his cohorts were probably themselves master artisans), but to the authorities and the community at large.

A memorable occasion for setting an example of free speech occurred in early 1897 during a town meeting convoked for the purpose of enlisting voluntary contributions of labor for the civic project of tearing down a portion of the ancient fortress walls, which were no longer of military significance and which hindered urban expansion in addition to shutting out light and air. Iglesias was in attendance and astounded both those presiding and the assembly by rising to speak, rather than to listen passively, by challenging the credentials of the chairperson, and by recommending refusal to labor voluntarily. In the melee that ensued, Iglesias retired to the roof of an adjoining building to watch the excited search for the Spanish "anarchist." The importance of the incident lies in the rejection, with impunity, of the paternalistic concept of "humble" labor.[29]

His ethnic immunity was short-lived, however. A half-century of political maneuver culminated in 1897 with the achievement of autonomy for Puerto Rico (precisely at the moment in history when expansionists in the United States were conspiring to take it away) and Iglesias's status changed from that of a reluctantly tolerated Spaniard to that of an undesirable alien.

Vested interests were threatened, and the press criticized the labor organizers for discussing socialism "not as a philosophical debating topic," as would have been acceptable, "but instead as yet another element of discord." The Church cautioned the workers to turn deaf ears to those who spoke of labor's rights and to remember that "the owner is at one and the same time the king, the priest, the confessor, and the pastor of the laboring man."[30]

The neophyte labor organizers, as they attempted to move from cooperativism to confrontation and from rhetoric to action, were fired, blacklisted, arrested, and generally harassed by the authorities. Iglesias attempted to convince his cohorts to take an anarchist position by refusing to support either of the two very traditional political parties then vying for control of the autonomous government. In what has become a pattern down to the present day, however, some of the working-class adherents of *Ensayo Obrero*, the recently established voice of organized labor, seized control of the periodical and editorialized in favor of the opposition party, while a dissident group created a rival periodical, *El Obrero Liberal*, and threw their support to the majority party.

What was probably the first mass, working-class meeting in Puerto Rico took place, with Iglesias as master of ceremonies, two days before the elections scheduled for March 25, 1898. A day later, on the eve of the elections, an order went out for the detention of Iglesias, who had been warned by the authorities that while "socialist ideals" might be appropriate for Spain, Puerto Rico was not yet ready for the propagation of that sort of doctrine. He attempted to flee the island, but was captured and imprisoned by the newly elected autonomous government of Luis Muñoz Rivera in April 1898.

Iglesias was still in prison when U.S. Naval Forces, in the early stages of the Spanish-American War, first bombarded the island fortifications and, in a symbolically significant adventure, almost escaped when a U.S. missile blasted a hole in his Spanish colonial prison wall. Released after seven months' imprisonment when the armistice was declared on October 5, 1898, Iglesias had to evade the local police who, only hours later, attempted to rearrest him. Like many other residents of the island, he expected the North American forces to be harbingers of social justice and fled San Juan in order to seek the protection of the U.S. army units approaching the capital from the other side of the island.

By this time, Puerto Rico had been blockaded for several months, the economy was in a shambles, political uncertainty reigned, and labor leadership's initial efforts to organize workers and protect their interests had disintegrated. Now, with the American military presence holding the insular employers temporarily at bay, and with what was to be a short-lived stimulus, efforts to organize the labor movement were redoubled.

2

Labor During the U.S. Military Occupation

"It wasn't much of a war, but it was all the war there was" (the military campaign in Puerto Rico lasted only seventeen days) was the way in which the ebullient Theodore Roosevelt later described the Spanish American War in which the United States seized colonial control of the island in 1898.[1]

As has been noted, although change was in the wind and crucial elements in Puerto Rican society had already begun to move into the industrial age, the society into which the invading troops marched was still substantially traditional: semi-feudal, still predominantly precapitalist, rigidly stratified. A small, literate minority of merchants, landowners, soldiers, and colonial administrators paternalistically controlled the 85 percent of the island's population who were illiterate, rural laborers. There were virtually no roads or other internal means of communication, few schools, even fewer newspapers, and meager and sporadic contact with the world beyond the island's shores. Patterns of behavior, although beginning to change, were still largely dictated by tradition and learned by experience.[2]

In 1899 General George Davis, the U.S. military governor, evaluated the possession for his superiors in Washington, just as Field Marshall O'Reilly had done for his in Madrid a century and a half earlier, and it is interesting to compare this extract with the excerpt from O'Reilly's report cited earlier and note how little change had occurred in the interim:

So great is their poverty that they are always in debt to the pro-
prietors or merchants. They live in huts made of sticks and poles
covered with thatches of palm leaves. A family of a dozen may
be huddled together in one room, often with only a dirt floor.
They have little food worthy of the name and only the most
scanty clothing. . . .A few may own a machete or a hoe, but
more have no worldly possessions whatever. Their food is fruit,
and if they are wage-earners, a little rice and codfish in addition.
. . .It is hard to believe that the pale, sallow, and often emaciated
beings are the direct descendants of the conquistadores who
carried the flag of Spain to nearly all of South America, and to
one-third of North America.[3]

The principal change in colonial administration turned out to be
the replacement of Spanish despotic neglect with exploitation by
the United States that was clothed in deviousness, confusion,
ambiguity, and pompousness.[4] Nelson Miles, the Commanding
General of the U.S. Expeditionary Force set the tone:

The people of the United States in the cause of liberty, justice
and humanity. . .come bearing the banner of freedom, inspired
by a noble purpose. . .[to] bring you the fostering arm of a
nation of free people, whose greatest power is in justice and
humanity to all those living within its fold. . .not to make war
upon the people of a country that for centuries has been op-
pressed but, on the contrary, to bring you protection. . .to give
to all. . .the advantages and blessings of an enlightened civilization.[5]

The U.S. Consul General in Puerto Rico, who had been present
on the scene prior to the arrival of the invading troops, was effusive
over the prize and its potential:

We can cause this island to be the Pearl of the Antilles. . . .We
can make it the diamond of the United States, and the almighty
will hold us responsible if we neglect to adopt the proper measures to make it such. . . .One year ago we never dreamed of
owning Porto Rico. In the providence of God she is ours to-day;
she will be ours forever, and there is no country nor people on
the face of the earth which could afford the United States a
better opportunity for showing the world the power of her institutions in developing a people and country than this island of
Porto Rico.[6]

Academicians, missionaries, teachers, bureaucrats, and businessmen began to arrive from the mainland and to reiterate the promises. "It is true," social scientist Leo Rowe commented in the early days of the occupation, "that we enter upon the work with an advantage which no other nation possesses; namely, the possibility of giving to these islands a degree of prosperity which they have not enjoyed. . . ."[7]

Tremendous prosperity did, in fact, prove possible, but was largely limited to investors from the United States and their Puerto Rican counselors and allies. The U.S. Consul General in San Juan, Philip C. Hanna, in December 1898 reported that his office had already been deluged with thousands of commercial inquiries

> from all classes of businessmen in all parts of the United States concerning this island, very many of them asking when the proper time will arrive for them to invest capital in Porto Rico. Several of them have said: "We propose to establish factories in this densely populated island, and teach the people there, who have been accustomed to labor at very low wages, to labor in the factories that we shall establish. We hope to be in a position," most of them say, "to pay them better wages than they have ever received in the past. We understand that they are not a class of people acquainted with strikes, and by giving them better wages than they have had heretofore and making labor respectable among them, we believe our factories can be successfully conducted in Porto Rico."[8]

In a model of how social and, specifically, labor movements develop, comparative industrial sociologist Henry Landsberger hypothesized that such "movements are likely to occur in societies where. . .objective economic changes in the place and structure of agriculture and/or. . .objective political changes such as war, have caused the traditional elites to lose ground relative to newer elites."[9] it is difficult to imagine a case more explicitly supportive of this hypothesis than that of the development of the labor movement in Puerto Rico following the takeover by United States forces and the subsequent transformation of the insular economy.

The changes resulting from the shift in sovereignty were abrupt, and they altered virtually every facet of human relationships—psychological, social, economic, political, legal, monetary, and, as we shall see, coincidentally, even meteorological. In combination, the changes dislocated but by no means entirely displaced the old society, especially its dominant class.

One alteration was psychological in that it involved the frustration of anticipated improvements in living conditions, which were already at so nearly subhuman level that further deterioration, which did occur, would have appeared impossible.

The U.S. Treasury Department, during the initial months of the military occupation, commissioned a study of the "island prize," and Commissioner Henry K. Carroll reported that in 1898

> daily wages of the common field laborer range generally from 35 to 50 cents, native money. . . .In the mills the day is from sunrise to sunset. . . .Almost no furniture is visible. . . .A good supply of pure water is almost everywhere wanting. . . .Few of the laboring class are robust. They are small and thin and generally anaemic. . . .More nourishing food can be said to be the universal need, and a less destructive drink than the native rum . . . .150,000 of the 900,000 inhabitants wear shoes regularly, and 50,000 irregularly, leaving 700,000 belonging to the barefoot class.[10]

The frustration of the "laboring class" thus described resulted from the understandably eager gullibility of the new subjects of the United States, who believed the invading military commander's promise that "the advantages and blessings of an enlightened civilization" were about to be bestowed upon them. Over and over again the reader of historical documents encounters the observation that Puerto Ricans quickly came to anticipate salvation from their new association with the United States. "The common people in the country look to the United States for help and guidance with a degree of faith and hope that is naively childlike," is a typical comment from a Brookings Institution Study published in 1930.[11]

Certain civic improvements did accrue from annexation, not enough to modify the social structure significantly, but more than enough to engender expectations. Moreover, the minimal improvements were not quick in coming—not nearly so quick as the arrival of the entrepreneurs, who did modify the economy, although not in the ways anticipated.

Under Spain during the latter part of the nineteenth century, the principal export had been coffee, because sugar had temporarily declined in importance. Change in sovereignty meant the immediate closing of the European markets, but without the simultaneous lifting of tariffs in the U.S. market. The transition from coffee cultivation back to industrialized sugar production was traumatic. "The war killed what little commerce the island had built up and, as a consequence, the working population, during the first year, was desperate."[12]

The source of the trauma was economic, but the results, were also social. Gordon Lewis describes the transition:

> The change in the production base entailed changes, inevitably, in the insular social structure. . . .As the family type hacienda was supplanted by the corporate central organization there went hand in hand with the change a quiet revolution in an entire category of folkways. A semi-feudal paternalism protecting the worker from the worst of the onslaughts of rural life, gave way to an impersonal wage system.[13]

In the political sphere the Puerto Ricans suffered another setback. Only months prior to the U.S takeover, during a transitory triumph of liberal government in Spain, the political maneuvering of decades had culminated in a grant of considerable autonomy to Puerto Rico. The disappointment over the negation of this achievement was temporarily assuaged by the illusion that the United States would soon substitute either independence or statehood for the lost autonomy. Frustration was intense and bitter when it became clear that the island had reverted to colonial status[14]—a carelessly and incompetently administered colonialism at that.

In the legal context the transition spawned yet another dislocation. The U.S. military government issued a spate of decrees involving a variety of issues from free speech to the eight-hour day, all without repealing the still applicable Spanish codes. In the subsequent confusion many of the newly proclaimed civil liberties were modified or negated by the civil governments that succeeded the military. Again expectations were encouraged, then dashed.[15]

Walter Weyl comments on this period in a U.S. Department of Labor study:

> The Americans have, moreover, tended to strengthen somewhat

the position of the workingman by giving him a vote, by defining his position before the law, and by recognizing to a less extent than did the Spanish the difference between the employer and the employed. Nevertheless, even at the present moment it is quite clear that the social and economic position of the Porto Rican worker is low, that he is held in small esteem, that there is a contempt for his work. . .and finally that the economic power and the political influence of the working man are extremely small.[16]

The change that most directly affected the working class involved the switch in early 1899 from the Mexican peso, which had been in use in Puerto Rico, to the U.S. dollar—at an exchange rate of sixty U.S. cents for one peso. Wages were immediately cut by forty percent although prices remained the same or rose. Azel Ames carried out a study of labor conditions in the new possession in 1901 and noted that "all amounts of wages have been reduced to United States currency. . ." but "prices of nearly all commodities involved in the cost of living have been much increased (temporarily) and some have been doubled."[17] The effect, contrary to Dr. Ames's prediction, was not temporary; it ultimately resulted in the calling of a general strike.[18]

Finally, as if all these manmade calamities were insufficient to dislocate the society, on August 8, 1899, less than a year after the invasion, a hurricane inflicted heavy damage. Rowe, writing in 1904 referred to it as "the most destructive hurricane in the history of the West Indies."[19] The coffee industry was virtually destroyed and a considerable proportion of the population made homeless.

Santiago Iglesias, by then a man without a country,[20] had reentered San Juan with the U.S. military contingent as a sort of spontaneous labor liaison to the occupying forces. In what must have been one of the more bizarre occurrences in a bizarre war, Iglesias found that a Puerto Rican who was serving the U.S. Army as an interpreter was an admirer of his. The interpreter introduced Iglesias to the U.S. officers as a public-spirited orator of renown and, as a result, at the "liberation" ceremonies in each municipality and hacienda, Iglesias was invited to speak and would deliver a fiery address urging the populace to go out on strike.[21] Circumstantial evidence indicates that Iglesias was effective in his efforts to arouse the workers to action. In November 1898 the U.S.

Consul General testified that

> the recent reports concerning the burning of plantations since
> our troops landed in the island are probably true substantially,
> but these burnings have mostly been committed by laborers who
> for years have been compelled to work at starvation wages
> . . . .the memories of persecution and low wages and of a condi-
> tion worse than slavery have caused these people, at this time
> and change of governments, to give vent to their wrath and re-
> sentment and to try to get even with their masters.[22]

Iglesias's influence, and that of other spokespersons for the
working class, were short-lived, however. Within days after the
beginning of the twenty-eight-month military occupation, the
administrative, entrepreneurial, and professional classes were
successful in disassociating themselves from the vestiges of Spanish
mores and in ingratiating themselves with the new dominance,
using their influence to counsel the North Americans against
moving too quickly in the implementation of political or industrial
democracy.[23] Iglesias summed up the transition in the following
terms:

> The ministers and subordinates who had sworn to stay in their
> posts and defend and die for the Spanish flag, calmly continued
> to carry out the same functions, at the same time swearing their
> allegiance to the American flag and enjoying the same powers
> they had obtained under the Spanish monarchy.[24]

Under "new management," it was business as usual for the
colony's local caretakers.

Nonetheless, the leadership of the incipient working-class
movement, heartened by the knowledge that Puerto Rico had
become the colony of a republic rather than of a monarchy,
attempted to regroup forces and take advantage of whatever
liberties might be afforded them. "*Porvenir Social*," the new
publication of Iglesias and his cohorts, came out on October 23,
1898, less than a week after the Spanish flag had been lowered in
San Juan. That same week, the *Federación Regional de los
Trabajadores de Puerto Rico* was formally established and the
founders swore to continue struggling "until the complete

emancipation of the proletariat is achieved.''[25]

The new federation's first resolution called for sending a delegation to Washington to lobby with the federal government and to confer with the representatives of the Socialist Labor Party and with the American Federation of Labor. In the meantime, before the delegation could find the means to make the journey, several labor conflicts took place, including a bitterly contested strike of printers, and before the year was out, in November 1898, Iglesias was again warned by the local authorities, this time in the person of Undersecretary José de Diego, to remember that San Juan was not Barcelona and that the Puerto Rican workers would need to be educated before being subverted by socialist and revolutionary doctrines.[26] The warning was ignored and Iglesias and Ramón Romero Rosa were subsequently jailed, only to be ordered released by the U.S. military commander on grounds of the right to free speech.

The military government called for new elections and by mid-1899 the newly revived *Federación Regional*, after having carried out an impressive conmemoration of May Day, was being fought over in a contest between those workers who favored one or the other of the political parties and those who favored a nonpartisan position. The adherents of the newly formed Republican Party managed to seize contgrol of the *Federación Regional* and Iglesias and several of his followers immediately split off and founded the *Federación Libre de los Trabajadores de Puerto Rico* (Free Federation of Labor) (FLT), which had representation of unions of construction workers, carpenters, painters, seamen and longshoremen, construction helpers, iron workers, food and drink workers, printers, tobacco workers, and general workers. The same group simultaneously founded the Socialist Party of Puerto Rico and subsequently received a charter from the Socialist Labor Party of Daniel DeLeon in the United States, with whom Iglesias and his cohorts had been corresponding for some months.

Early in 1900 the Socialist Party of Puerto Rico sent delegates Eduardo Conde and Santiago Iglesias to New York where they were hosted by Julius Gerber, Henry Slobodin and Morris Hillquit of the anti-De Leon faction of the socialist movement in the United States. One of the principal issues that divided Socialists at the time was whether the socialist movement should cooperate with or combat the American Federation of Labor. The delegation from

Puerto Rico chose to make common cause with the faction opposing dual unionism, that is, to cooperate with the established labor movement.

On May 1, 1900, the military occupation ended. President McKinley sent the first American colonial governor to Puerto Rico and the FLT, for the second year, conmemorated the martyrs of Chicago's Haymarket Massacre, an indication of the labor federation's radical inclinations. By mid-year, precipitated by the calamitous decline in real wages caused by the arbitrary imposition of devaluated currency and complicated by the entrepreneurially fomented divisions in the labor movement, the island's labor relations were in a state of chaos, which culminated in a series of work stoppages and the calling of a general strike in July 1900. By August, Iglesias and most of the leaders of the unions affiliated with the FLT were back in jail. As already noted, living and working conditions had deteriorated rapidly, going from bad to worse. The record of that year is one of strikes called and strikes broken, of workers being incited to attack other workers, of transitional chaos as colonial dominance was haphazardly shifted.

Iglesias, physically spent as well as emotionally despondent over the American dream-turned-nightmare, was encouraged to leave the island by functionaries of the Carpenters' Union in the United States. A colonial official counseled Iglesias to leave Puerto Rico "for ten years," thereby supposedly allowing time for the new educational system to influence the population so that the concept of self-help would become understandable to the working class.[27] In September 1900, in what was eventually to become a pattern and a strategy for frustrated colonials, Iglesias took advantage of the metropolitan "escape valve" and journeyed to the mainland to seek solutions for the problems of Puerto Rico.

Regaining health and spirit in short order, Iglesias found employment as a carpenter in New York City and, in late 1900, joined the Brotherhood of Carpenters and Joiners, which was then one of the bulwarks of the AFL. He simultaneously enrolled in the Cooper Union, a working-class night school where Gompers had earlier studied, and became active in socialist and labor circles. This was a time when a faction of the Socialist Party in the United States was seeking accommodation with the craft unionists.[28] Iglesias apparently became persuaded that the path to salvation for the working class in Puerto Rico would be through soft-pedaling radicalism and gaining the support of the AFL, which had initially taken an anti-imperialist stand following the American occupation of the island.

The AFL, by the turn of the century, had already become the dominant labor organization in the United States. The Knights of Labor had faded from the scene a decade earlier (in the aftermath of the Haymarket Massacre of 1886 and other setbacks), and the Industrial Workers of the World would not gain prominence and strength until nearly a decade later.

The AFL had been in existence for only fourteen years at the turn of the century, but had already demonstrated its staying power by surviving a depression, something no previous national labor organization in the United States had been able to do. The AFL, under the cautious (or opportunistic) leadership of Samuel Gompers, had not only survived the depression and industrial crises of 1893-97, which preceded the Spanish-American War, but showed a steady growth in membership and strength at a time when rival labor groups, undercut by armies of unemployed workers, were being driven out of existence by formidable employer assaults.

The historic and bloody confrontation with Carnegie Steel at Homestead, Pennsylvania, in 1892 had ended with the union so thoroughly smashed that forty years would pass before concerted action by steelworkers could be successfully undertaken. The Pullman strike of 1894, which had taken on revolutionary dimensions, eventually involving tens of thousands of railroad workers and twenty railway lines and bringing about pitched battles with federal troops, ended with the destruction, from which it was never to rise again, of Eugene Debs's American Railway Union. The coal miners' organizational efforts had been so severely thwarted during the 1870s and thereafter that it was not until the early 1900s that the United Mine Workers were able to achieve anything approaching a standoff with the nation's coal operators. During the "gay nineties," the working-class movements in all of the nation's principal industries had been systematically crushed.

Through all this, the AFL survived and even grew. The success of the skilled workmen who founded the AFL was based on a formula that came to be known, variously, as "business unionism," because of the conduct of union affairs on the model of the capitalist firms with whom the union officials dealt; as "bread and butter unionism," because of the policy of limiting demands to readily achievable, short-run economic gains for organized workers; and as "pure and simple unionism," because of the workmen's policy of not questioning the political, social, or economic system itself but instead seeking job-related gains for organized workers within the system. Indeed, Gompers, who made much of the lessons he claimed to have learned as a young Marxist participant in the social upheaval of the 1870s that had been ruthlessly crushed by the authorities, went much further than simply not questioning the established order. He continually chided radicals as being hopelessly utopian while himself making common cause, in such organizations as the employer-dominated National Civic Federation, with the nation's leading industrial and governmental figures.

The AFL also followed a strategy of concentrating their efforts and resources on the organizing of craftsmen whose strikes were effective to the degree that their difficult-to-replace skills made them impervious to labor-market pressures. In addition, the AFL guaranteed the autonomy and exclusive jurisdiction of national unions in each trade or craft, avoided ideological commitments or controversies, and eschewed partisan politics (following instead a policy of punishing the enemies and rewarding the friends of organized labor in either political party). The AFL also "voluntaristically" resisted governmental regulation of employment relations (opposing such measures as unemployment compensation, for example) in labor's version of capital's policy of laissez-faire. An additional element of AFL policy, which probably accounted in large measure for the AFL's interest in Puerto Rico, involved opposition to immigration laws that could have the effect of swelling competition for jobs in the United States.

Iglesias was introduced to Gompers in New York in late 1900, the two former radicals-turned-trade-unionists hit it off immediately.[29] Iglesias penned a formal request for aid, in representation of Puerto Rico's fledgling Free Federation of Labor, which a Socialist friend in New York translated and forwarded to Gompers. The AFL convention acted favorably on the request in December of 1900, urging affiliated unions to disseminate information in Spanish among workers in Puerto Rico and authorizing an expenditure of three thousand dollars.

Iglesias apparently went on the AFL payroll in early 1901 and spent most of the year learning English, translating AFL documents into Spanish, and writing articles urging affiliation with the AFL.[30]

In October 1901, after having taken him to the White House to meet the hero of San Juan Hill, President Theodore Roosevelt, Gompers handed Iglesias the AFL's charter for the Free Federation, the AFL's Executive Council's appointment of Iglesias as its "General Organizer for Puerto Rico and Cuba," and dispatched him to the island with a letter to the new civil colonial authorities. A new chapter in the struggle of organized labor in Puerto Rico was about to begin.

3

Labor during the Early U.S. Colonial Period

The U.S military government ended in early 1900 with the adoption by Congress of an organic act[1] stipulating a civil administration for the island possession, the spirit of which was

> not to give those people a complete local self-government, but a government republican in form, and to confer upon them the right to as much participation in that government as we thought, in view of the testimony submitted to us, it was safe to give them.[2]

The Foraker Act, as this law is referred to, provided that the president would appoint the governor, the members of an executive council, and the justices of the insular Supreme Court. The Puerto Rican subjects would elect a resident commissioner, who would have voice but no vote in the U.S. House of Representatives, and the members of an insular House of Delegates—the legislation of which body could be vetoed by either the governor or the U.S. Congress.

Iglesias's return to Puerto Rico as the AFL's agent coincided with the reinplacement of the commercially naive (relatively speaking) military governors by civil, colonial administrators from the United States, who were more in tune with "the realities of development." The recognition of these "realities," then as now, meant the imposition of austerity and restrictions for the working class and the encouragement of affluence and opportunities for the entrepreneurial class in the implementation of what was seen as the optimum economic policy for capital formation, industrial growth, and the creation of employment.

Politically, it was a frustratingly ambivalent period for labor in the sense that the insular society's mores were rapidly becoming American without ceasing to be fundamentally Hispanic. The clearest and most crucially important example of this superimposed, transitional confusion is found in that no sooner had Iglesias again set foot on the island in late 1901 than he was arrested on an old charge arising out of participation in a dock and construction workers' strike during the preceding period of military occupation. Convicted by local magistrates of having "conspired to raise wages" (with the lone American judge dissenting) he and Eduardo Conde, Juan Guerra, Sandalio Sánchez, Teodoro Rivera, Adolfo Cora, Luis Ventezal, and Román Fuentes were sentenced to several years' imprisonment. The only recently founded *Federación Libre de los Trabajadores* (FLT) was also decreed dissolved, all in accordance with Spanish criminal conspiracy codes that no one in the new regime had got around to repealing or replacing[3] (and that were no longer applicable even in Spain!).

Iglesias and his cohorts spent several days in jail before Gompers could complete arrangements for bail. The threat of long prison terms was present for nearly six months while the appeals were processed. The intent of the local government, then in control of the insular Republic Party under the uneasy tutelage of the colonial overseers, was to nip Iglesias's organizational campaign in the bud and put the FLT out of business, thereby clearing the way for the rival *Federación Regional*, which Iglesias and his followers had earlier founded and then abandoned when it became dominated by the Republic Party.

Paradoxically, under Gompers's astute orchestration, the intended persecution backfired, quickly becoming a cause célebre in both Puerto Rico and the United States as support for acquittal of the labor organizers and for repeal of the Spanish conspiracy codes gained in momentum. An editorial crusade ensued, protest rallies were organized, and labor groups from far and wide pledged support. The relatively unknown Iglesias became a center of attraction and his "most eminently American mission" of uniting Puerto

Rican workers under the banner of the AFL was widely publicized. The revitalized supporters of the until then virtually defunct FLT ignored the decree to dissolve, instead holding a mass meeting on December 6, 1901, and voting to affiliate with the AFL.[4]

In early 1902 Theodore Roosevelt's appointee as colonial governor, William H. Hunt, addressed the insular legislature and, referring directly to the cases under appeal, explained that

> there is no room for lawlessness in Porto Rico, but the right to organize to secure better wages by peaceable measures is perfectly lawful and consistent with good government. Ambition to better one's condition is intensely American and oftentimes only gratified through organized effort; and where the purpose of an organization is merely to increase the profit of labor or dignify its worth through peaceful ways, a law which is susceptible of a construction forbidding the execution of such purpose is unworthy of an American government and should be abrogated.[5]

Governor Hunt followed this admonition with a note to the Supreme Court of Puerto Rico, when the cases were heard on appeal in April 1902, in which he pointed out that the convictions had been a violation of the personal liberty of those involved and contrary to the fundamental right of free assembly. The Supreme Court justices, although probably very dubious about such notions, nonetheless reluctantly agreed and overturned the sentences of the lower court.

Revealingly, a crucial role in this precedent-setting episode was played by the *San Juan News*, a Puerto Rican daily that was published in parallel columns of English and Spanish and that had an important mission at the time of helping Puerto Rican elites to understand metropolitan mores (much as the *San Juan Star* currently does). The city editor of the *News*, Sidney S. McKee, acted, in fact, as Gompers's agent throughout the incident. McKee served as the conduit for the AFL's funds deposited as bail, kept Gompers informed, publicized the case, and editorially denounced the persecution, always carefully emphasizing that Iglesias was a reformed radical who counseled "order instead of disorder." McKee was eventually paid one hundred dollars by the AFL for his invaluable services, a relatively substantial sum at the time.[6]

There can be little doubt that Iglesias and his codefendants would have been imprisoned and their organizing efforts thwarted had it not been for the combined advocacy of the AFL in the United States (Gompers personally petitioned President Roosevelt) and the *San Juan News* in Puerto Rico (other, Spanish-language, more traditional, periodicals in Puerto Rico attempted to sway public opinion against Iglesias).

The incident is illustrative of the central role that North American interests have played in Puerto Rico in general and in labor relations in Puerto Rico in particular. "Many of the country's labor issues are studied and decided in Washington," is the straightforward comment of Félix Mejías, author of one of the best treastises on labor in Puerto Rico.[7] A system of appeals to mainland interests by conflicting groups within the colony has played a key role in labor relations over the years, beginning even before the U.S occupation.[8]

In the waning days of the Spanish Empire in the Americas, it had become clear to opportunists in Puerto Rico that U.S. destiny manifested an inevitably pervasive presence in the entire hemisphere and that North American support and cooperation would be essential for the advancement of any particular colonial interest group.

Spanish colonial policy had neither permitted democratic development nor encouraged economic growth, and the demise of that regime was therefore largely unlamented in Puerto Rico—for difference reasons—by either the incipient industrial proletariat or the eager-to-emerge entrepreneurial class. The switch in sovereignty kindled very different hopes within these groups, who were about to see their semifeudal, paternalistic relationship of subsistence and dependency transformed into one of rationalized, industrial relations of a calculating sort.

The conflicting classes began to see in the sometimes pluralistic, sometimes unitary Colossus of the North the potential champion of their respective aspirations. The buddingly expansive Puerto Rican entrepreneurs were suspicious and fearful of the extension and amplication of civil liberties, but were avidly interested in the U.S market and consequent commercial opportunities. The representatives of the new wage-earning class, who were becoming conscious of the terrible implications of a laissez-faire economy for the sellers of surplus labor, were principally interested in the U.S. system as constituting an erratic but occasionally serviceable court of appeals for civil injustice, and as a means of restricting the freedom of enterprise in exploiting labor.

Compare, for example, the statement made by Luis Muñoz Rivera, the leading Puerto Rican politician of the time, to U.S Commissioner Henry Carroll in 1898 that "it would be extremely dangerous to hand over our future to the masses, who are entirely without civic education and who might be wrongly directed by the audacity of the agitators who would make them their tools," with the statement of Iglesias in reference to the same period: "It was from these times on that there began to be organized a colonial factory of cheap laborers, sick and servile in their homeland, combating at the same time the democratic ideas represented by the United States."[9]

Both competing, dependent groups have consistently been able to find their collaborators in the metropolis—the colonial entrepreneurs with the American financiers and the colonial labor leaders with the mainland socialists, radicals, and liberals of one degree and persuasion or another. Both groups, through their allies, attempted (and continue to attempt) to influence the center of power in Washington. (Significantly, both Muñoz Rivera and Iglesias Pantín ended their respective careers far from home, but close to the center of power, both having been elected to the office of Puerto Rican Resident Commissioner in the U.S. Congress.)

The inadequacy of this competitive appeals system for Puerto Rican labor grew out of the disproportionate influence of their opponents the industrialists, coupled with the initial, relative impotence of colonial labor's friend at court. Organized labor in the United States, even though the AFL won the opening round in the Igelsias criminal conspiracy case, was unable even to defend itself adquately until thirty years later (when the scare of the depression of the 1930s led to the concession of legal recognition for labor and the statutory obligation to bargain in good faith), let alone provide significant protection for their colonial protége.

To cite only one manifestation of this imbalance, the U.S Congress in 1900 had provided that no single entity could control more than five hundred acres of land in Puerto Rico.[10] Notwithstanding, by 1910 U.S interests had invested more than ten million dollars in the acquisition of vast holdings for the exploitation of sugar. The law simply remained unenforced despite protests. In an example of the interchangeability of the representatives of capital and government, the secretary of the first civil colonial government in Puerto Rico, Charles Hartzell, resigned his governmental post to become counselor for the sugar corporations. In 1905 Hartzell appeared before the court to request (and obtain) the first injunction in a labor dispute in Puerto Rico (in the sugar workers' strike during the 1905-6 harvest).[11]

An additional shortcoming of this "fraternal" (big brother-little brother) relationship for workers in Puerto Rico was that mainland and Puerto Rican labor interests coincided only as long as protection of labor in the colony posed no threat to labor standards in the States, and as long as overriding national interests—as perceived by the AFL—were not in conflict with the interests of their colonial protectorate.

Angel G. Quintero Rivera has hypothesized that the AFL's support for Puerto Rican labor can be best explained as part of American labor's very understandable policy—understandable from the standpoint of what happens to domestic labor standards when supplies of labor are unlimited—of restrictions on immigration. AFL assistance for their brothers in Puerto Rico was predicated, it is hypothesized, on the hope of raising standards sufficiently in Puerto Rico so as to stem migration from the mainland (Puerto Ricans, it is important to understand, are migrants, not immigrants, and cannot be excluded).[12] An exclusionist policy of this sort, of course, inevitably has racial implications, an aspect of AFL policy that has repeatedly engendered difficulties with Puerto Rican labor.[13]

The currently close identification of the AFL-CIO with the foreign policy position of the U.S. government has venerable origins. The foreign-labor protégés of U.S labor everywhere soon learn that continued subsidization is contingent on their support for U.S foreign policy goals within their own countries. Gompers, for example, in 1904 had little difficulty in persuading Iglesias and his followers not to oppose the establishment of a U.S naval base on the island.[14]

This tradition, growing out of the awareness of the limitations of genuine insular autonomy, has grown over the years and developed into a ritual. Antonio J. González has provided a fascinating

account of one of the representations of this rite in his description
of the pressures and counterpressures on the National Maritime
Board in 1921 that eventually converted a 40 percent pay cut into a
10 percent increase for Puerto Rican dock workers. The shipping
companies and the dock workers' union engaged in virtually no
face-to-face negotiations, instead separately lobbying before the
authorities in Washington.[15] The perennial lobbying by labor and
management in Washington in opposition to and in support of the
extension of minimum-wage legislation to Puerto Rico provides the
clearest, modern example.

The strings were pulled from the mainland, but the action
occurred and the repercussions were felt on the island. Iglesias had
initiated the FLT's organizing campaign early in 1901, long before
his conviction was overturned, and the expansion of organized
labor coincided with the explosive industrialization of sugar
production. Between 1896 and 1928 the percentage of land devoted
to sugar cane increased 263 percent while that devoted to food
crops *decreased* by 31 percent.[16]

American industrial enterprise succeeded in accelerating
commerical production, but actively inhibited the modernization of
other aspects of the insular society not directly or indirectly
connected with the exploitation of agribusiness. Production of
sugar rose to 284,000 tons by 1910 (an increase of 473 percent over
the last year of preinvasion production) and to 606,000 tons by
1928, with similar organization and growth of tobacco production.
Between 1901 and 1910, for example, the sugar corporations built
more than a thousand miles of railroad in a country only ninety-
five miles long and thirty-five miles wide.[17]

The labor force, which the Spanish colonial government had
attempted to force into abandoning subsistence agriculture in favor
of plantation employment through a series of coercive measures,[18]
was progressively absorbed into commercial agriculture after 1898.
See Table 2 which indicates that betwen 1910 and 1940,
employment in sugar, tobacco, and coffee increased by 30 percent
while employment in "other farming" decreased by 45 percent.
These statistics are approximate at best in a situation where salaried
employment in a given crop rarely lasted more than a few months
and where laborers were shunted back and forth between paid
labor, subsistence farming, and destitution.

TABLE 2

EMPLOYMENT BY INDUSTRIES, SELECTED YEARS,
PUERTO RICO, 1910-1940
(in thousands)

Industry Group	1910	1920	1940
Sugar cane	84	85	124
Tobacco	7	30	18
Coffee	38	48	26
Other farms	111	81	61
Manufacturing and handicraft	45	62	101
Trade and transport	35	35	74
Construction	8	9	16
Services (including government)	61	49	85
All other	4	7	7

SOURCE: Harvey S. Perloff, *Puerto Rico's Economic Future*, (Chicago, Ill.: The University of Chicago Press, 1950), p. 64.

Gordon K. Lewis, the best chronicler and commentator of this crucial, formative period, sums up the transition as "the replacement of a rudimentary rural capitalism by an industrial, high-finance capitalism. The characteristic social type of the former economy—the individual and independent hacendado working his family farm—gave way to the managerial hierarchy of the corporate sugar factory."[19] "Under America as under Spain," Lewis goes on, "Puerto Ricans were goverened by an alliance of business corporations, high officials, and local professional politicians; and the burden was perhaps made even more intolerable because of the self-righteous attitude that the American government and people brought with it."[20]

The rationale, then as now, for this massive capital investment was alleged not to be the extraction of fabulous profits, but instead the "development" of Puerto Rico, presumably implying by this the improvement of the living standards of the inhabitants of the island. This was not immediately the case. Seven years after the landing of troops, the U.S. government commissioned Walter Weyl to perform a study of labor conditions in the new colony. He found that the early optimism of the Puerto Ricans about the benevolence of their invaders had been excessive:

> Such a policy of improving the conditions of the Porto Rican population, or what is almost the same thing, of the great mass of Porto Rican laborers, will necessarily run counter to the interests of many individuals—Spanish and American— financially interested in the island. Many of the absentee owners consider the island and its population as equally fit for the crassest exploitation.

Weyl further observed that "prosperity" had increased, but that "to what extent, however, this improvement has filtered down to the laboring population is somewhat problematical."[21]

"Problematical" it was, but for the labor force, not for the investors. In Eric Williams's succinct appraisal of the sugar industry of the West Indies, "tremendous wealth was produced from an unstable economy based on a single crop, which combined the vices of feudalism and capitalism with the virtues of neither."[22] Within a matter of months, thousands of rural laborers had been converted into an industrial proletariat subject to "the crassest exploitation." Four or five years were to pass, however, before the labor movement of Puerto Rico could gird itself for the inevitable confrontation with the capitalists from the mainland.

Iglesias and his fellow organizers first attempted to gain legal protection for labor, an effort they soon recognized to be sterile. "Development" was the watchword, and governmental interference in the labor-management relationship was seen as an intolerable hindrance in the drive for production. They turned instead to the organization of the unorganized, with or without legal sanction. The unorganized at the time constituted virtually the entire labor force, with the exception of handfuls of skilled artisans in the few principal towns. These "aristocrats" of the working class formed the nucleus and turned to the task with missionary zeal.

The term *aristocracy* in reference to the urban artisans is used relative to the conditions of the unskilled, rural workers. An indication of the comparatively superior position of the artisans of San Juan, for example, can be gathered from the report of Henry K. Carroll who, during the military occupation, observed that the artisans were literate and "neatly dressed," while the rural workers were "usually illiterate" and meagerly dressed. "The artisans are better educated, have better food, and wear better clothes." Commissioner Carroll, for example, took testimony in 1898 from numerous spokesmen for the urban handicraftsmen, but was apparently able to find only a school teacher to speak in behalf of the farm workers.[23]

In retrospect, although it was a time of considerable educational and organizational activity of labor, those first four or five years at the turn of the century, when the sugar corporations were investing millions of dollars in preparation for massive extractive operations, can be seen as a period of relative calm before the storm of industrial conflict that was to descend on Puerto Rico in the decades preceding and following World War I.

It was also a period in which Iglesias, backed by an extraordinarily selfless group of laborites, of whom Eduardo Conde was one of the most active, consolidated his position as insular labor's principal spokesman.[24] At the same time his own rudimentary ideas of anarcho-syndicalism—if not those of all of his colleagues—were being rapidly replaced by Gompers's voluntaristic, trade-union philosophy. Iglesias's ideological conversion included his individually exchanging Spanish for U.S. citizenship in 1900, many years before the mass of Puerto Ricans became citizens en masse legislatively, a status the uniqueness of which provided him with advantages vis-à-vis the metropolitan power much as had been the case previously with the Spanish authorities.

The relationship was reciprocal. The AFL provided financial support in addition to Iglesias's salary and quantities of organizing materials in Spanish. An allocation of three thousand dollars was made by the AFL Convention of 1900, another five thousand dollars was provided to support a strike in 1905-6, and another twenty thousand dollars in 1908-9.[25]

Samuel Gompers and Santiago Iglesias in 1904. *Courtesy of the Free Federation of Labor of Puerto Rico.*

Gompers paid a visit to the island in 1904, and by that time Iglesias was able both to act as his mentor's interpreter and to address the AFL Convention in English for the first time. By 1907 May Day with its revolutionary connotations was no longer observed by the labor movement, having been officially replaced by "Labor Day," in September, in accordance with United States custom.[26]

4
The Metamorphosis of Labor's Ideology and Strategy

Early organizers of labor in Puerto Rico emerged militantly into the new industrial order as radicals ideologically dedicated to the total transformation of that order.[1] The labor movement's resources and the surrounding circumstances were such, however, that simple self-survival in the face of the highly efficient onslaught of the entrepreneurial class became sufficiently engrossing, and plans for the elimination of that class began to be compromised and postponed. Labor was only briefly on the offensive, soon adopting a defensive, responsive role.

A principal environmental factor that served to temporize radical posture was the nature of labor's alliances. The first international contacts of Puerto Rican labor under American rule had been with the Socialist Party of Daniel De Leon. The neophyte radicals of Puerto Rico had achieved affiliation via correspondence in 1899 as part of their attempt to found simultaneously a labor federation and a labor party with international, working-class orientation on the Marxist model. Iglesias and Eduardo Conde in early 1900 attended the convention of the Socialist Party in the United States with Morris Hillquit acting as their interpreter.[2] As we have seen, however, the financial and lobbying support came from the AFL, an organization that a contemporary Puerto Rican legislator aptly described as "one of the most progressive movements in the world, although conservative,"[3] meaning that the AFL was progressive in economic, reformist terms, but conservative ideologically.

The switch in sovereigny left unchanged the insular balance of power between capital and labor. The island's entrepreneurial and professional classes managed to remain in firm control of local government, which, it turned out, could administer employment relations with a considerable degree of freedom from the often oblivious colonial overseers. Consequently, one aspect of Puerto Rican labor's gradual move from a radical stance to a more pragmatic position was a growing opposition to independence for Puerto Rico, the most "extreme" of the status alternatives. This opposition, was in part, based on the perception that the severance of surveillance from Washington would leave working people at the total mercy of the island's employing class.

General organizer Iglesias, as Puerto Rico's delegate to the AFL's twenty-sixth convention, had been obliged to present an FLT resolution calling for self-government for the island, but in 1907, in his subsequent report to the FLT on his attendance at the AFL convention, he specifically developed the contrary philosophy of metropolitan dependency that ultimately prevailed. Iglesias summed up his opposition of independence by posing the following questions:

> What practical benefits will the workers obtain from putting their energies and their influence to the test in order to deposit in the hands of the elites of Puerto Rico the absolute and un-hindered direction of the political, administrative and judicial matters of Puerto Rico? What has been the behavior which these persons have generally demonstrated with the working classes? . . . . Will it be wise for the Free Federation and affiliated labor organizations to carry out a campaign of popular agitation in the United States . . . in order to obtain a larger measure of "self-government" for Puerto Rico while our organizations are combatted, our protective labor laws trampled on; when venal and corrupt Puerto Rican judges commit terrible and irreparable injustices against our unfortunate striking farmworkers, and all this is done with the approval and sanction of the people of Puerto Rico who now possess a measure of "self-government" and with the approval of the capitalists who inescapably would come to have in their hands greater power to continue with their work of popular repression?[4]

Considerable opposition to this strategy of dependency existed within the Puerto Rican labor movement during the formative years, but the anti-independence elements clearly prevailed. The dissidence was never entirely eliminated and this lack of unanimity on the status question, as we shall see, in part led to the ultimate disintegration of the FLT.[5]

Affiliation of the FLT with the AFL, and the pervasive presence of AFL organizer Iglesias as the only full-time, paid union representative on the island for many years during the critical, formative period, contributed heavily to changing Puerto Rican labor from radical to reformist. Gompers, for example, specifically assured Theodore Roosevelt, when he took the new Caribbean organizer on a courtesy call to the White House in 1901, that Iglesias would devote himself wholly to trade-union activities, not to fomenting revolution.[6] In 1902 Iglesias assured the American colonial governor in Puerto Rico that his mission was the *"americanización obrera"* in accordance with instructions from the AFL.[7]

It should be emphasized, however, that the abandonment of revolutionary goals was by no means simply the result of expedience or opportunism, but rather also resulted from a rational calculation of the relative feasibility of the alternatives of revolution or reform, given the objective situation prevailing at the time, including especially the overwhelming capacity of the ruling regime for repression. Iglesias and colleagues were repeatedly jailed, assaulted, and otherwise harassed, including even attempted assassination. Despite their best efforts, the accomplishments for labor were essentially negative until, on the verge of total annihilation, they were forced to learn the lessons of what Charles Anderson has termed the "prudence model of politics." In Anderson's model, applicants for inclusion in the decision-making establishment of a given society are permitted entry into the power structure only on condition that the status of prior members not be fundamentally threatened.[8] In other words, the representatives of the working class in Puerto Rico, finding themselves without effective bargaining power, were faced with what they judged to be the choice between playing the game according to the rules of the existing oligarchy or not playing at all. They decided to play by the establishment's rules.

Given the ideological shift from revolutionary confrontation to reformist cooperation, it would seem to follow that the operational strategy subsequently adopted by the Puerto Rican labor movement would have emphasized economic rather than political action. The reverse was true, however, and the theory of labor movements developed by Adolf Sturmthal is helpful in understanding the reasons. Sturmthal explains that in those situations in which a labor movement is based on "unskilled working class groups, the emphasis on political action is rational, just as the use of market power is perfectly reasonable for an organization limited to scarce higher skill groups."[9]

The leaders of the labor movement in Puerto Rico, seeing the working class at a terrible disadvantage in an economic struggle because of the unlimited supply of unskilled, easily replaceable labor, became persuaded that the best chance for social reform was through use of the power of numbers politically. The hope was that of obtaining measures protective of minimal labor standards through legal enactment rather than through either confrontational syndicalism or collaborationist collective bargaining.

The Puerto Rican labor movement had almost from its inception adopted a policy of backing candidates from its own ranks for the insular legislature, a phenomenon—given the affiliation with the AFL and the intimate relationship with Gompers—that has long perplexed observers at a loss to understand the AFL's tolerance for this apparent deviation from its nonpartisan, seemingly apolitical norms. Ramón Lebrón Rodríguez, one-time Assistant Secretary of the Puerto Rican Bureau of Labor, summed up the question as well as anyone.

> The American Federation of Labor is of purely economic character and its politics are non-partisan. . . .The American Federation of Labor. . .has declared itself to be absolutely opposed to the Socialist Party. . . .Therefore, those who observe closely the political movement in Puerto Rico and who understand that Puerto Rico's Socialist Party is intimately linked with the Free Federation of Labor while in the United States the organizations denominated as Federation of Labor and Socialist Party are antagonists, are at a loss to explain this dual tendency.[10]

The explanation of this apparent contradiction, as William Knowles has pointed out, is that the economic situation in Puerto Rico rendered collective bargaining (on the AFL skilled-worker model) unfeasible. The labor organizations, unable to prevent their strikes from being broken because of the availability of hordes of unemployed workers, and legally unprotected by a mandate requiring employers to recognize them and bargain directly in good faith, attempted to deal with their employers indirectly via the government.[11]

Iglesias, in his report to the Sixth Congress of the FLT in 1906, enunciated the policy of pressuring for legally enacted, rather than negotiated, protection when he explained that

> for ten years we workers have requested from the Legislature that which the body cannot grant, and that which cannot be obtained in any other way, given the conditions of the laboring masses of Puerto Rico.[12]

Gompers, unlike the current foreign-policy makers of the AFL-CIO with their single-minded insistence on apolitical unionism for their foreign protégés (thereby ignoring even their own domestic experience), seems to have understood the impossibility of controlling job markets in the labor surplus environment of the early stages of agricultural industrialization in Puerto Rico. William Knowles, who interviewed the leaders of the remnants of the original FLT, some of whom have been active in the labor movement since the 1920s, has written that his sources claim that "Gompers himself defended the union-party alliance in Puerto Rico and argue that pure and simple unionism was impossible under the circumstances."[13]

Moreover, the Puerto Rican labor movement's practice of sponsoring candidates from its own ranks was not a deviation from the AFL strategy of rewarding its political friends and punishing its enemies in the sense that in Puerto Rico the working class had plenty of enemies and virtually no rewardable friends in either of the contending parties.[14] The elitist political parties differed to a degree in the area of allowable civil liberties and on the relationship with the United States, but were virtually unanimous in opposing industrial democracy and brooked no indiscipline internally.

Bolívar Pagán, in his history of political parties in Puerto Rico, explains that the leaders of the AFL understood that Puerto Rico's political situation, where party discipline was always more strict than in the United States in determining the line of conduct of the elected legislators, and, for all practical purposes, left the labor movement [in Puerto Rico], affiliated with the American Federation of Labor, with a free hand to work out its own local arrangements for achieving legislation which would improve the working and living conditions of the workers. This explains those outbursts of political activity which we have related [on the part of the labor movement].[15]

Pagán also explains that until about 1906 the Puerto Rican labor movement made an effort to emulate the AFL strategy of emphasis on collective bargaining and avoidance of identification with a particular political party. According to Pagán, the working-class representatives found themselves rebuffed by both parties and simultaneously accused by both of tacitly collaborating with the opposition. It was therefore decided that the labor movement had no alternative but to form their own electoral effort and go it alone.[16]

Robert W. Anderson offers a similar explanation:

This apparent contradiction of Gomper's (*sic*) ideas was probably just a manifestion (*sic*) of the traditionally partisan nature of Puerto Rican political life, reinforced in this particular instance by the undeniably powerful figure of Iglesias.[17]

An additional explanation of the AFL's tolerance for its Puerto Rican affiliate's partisan political stance can be deduced from Gompers's apparent understanding of the distinction between political action by labor in pursuit of ideological *social* goals (the radical transformation of the system, which Gompers considered utopian), and political action by labor in pursuit of reformist, nonideological, *labor* goals (the evolutionary reform of the system, which Gompers considered practical).

This is a distinction that many observers of labor movements have not grasped, as is evidenced by simplistic distinctions of collective bargaining versus political action, failing to understand that *both* collective bargaining *and* political action are utilized in pursuit of the goals of a given labor movement. The meaningful distinction is between those labor movements with the goal of transformation of society and those labor movements with the goal of achieving more for wage earners within the society.

Evidence in support of this hypothesis is discernible from Gompers's unswerving rigidity in opposing "political," i.e., ideological, unionism in other Latin American labor movements within the Pan-American Federation of Labor (where the AFL had considerably less influence), and his permissiveness of non-ideological "political," i.e. union pressure for legal enactment, in Puerto Rico (where the AFL had considerably more control).

This special consideration for the special case of Puerto Rican labor within the American house of labor existed from the beginning of the affiliation and continues to the present although with decreasing tolerance. The essence of the relationship has been that of flexible ambiguity: in certain aspects the Puerto Rican affiliation with the AFL then and the AFL-CIO today is like that of any other "state" federation of labor while in other aspects it is like that of an independent republic. Rafael Alonso Torres, who for many years was Secretary General of the FLT, has explained that despite the fact that the Puerto Rican central labor body was affiliated with the AFL, the national labor center of the United States, that the Puerto Rican affiliate always "appeared on its own before international bodies..."[18]For example, although the FLT was affiliated with the AFL, both the AFL *and* the FLT were affiliated with the Pan-American Federation of Labor,[19] and, although the *Federación de Trabajo de Puerto Rico* (FTPR) is currently considered a "state" federation of the AFL-CIO, both the Puerto Rican affiliate *and* the AFL-CIO are affiliated with the *Organización Regional Interamericana de Trabajadores* (ORIT), the Western Hemispheric regional organization of the International Confederation of Free Trade Unions (ICFTU).

Most attempts to explain Puerto Rican labor's reformist philosophy are based on the premise that the original movement was not genuinely revolutionary, that no retreat to pragmatism was involved, inasmuch as, indeed, the Puerto Rican labor movement had been radical only rhetorically. Gordon Lewis, for example, describes the early ideology as "nothing much beyond an eloquent confusion of disparate and ill-digested ideas gathered in-discriminately from Marxism, Spanish syndicalism, and American labor of the Gompers's style,"[20] but he thereby makes no distinction between the original and modified ideological stances. William Knowles has maintained that the early Puerto Rican socialists were "never extreme" and merely accepted "democratic socialism as a general altruistic principle."[21]

Such interpretations, however, are perhaps based on revisions as gleaned from Iglesias's memoirs of the initial ideological positions of the labor movement in Puerto Rico. Writing thirty years after the fact, Iglesias recalled the affiliation of the Socialist Party of Puerto Rico with the Socialist Party of the United States and claimed that the founders had declared themselves "in favor of the international program of Karl Marx without sufficient knowledge or opportunity for analysis." Iglesias went on to allege that, for Puerto Rican workers of that time, socialism meant something vaguely similar to the emancipating doctrines of early Christianity.[22] Similar evidence of the confused impurity of early Puerto Rican radicalism is readily available. In 1902, for example, when insular politician Rosendo Matienzo Cintrón was seeking labor support for the newly formed Union Party, he explained that he was a "socialist" just as "Lincoln and Washington had been."[23]

This sort of naivete, however, dates from the period after accommodation with the established powers had begun and after Iglesias had found it politic to reinterpret history. Iglesias recalls, for example, having become aware, while still a youngster in Spain, of the "suicidal" tactics of the left, but this was clearly an autobiographical reconstruction. For one thing, the passages in which Iglesias recants his youthful, radical ideology[24] closely parallel the similar recollections of his mentor Gompers, who in his youth had also learned "the weakness of radical tactics."[25] Gompers's autobiography was published in 1925, four years before Iglesias's autobiography, *Luchas Emancipadoras*.

Whether or not Iglesias was confused about the nature of radical ideology, many of his contemporaries were not. Angel Quintero Rivera and Gervasio Rodríguez have delved into documents produced by labor activists long before the post-facto recollections of Iglesias and have demonstrated that a significant sector of Puerto Rican labor leadership had a reasonably clear understanding of the nature of capitalism and were unwavering in their reluctance to collaborate with the system. Quintero Rivera has succinctly described the two opposing ideologies that eventually emerged:

> On the one side were those who saw in the Socialist Party an instrument for the transformation of the social order. . .represented by the most radical sectors of the labor organizations; and, on the other side, those who saw this transformation as more distant and who limited themselves to opposing injustice or, basically, to improving the living conditions of working people. Among the latter predominated those who were most closely associated with the North American labor organizations and who were most directly connected to the process of appealing to the metropolitan powers in their struggles with the local bourgeoisie.[26]

It must also be pointed out that there is an important distinction between not understanding and not being able to implement radical ideology. Extremely heroic efforts were made, as we shall see in the next chapter, to carry out a class struggle. Although it is accurate to note that this confrontation eventually became class collaboration, it is both unfair and inaccurate to deny that the class nature of society was universally misunderstood or that the struggle was never attempted. A great deal took place before Iglesias and his fellow organizers threw in the towel. This is getting far ahead of our story, however. What took place next, indeed, was the most heroic chapter in the annals of organized labor's struggle with capitalism in Puerto Rico. To that brief but significant period we now turn our attention.

5
The Early Confrontations with the New Industrialists: 1898 to World War I

The period up to and including World War I was characterized by the expansion of the sugar and tobacco industries and consequent proletarianization of the agricultural labor force. FLT organizers made rapid progress in the urban centers, converting the existent guildlike associations into craft unions, founding trade unions where none had existed, and duly affiliating all with the AFL.[1]

The FLT was not the only labor central attempting to organize the labor force in Puerto Rico. A rival, less militant group, the *Federación Regional*, from which the FLT founders had split after alleging domination by the Republican Party, also existed. As mention earlier, Azel Ames carried out a study for the United States Department of Labor in 1901 in which he predicted that the "socialistic" FLT would "soon wither away" and that the "antisocialist" rival organization would not.[2] Contrary to his prediction, the *Federación Regional* soon disappeared from the scene while, nearly eighty years later, vestiges of the FLT still survive. In fairness to Ames, the price the FLT was ultimately to pay for survival was moderation of its original, socialist goals.

Ames, again in 1901, found "several *gremios*" in existence. These were workingmen's associations that were attempting to regulate wages and hours, procure work, and maintain sick and death benefits plus similar functions common to mutual aid societies everywhere at the outset of industrialization.[3] Skilled labor was in short supply then as later, and it became possible for craftsmen to engage in a rudimentary form of collective bargaining without altogether abandoning traditional mutual aid functions.

Most employed workers, however, were neither skilled nor in short supply. Neither were they concentrated in the minuscule urban centers, nor did there exist in the rural areas the organizational structures or guild traditions on which to build trade unions. Unemployment was estimated at about 18 percent from 1899 until 1910, 20 percent in 1920, and 30 percent in 1926, and it rose to 35 percent by the height of the depression in 1934.[4]

It was clearly not propitious ground for organizing. Walter Weyl, who made a study of labor in Puerto Rico at about this time, compared the FLT with the AFL and found them to be similarly structured, but with one important difference. The federation in the United States was a creation of its component unions and had been built from the ground up. In Puerto Rico the situation was reversed. The FLT (which in the beginning "federated" nothing) was first chartered, and then proceeded from the top down to organize affiliated unions.[5] The shakiness of this foundation proved significant in the coming years.

Nonetheless, in 1903, having by then organized many of the skilled workers on the urban fringes of the main, agricultural, labor force, the FLT formally resolved to organize the rural proletariat and sponsored a vigorous campaign of proselytization known as the "*Cruzada de la Ideal*." The organizers were extraordinarily successful in chartering "unions." One admirer of Iglesias claims that they organized sixty thousand agricultural workers in the first year of the campaign.[6] Furthermore, the workers were in such desperate straits that it was not difficult to generate support for strikes in the new agricultural industries, notably in tobacco where the traditional sheds or "*chinchales*," in which cigars had been handmade in semicooperative fashion for local markets, were being consolidated into cigar factories.[7] To charter organizing committees and agitate workers into sporadic protests were objectives that were relatively easier to attain than the more meaningful building of permanent bargaining units and achieving recognition and concessions from employers.

The first associations of industrialized agricultural workers were formed in the early 1900s—several were chartered during Gompers's first visit to the island in 1904[8]—and the first major strikes of sugar workers took place during the harvest season of

1905-6.[9] FLT organizers, in an editorial calling for the strike, included a passage before the stoppage had even begun, declaring: "So the strike may be lost? Well, so what?" The author, Eduardo Conde, went on to explain:

> If this beautiful movement should fail, if this strike should be lost, the farmworkers will gain experience, because if fear or other causes shall oblige them to be weak, in this occasion, they will know how to become strong in order to arrive at victory.[10]

The editorial was prophetic in that the strikes of that period were clearly not "won" by labor, since few concessions were obtained from employers, nor were contracts signed in the sugar industry (although some benefits were obtained by the more skilled tobacco workers), and no lasting organizations of sugar workers were established until decades later.

The record during the early years of labor organizing in the sugar industry is one of nearly annual conflict during the harvest seasons, because the leadership attempted to improve barely tolerable working conditions through concerted action. Their efforts were frustrated by an environment in which (l) a large proportion of the potential labor force was totally unemployed and eager for employment at almost any wage, despite the fact that thousands of nearly destitute agricultural laborers were transported by the shipload to Hawaii and to other plantation economies during this period; (2) the vast majority of the rural workers were only seasonally employed; (3) wages were so low as to preclude savings, payment of dues, or accumulation of a strike fund; (4) the employers were the landlords, commissary owners, and the sole source of credit; (5) protective labor legislation was not enforced; (6) the government was passing rapidly into the effective control of the agribusinesses; and (7) the craft union orientation of the FLT-AFL was not well adapted to an increasingly complex division of labor in the industrializing work force.

Joseph Marcus, a special agent of United States Employment Service at the time, described his personal observation of strikebreaking activities in violation of insular law. His report stated that "the employers have no difficulty in breaking strikes ...

the presence of thousands of unemployed...provides a ready supply of labor whenever a strike is declared, for if labor is not available immediately at hand an agent is usually sent to another district and men are brought in by the trainload."[11]

In 1910 the insular legislature promulgated a law providing police protection to haciendas and corporations whose employees were on strike, the police being housed and subsidized by the employers.[12] The period's industrial relations were characterized by shootings, beatings, jailings[13] and, finally, the gradual decline of concerted activity in agriculture as strike after strike was crushed and as the organizations, conceived in protest, failed to survive, the "dead season" of several months unemployment between each harvest. Carmelo Honore, Chief of the *Negociado del Trabajo* of Puerto Rico in the 1920s, looked back on this period and observed that

> thus far the farmworker, in order to try to achieve a wage increase, has followed no road other than the strike: when we examine the statistics we find that 98 percent of the protest movements have been resolved in favor of the employers.[14]

Excerpts from the Annual Reports of the governor of Puerto Rico for some of those pre-World War I years provide insights into the magnitude, tactics, and attitudes involved in these perennial struggles:

> As soon as the outside agitators began to take part in the strike and to preach violence and lawlessness as a means for securing higher wages and shorter hours of work, fires were started in the cane fields at different parts of the island and great damage was done to the properties of the owners.

> The government could not ignore the appeals for protection against such acts of lawlessness and disorder, and in the attempts made by the insular police to restore order and to prevent the wanton destruction of property clashes between police and the strikers occurred at Juncos, Vieques and Ponce, which unfortunately resulted in the killing of five or six strikers and the serious wounding of two policemen.[15]

[The strike's] purpose was to try to secure for the workers in the fields higher wages and shorter hours of labor as their fair share of the extraordinary prosperity of the sugar industry. The movement involved from first to last some 30,000 to 40,000 laborers.[16]

The FLT had unsuccessfully attempted to obtain an industrywide agreement with the Association of Sugar Producers in 1916, a year in which more than a hundred million dollars of sugar was exported, but it was finally obliged to settle individually with some of the producers. The contracts were signed only for the duration of the harvest in progress, were tied to the price of sugar, varied from sixty cents to a dollar for a day's labor, and were invariably ignored when the following year's harvest commenced.[17] Nevertheless, a beginning had been made, precedent set, and the possibility of bilaterally negotiated working conditions in agribusiness grudgingly accepted. This period of bitter struggle also ended with at least a partial gain achieved by the other segment of Puerto Rico's industrialized agricultural labor force as the more skilled and therefore less easily replaced tobacco workers managed, in 1915, to hold out for four months in a strike against the Porto Rico American Tobacco Company.

Industrialism had become firmly entrenched in Puerto Rico within the first decade of the American takeover, but only those "industrial men" on the fringes of the island's principal economic activity were organizable. The Sixth Congress of the FLT in 1910 reported that charters had been extended to 267 unions in the preceding decade, but that less than 150 were still functioning with a total membership of only 4,143. Fifty-five delegates attended the FLT Congress that year, representing tobacco workers and the various trades. Not a single union of sugar workers, from what was far and away the island's predominant economic activity, was among them.[18]

Two U.S. Department of Labor investigators, in 1905 and again in 1919, described the futility of attempting to build lasting, solvent organizations with workers who were paid only a few cents an hour (often in the form of credit vouchers) during the six months or less of employment each year.[19] At one point, literally adding insult to injury, the sugar corporations refused to sign labor agreements with their employees and based their refusal on the ground that the workers were not formally organized and could not, therefore, be held legally responsible for compliance with the contract.[20]

In this sense, the reports of the governor of Puerto Rico during the pre-World War I period were quite accurate: the labor conflicts in industrialized agriculture could, in part, be traced to "outside agitators." The great mass of only occasionally employed agricultural workers were not union members in the permanent and continuous sense specified by the Webbs. Driven by desperation and encouraged by leadership drawn from the ranks of the relatively better-off urban craftsmen,[21] they could be relied on only to strike briefly and sporadically, but nothing beyond that organizationally until the provision of governmental safeguards many years later.[22]

6

Labor between the Two World Wars: Frustration, Coalition, and Dissolution of the Free Federation of Labor

> Plantation strikes were accompanied in some instances by intimidation, murder, cane fires, and other forms of lawlessness and violence...waves of labor agitation...rise and subside as if they were the result of psychic contagion...it is not strange...that they have little observable effect upon the material conditions of the working people.

The above is the way in which a team of researchers from the Brookings Institution[1] summed up the results of a quarter century of attempts by labor to introduce a modicum of human decency into employment relationships in Puerto Rico. All attempts to bargain collectively were ruthlessly suppressed and the violation of civil rights subsequently ritualistically "investigated" by boards of inquiry after the strikes were broken and the harvests safely completed.[2]

For labor the situation had improved somewhat during the relative prosperity of World War I, moving from very bad to slightly less bad only to revert to much worse, with the Great Depression coming to Puerto Rico earlier than on the mainland and lasting longer (there is an old saying in Puerto Rico to the effect that "if the United States has a cold, Puerto Rico sneezes). The cost of living rose, unemployment increased, and income plummeted, averaging $82 per family annually in 1933 (by 1941 it was still only

$117 annually per family, one dollar more than in 1929, a dozen years earlier, giving some idea of the extreme stagnation).[3] In 1937 agricultural workers were averaging less than twelve cents an hour, when employed.[4]

Organized labor's attempts to achieve protection indirectly via legislation ultimately proved as frustrating as had their earlier efforts to bargain collectively directly with employers. The authors of an extensive study conducted during this period were succinct in their appraisal of Puerto Rico's government: "Sugar interests have taken charge of the legislature and of the Bureau of Insular Affairs, and rendered the people impotent to help themselves." Antonio Barceló, president of the insular Senate for many years, calculated the political strength of the four principal sugar companies as "greater than the Government of Puerto Rico."[5]

By 1920, after more than two decades of massive investment and intensive industrialization, an observant Caribbean traveler could note that the Puerto Rican worker had sunk to a level of poverty more abysmal than that of the traditional economy of neighboring Haiti.[6] Labor leaders after more than twenty years of futile struggle and sacrifice, apparently powerless to defeat their employers, decided to join them.[7] The marriage of convenience took place in the political rather than the economic arena.

The electoral process in Puerto Rico under North American colonial dominion revolved around attempts by opposing factions to control the locally elected, insular legislature. Each of the factions also espoused an alternative solution for the perennial status question—eventual statehood, autonomous association with the United States, or independence—an issue which the U.S. Congress had left ambiguous.[8]

Political maneuvering in the years prior to World War I was an activity in the virtually exclusive domain of the dominant class of property owners, businessmen, and professionals. These different segments of the privileged class—all with close alliances with the metropolitan power—differed opportunistically on the status question but were unanimous in their economic conservatism. Henry Wells, in an instructive study of changing values in Puerto Rican society, describes the political elite of the early twentieth century as:

largely indifferent to the distress of their humbler fellow citizens. Such problems as miserably low wages, seasonal unemployment, endemic diseases, mass illiteracy, inadequate housing, and the like, received little more attention than the lip service occasionally paid to them in party platforms.[9]

The working class, its incipient central organization linked self-protectively with the AFL, dutifully adhered to the Gompers strategy of shunning formal party alliances, but occasionally sponsored laborite candidates for the legislature or municipal assemblies. These haphazard efforts, under the banner of the Socialist Party, initially met with sporadic but gradually increasing success, eventually shocking the power brokers by electing a majority in Arecibo, an important municipality, in the 1914 elections.[10]

The principal political parties of that era had consistently failed to fulfill campaign promises designed to attract working-class support during the period prior to World War I, a time when the propertied classes were in transition from commercial ties with Europe to industrial collaboration with the United States. By the end of World War I, the insular power elite had become clearly linked, if not totally subservient, to the sugar corporations, which were extending their dominance from the economic to the political sphere. Henry Wells has described the traditional parties' "increasingly overt alliance with the big landowners and the representatives of corporate interests," and noted that by the early 1920s the presidents of both parties were either related by marriage to sugar corporation executives or were on sugar corporation payrolls.[11]

Even before World War I, however, the radical elements in the labor movement had been reduced from decisive majority to articulate but largely powerless minority. Labor's established leadership was increasingly heard to complain that workers were too quick to strike and that rank-and-file demands had an unacceptably "radical flavor."[12] By 1912 Puerto Rican labor's official spokesman—in cooperation with representatives of the insular legislature, the sugar corporations, and the Puerto Rican Chamber of Commerce—was attempting to convince the United States Congress that what was good for the sugar corporations was good for the workers. In Iglesias's sentence, "when a country—as is the case in Puerto Rico—is entirely dependent on one industry, the prosperity of that industry becomes the prosperity of the working people."[13] It was symptomatic of labor's metamorphosis that Iglesias, who had become an official spokesman for the sugar industry and who had stayed on alone in Washington to lobby for repeal of the sugar tariff, in recalling the episode, emphasized the inadequacy of his personal expense account.[14] In the same vein, by 1913 the principal labor leaders were being invited to comment on the governor's annual messages to the insular legislature *prior* to their presentation,[15] an indication of the transition from rebels to collaborators.

Frustrated by their inability to enforce compliance with the platforms of the traditional parties, encouraged by the localized success of working-class candidates, and granted a degree of absolution from AFL strictures on partisan political activity,[16] FLT leaders in 1915 revived a pragmatic "socialist" party, an earlier version of which had been stillborn in 1899. The Socialist Party of Puerto Rico, as reformulated in 1915, pushed a program of social and economic welfare which, as Robert W. Anderson has observed, was "a markedly undoctrinaire and nonideological party."[17] The party's platform was developed within the guidelines of the AFL,[18] and the flavor of the "socialism" sought by the new party, at any rate after a number of years of degeneration, can be appreciated by recalling that its president once attacked colonial Governor Rexford Guy Tugwell as a "sworn foe of free enterprise."[19]

The revamped party was hampered by a restrictive electoral law, no representation on the Electoral Board, and notorious corruption of election officials; it was further denied surveillance of the polling places.[20] Nonetheless, the revamped Socialist Party's laborite candidates garnered 14 percent of the popular vote in 1917 and more than doubled that proportion in 1920, managing to place their representatives in several municipal assemblies and in the insular legislature.

Thoroughly shaken by the growing electoral strength of the working-class party, the traditional parties—as so often occurs when a superior external force is perceived as more threatening than internal differences—formed an *Alianza* (alliance) in the mid-1920s for the subordinate goal of presenting an elitist united front as an obstacle to working-class aspirations. Dissident vestiges of both traditional parties remained outside the merger, however, and the availability of these potential electoral allies was too great a temptation for the budding Socialist Party. A *Coalición* (coalition) was created with these leftover opponents of the working class and the merger did enhance electoral success, but also served to undermine the Socialist Party's short-lived credibility as an uncompromised vehicle for social justice.

Félix Mejías, writing on labor in Puerto Rico in the 1940s soon after Iglesias's death, empathetically suggested that when the biography of Iglesias is written it should be divided into two parts in such a way that his activities as the compromised politician in power are not permitted to "becloud" his accomplishments as the uncompromised trade unionist and politician of the powerless class.[21] Iglesias, from the moment he arrived in Puerto Rico in 1896 until his death in 1939, personified the dominant trends in the Puerto Rican labor movement. From 1896 until World War I and shortly thereafter, the record was one of struggle and sacrifice but very few gains. From World War I and the coalition with the conservatives until World War II, the record becomes one of accommodation, compromise, corruption, and hollow victories. The tragic ignominy of the last chapters of Iglesias's life should not wipe out the memory of the heroic earlier chapters.

In accordance with Charles Anderson's model, as indicated in the chapter on the metamorphosis of the ideologies and strategies of the labor movement, the leaders of organized labor in Puerto Rico were permitted access to the power structure and granted the official franchise, as it were, to represent the working class in the legislature, but with the implicit understanding that none of the prior members of the dominant class be fundamentally disturbed.

The clearest evidence of the cooperative arrangement can be seen in the area of protective labor legislation. The bills, including wage and hour regulations, health provisions, safety regulations, social security, and similar measures, all of which had been bottled up in committees for many years, were taken out of storage, amended, and duly promulgated as soon as the coalition came to power in the early 1930s—and then not rigorously enforced. The Department of Labor of Puerto Rico was headed and staffed by Socialist Party members during the coalition period. After the takeover of political power by the Popular Democratic Party in 1940, for example, the

Labor Department collected forty-three percent as much money in wage claims in a single fiscal year, 1941-42, as the Socialist Party administration had collected in the ten previous years from 1931 through 1941.[22]

The principal achievement during this sorry period for the FLT and the Socialist Party came in the form of access to public office and the patronage that the posts controlled. Santiago Iglesias became resident commissioner in Washington, several FLT militants became legislators or municipal assemblymen, and Prudencio Rivera Martínez, who had led the tobacco workers for many years, became Commissioner of the Department of Labor.

The gradual dissolution of the FLT and the eventual destruction of the Socialist Party were consummated in the act of coalition in the 1920s and became manifest in a variety of ways during the decade of the 1930s. Sterility of legislative accomplishments played an important debilitating role, as did internal competition for sinecures on the public payroll for the party faithful. The struggle for government jobs reached a point at which Antonio J. González could describe it as "a contagious disease,"[23] and an FLT editorialist, writing under the title "Good Socialist Today; Better Organizer Yesterday," could refer to the job competition as the "current madness."[24]

Of considerable importance also in the process of dissolution was dissension over the issue of class collaboration, which had been present within the Federation for years, but which became irreconcilable during the coalition period. An illustration of the conflicting positions can be seen in the philosophical transformation of long-time FLT officer Manuel F. Rojas. In 1905 Rojas was counseling caution, explaining that progress is a long, slow process (and "doesn't require pushing from anyone"), and urging his fellow workers to conduct their campaigns in the "softest possible terms. . .without wounding sensibilities, without causing bad feeling, without hurting anyone's feelings."[25] But by 1919, apparently thoroughly disillusioned with gradualism, he was voicing premature[26] suspicions of possible collaboration with the capitalists, and taking the position that the workers had too long been overly

> tolerant with the disembowelers of children, with the disembowelers of women, with the torturers of unfortunate old

people; we have been condescending with the serpent, permitting it to sink its poisonous fangs into our defenseless flesh whenever it wishes. Because of our carelessness we have seen entire generations die after slow and horrible agony. . . . There can be no peace as long as the demonical social organization, encouraged by the system of usurpation and by its unlimited anxiety for exploitation and by its insatiable selfishness, is not totally changed.[27]

By 1934 the ambivalence of a "socialist" party in active collaboration with the capitalists had become so awkwardly apparent that the party leadership found it necessary to purge those who insisted on calling attention to the contradictions.[28] The most outspoken external critic of the Socialist Party was Iglesias's long time adversary Andrés Rodríguez Vera, who apparently suspected the *de facto* existence of the coalition long before it was publicly announced. Rodríguez Vera, as have so many others before and since, pointed to the paradox of AFL support for a socialist political party and concluded that the entire operation had been a facade for United States colonial domination:

Thus are the men of the American Federation of Labor: they take part in political campaigns in the United States side by side with the National Democratic Party, which is the party to which President Gompers is affiliated. There they are the enemies of socialism, while here in Puerto Rico they defend, patronize and pay propagandists for the establishment of an International Socialist Party. They have their objective; and in the same way that they behave politically above and below board in the dominions of Uncle Sam, they do likewise in Mexico calling themselves Liberals, in Columbia Nationalists, and in Cuba Opportunists, as the case may be, in order to insinuate themselves with the popular masses and in the governments of these countries, with the only goal of favoring the domination of American capitalism.[29]

The machinations of the AFL may not have been so consciously Machiavellian as Rodríguez Vera charges. Be that as it may, the AFL's tacit support of the predominant thrust of United States policy in Latin America—the provision of security for North American investment—and the AFL's support of the FLT, and through the FLT the Socialist Party of Puerto Rico, is an element that cannot be ignored in analyzing the discrediting of the FLT as a legitimate advocate of working class interests.

Gordon Lewis's thoughtful analysis of United States influence in Puerto Rico makes it clear that there was no deliberately preconceived grand design of imperial policy, the colonial administrators preferring instead, often haphazardly, to dominate and control indirectly, through indigenous collaborators, rather than to rule directly in British fashion. Lewis explains how the material benefits of imposed modernization—improvements in health, education, communications, and the like, which were often introduced by dedicated and well-intentioned metropolitan technicians—unquestionably served to improve living standards. But he remarks that the improvements invariably directly enhanced United States commercial interests at the same time that the populace was incidentally affected, and that the measures "lacked the base of a popular support . . . an absolute necessity were they to become anything permanent."[30] In the end, it was this alien and artificially imposed character of the FLT and the Socialist Party that led to their decline.

Meanwhile, back at the sugar plantations, the results of the contradictions implicit in the coalition were taking their most tangible form in decreasing militance in labor contract negotiations and in declining wages.[31] Robert Alexander sums up this development with unadorned understatement:

> In 1932 the Socialist party entered a coalition government with the Republican party, the principal spokesmen for the sugar interests. The union leaders and plantation owners had for a decade and a half been negotiating on a friendly basis in the economic field. During the decade of the 1930s they extended their cooperation to the area of politics.[32]

The FLT, citing the provisions of the National Industrial Recovery Act and negotiating under the auspices of the Commissioner of Labor, finally achieved in 1933, for the 1934 harvest, a semblance of the goal it had been seeking for three decades: the acquiescence of the sugar corporations in the signing of an island-wide labor agreement. The victory, such as it was, came much too late, however, for the substandard contract, which smelled of collusion, was spontaneously and massively rejected in a short-lived, but furiously militant stoppage that Quintero Rivera has described as the first strike of workers in Puerto Rico against their own leadership. The strike was significant also in that non-FLT labor leadership made its first appearance. Some of the new leaders were farm workers who were later to be sponsored by and ally themselves with the Popular Democratic Party; others came from the urban centers, notably the charismatic Nationalist Party leader, Pedro Albizu Campos; still others were later to found the Communist Party in Puerto Rico.[33]

The FLT never fully recovered from the repudiation of 1934, although it continued to negotiate with the Association of Sugar Producers for several years (in 1942 a period of rising cost-of-living, the FLT signed a three-year contract as a gesture of "support for the war effort")[34] and in the 1970s a pathetic semblance of the original organization still existed. One of its principal activities, since its announcement in the late 1950s of the "obsolescence of the strike weapon," has been the sponsorship of annual "Labor-Management Peace Banquets."

The pattern of labor leadership until this point in history had been one of dominance by the most adept of the tobacco workers and urban skilled craftsmen, all under the tutelage of the AFL's Iglesias. This period ends with an important strike of dock workers in 1938, which was uncontrolled by the FLT—always the bellwether—with the death of Iglesias in 1939. It is especially symbolic—and somewhat pathetic—that Iglesias, in his last address to an AFL convention in 1939, made the same request that he had made at the first convention he attended in 1900: that President William Green, who has replaced Gompers, should visit Puerto Rico at his earliest convenience. Iglesias apparently died still convinced that the key to the security of Puerto Rican workers was not in their own liberation but instead in their role as perpetual protectorate of their "big brothers" in Washington.[35] The old FLT leaders faded away, and with them the unity of forty years, thereby creating a leadership vacuum and consequent indirection of the labor movement, which still remained in the 1970s.

7

Labor and the New Deal: The Rise of the Popular Democratic Party and the General Confederation of Labor

During the Great Depression, a full thirty years after the switch in sovereignty and the promises of the "advantages and blessings of an enlightened civilization" by the invading military commander, the Brookings Institution commissioned a painstaking survey of the island. It is pathetic to note that, if anything, the living standards of most Puerto Ricans had degenerated since the similar survey conducted for the Spanish crown in 1765 by Field Marshall Alejandro O'Reilly. The following are excerpts from the study conducted at the beginning of the period on which this chapter focuses:

> Only about one person in four . . . lives in a town or village... the Island is not a farming community ...but, instead a community of agricultural laborers. A great majority of the country people are tenants-at-will, dependent upon wages for their livelihood. They own neither the land that they till nor the crops that they raise. The fact that nearly four out of five of those living in the country are landless, presumably own no home, possess few or no animals, and none but the most primitive agricultural implements . . . lies at the root of the structure of the rural community. It is a country where the masses depend . . . upon the good will of the land-owner whose property the little single-partitioned hut happens to be built. . . . the typical agricultural unit is the commercial

plantation which produces one or more of the great staple crops—sugar, tobacco, or coffee.

These plantations produce for the outside market, and each employs a large number of wage workers. . . . The commonest type of . . . house today is a framework of poles or scantling, nailed or tied with native fiber. The walls may be of boards, thatch, or the bark of the royal palm, and the roof is of thatch, bark or galvanized iron. The floors are made of boards and generally raised a few feet from the ground. . . . It has no ceiling. It has no kitchen, except a lean-to on the outside. . . . the torrential rains and strong winds break through the light construction and make it an uncomfortable and unhealthful place of residence. . . . Nearly all of the money earned as wages is spent for food . . . . By importing a very large proportion of its food, the Island is able to export the maximum amount of the staple crops to the production of which it is expecially fitted. Whatever may be the net financial gain from this specialization, it has clearly encouraged the use of a monotonous and debilitating diet by a large proportion of the people . . . . There is . . . submissiveness to misfortune and a lack of class feeling.[1]

It was during this period, to use David Ross's terminology, that the "agricultural laborer who, a few generations before, had been a small subsistence farmer, was now becoming increasingly a rural vagrant." (In Ross's analysis the casualties of industrialization are pejoratively described, implicitly, as being culpable for their own misery.) Ross goes on to describe the effect of the depression of the 1930s on the agro-industrial labor force in Puerto Rico:

The boom that Puerto Rico had experienced during the first 20 years of American possession, when the great sugar properties were being developed . . . had been spent . . . Many able-bodied men and women now lived in rural areas, often on the property of commercial plantations, whose labor was superfluous. In an economy based on subsistence agriculture, the problem could have risen too, and frequently does; but in such an economy, everyone is employed even though many are superfluous. . . . A commercial agricultural enterprise . . . is in a different position. It is no reflection on its motives that it does not assume responsibility for the economic welfare of

Cutting sugar cane. The proportion of the labor force engaged in agriculture dropped from 45 to 7 percent between 1940 and 1975. *Courtesy of Office of Information, Puerto Rico; Jack Delano, photographer.*

all who happen to live with its vicinity. The fact that unsuccessful applicants for employment have no alternative source of income is not its responsibility, nor its proper concern. It is the proper concern of the state. . .[2]

The "state" in Puerto Rico, however, was totally unequipped to deal with the problem of human beings rendered "superfluous" by economic "development." Ross neglects to mention that the principal reason the state was not modernizing was that the American sugar corporations and their insular abettors actively and efficiently opposed representative democracy, collective bargaining, and diversification of the economy. This opposition was carried out through a process of corruption of the insular legislature, the crushing of labor organizations, and the open violation of the federal law limiting land tenure to five hundred acres.

Tobacco strippers weighing their day's production. *Courtesy of Office of Information, Puerto Rico; Edward Rosskam, photographer.*

Periods of total unemployment during the non-harvest seasons stretched into months. Wages, when employment was available, varied from fifty to seventy-five cents for a day's labor. Diet, health, living conditions, and educational facilities were grossly inadequate. "The agricultural workers of Puerto Rico had, in short, most of the disadvantages of an urban industrial worker, and none of the advantages."[3]

Luis Muñoz Marín, prototypical of a new bicultural Puerto Rican, growing up ambivalently and bilingually during this period, was the son of Luis Muñoz Rivera, who had been instrumental in obtaining a measure of autonomy from Spain for Puerto Rico, Muñoz Marín, who would himself untimately be instrumental in obtaining a similar measure from the United States, bitterly described "The Sad Case of Puerto Rico" for the *American Mercury* in 1929 in a much quoted condemnation:

the development of large absentee-owned sugar estates, the rapid curtailment in the planting of coffee—the natural crop of the independent farmer—and the concentration of the cigar manufacture into the hands of the American trust have combined to make Porto Rico a land of beggars and millionaires, of flattering statistics and distressing realities. More and more it becomes a factory worked by peons, fought over by lawyers, bossed by absent industrialists, and clerked by politicians. It is now Uncle Sam's second largest sweat-shop.[4]

The situation, clearly, had never been worse. Yet, at the same time, the situation was beginning, relatively speaking, to improve and expectations were beginning to rise. Political scientist Murray Edelman has observed that when labor as a class can demonstrate that working people enjoy far more public support than is reflected in existing institutions, it becomes inevitable that workers "will grow increasingly restive until new institutions and a major status realignment" occurs.[5] This is, in fact, what took place in Puerto Rico in the late 1930s. Not only the FLT and the Socialist Party, but *all* the institutions existent in Puerto Rico about the time Franklin D. Roosevelt came to power in the United States, had become unsalvageably unresponsive to the great mass of the population.   The Popular Democratic Party (PPD), the "*Populares*," a reformist, populist party of the "democratic left" type that was coming to power in several Latin American countries during this period, was founded in 1938 and came to partial power in 1940. The PPD proceeded to sweep the elections thereafter for the next quarter century, orginally not so much because of its own democratically socialist promise as because of the utter obsolescence of the prevailing institutions.[6]

The compromises described in the last chapter that had led to the merger of the then existing political parties, turned out to be as lethal for the Alliance (of the conservative parties) as it had been for the Coalition (of the "progressive" parties). By the mid-1930s, fresh political personalities were emerging from the mire of the despair of the previous period. New political alignments were being forged and, most important, new ideologies deemphasizing political status were being formulated. The dominant political force to emerge as indicated, was the PPD, with the charismatic *caudillo* Luis Muñoz Marín in the forefront on a platform of subservience of the status question to the goal of economic growth, with the slogan of "self-respect versus money."[6]

Edelman explains that "the trigger for such realignment is never repressive objective conditions in themselves, but rather a discrepancy between public values and the values realized through existing institutions."[7] This again describes the impetus for the power realignment in Puerto Rico in that the rebellion came, not when conditions were worsening, but at a time when the situation, relatively speaking, was improving—a time of rising expectations which engendered a higher level of demands, a circumstance to which Maslow's "hierarchy of human needs" clearly applies.[8]

Expectations were rising and material conditions relatively improving in the 1930s largely as the result of federal relief programs administered by the Emergency Relief and Reconstruction Administrations. These offices, together with the host of other New Deal agencies such as the Public Works Administration, the Civilian Conservation Corps, and the Food Distribution Administration, pumped millions of dollars into the island's economy, beginning in 1933.

The laws of the United States apply to Puerto Rico unless a given statute specifically excluded the island. Federal labor relations legislation (the National Labor Relations Act, the "Wagner Act" of 1935, as subsequently amended by the Labor Management Relations Act, the "Taft-Hartley Act" of 1947) applies only to enterprises engaged in interstate commerce—including commerce with territories such as Puerto Rico—and excludes the employees of governmental agencies and agricultural workers. Puerto Rico's economy, however, unlike that of the United States, was still overwhelmingly agricultural at the time of the initial application of the National Labor Relations Act. In 1940 thirty-two percent of insular net income derived from agriculture, compared to twelve percent from manufacturing. More important, fully four times as many workers were employed in agriculture as in manufacturing (in 1940 in the U.S., nineteen percent of the labor force was engaged in agriculture and twenty-four percent in manufacturing).

Still more important, Puerto Rican agricultural workers were not predominantly the hired hands of family farms, having for decades been industrially employed in salaried relationships with corporate enterprises. Also unlike on the mainland, where a significant portion of agricultural labor was migratory, the labor force in Puerto Rico was geographically stable and had been intent on bargaining with their corporate employers for many years. It was clear that the National Labor Relations Act would need to be supplemented locally and, in 1945, the insular legislature followed the model of the Wagner Act and enacted the Puerto Rico Labor Relations Act (PRLRA), but with very important modifications. Agricultural workers were included by the straightforward device of defining an "employee" as "any employee" and excluding from that definition only executives, supervisors, or persons employed in domestic service or by parents or spouse.

The New Deal administrator who had been appointed governor of Puerto Rico, Rexford Guy Tugwell, joined forces with PPD leader Muñoz Marín, and the subsequent transformation of the insular government has often been referred to as constituting a "peaceful revolution." Whether or not the results have been as geniunely revolutionary as anticipated, there can be no doubt that the revamping of public administration was profound. Key executive and legislative innovations of the early 1940s, in an effort reminiscent of the legendary first one hundred days of the New Deal in Washington, included the rapid-fire creation of a planning board, a budget bureau, a higher education council, a governmental development company and bank, the passage of the Puerto Rico Labor Relations Act (PRLRA) on the model of the Wagner Act (National Labor Relations Act of the United States), as indicated, and, most significant of all for future labor relations, a series of public corporations on the model of the Tennessee Valley Authority (TVA).

The public corporations (or authorities or instrumentalities, as they are variously referred to) have all been created since 1940, with the exception of the University of Puerto Rico, which was founded in 1903, and their proliferation is of utmost importance. Although structurally situated within the executive branch, their operations are carried out with considerable autonomy. These hybrid entities, which combine characteristics of both public and private enterprise—the Federal Deposit Insurance Company is an analogous example—are in other political jurisdictions ordinarily created as emergency devices and subsequently absorbed into the traditional bureaucracy. The reverse has been the case in Puerto Rico. The original eight corporations, which were founded between 1940 and 1945 in such classic public utilitarian fields as water, sewage, electric power, communications, and transportation, had by 1972 been joined by seventeen additional autonomous authorities in such diverse fields as public housing, agricultural credit, prison industries, Puerto Rican culture, and highway construction.

This socialization of services had in some cases involved the expropiation of private enterprises in which collective bargaining had previously taken place. The Puerto Rican legislature, faced with a situation in which existing labor organizations with considerable bargaining power in such crucial industries as electric power were adamant in retaining their right to bargain collectively, "resolved" the situation by accommodating within the definition of "employer" in the PRLRA those "corporate instrumentalities" already established (except for the University of Puerto Rico) "as well as such other government agencies as are engaged or may hereafter engage in lucrative businesses or activities for pecuniary profit."

At the same time, however, the Act excluded from the definition of "employer" the government of Puerto Rico or any political subdivision other than the aforementioned corporate instrumentalities. The legislature thereby created for the regular employees of the commonwealth and municipal governments, and for government itself, a situation that was to become increasingly untenable over the years. It is apparent in retrospect that the employees of the governmental agency monopolistically providing electric power, for example, were granted the right to bargain collectively—including the right to strike—while the same rights were withheld from, for example, the employees of the Park and Recreation Commission, clearly not because the services of the former are less essential, but principally because the employees of the traditional agencies were not yet organized and were thus incapable of exerting pressure on the legislature.

The working class, organized and unorganized, employed and unemployed, was in a state of rudderless, chaotic, nonconformity. A dock strike that occurred in 1938 marked the emergence of a dynamically disruptive new element: Puerto Rican "labor agitators" loosely allied with the incipient industrial union movement in the United States, who were labeled the "CIO communists" by the panic-stricken old guard of the FLT. The Nationalist Party became increasingly defiant during this period, and in 1937 twenty persons were killed and more than one hundred wounded in an incident involving the "*nacionalistas*" that the United States Civil Liberties Union accurately described as a massacre. Thousands of unemployed workers participated in a hunger march in San Juan in 1939.

As part of the process of realignment, a new labor center, created to supplant the FLT and challenge the employers, the *Confederación General de Trabajadores* (CGT),[9] was formally constituted in early 1940 after several months of agitation and organization—often in indistinguishable cooperation with the founders of the PPD.

The CGT, during its meteoric existence as an entity independent of PPD domination, made an indelible mark on the history of labor's struggles in Puerto Rico. The new labor central, which in many ways was similar to the Industrial Workers of the World in the United States a few years earlier, took shape with the impetus of the *Asociación de Choferes* (Transport Workers' Union), an industrial union of drivers, mechanics, and others, both independent and salaried, who provided most of the jitney-based transportation (and much of the oral communication) to the working-class public. The members were mainly urban refugees from the depression-desolated rural areas, displaced small landholders and plantation workers who were well aware of the nature of industrial exploitation and the political power of capitalism. The "*choferes*" reversed the earlier thrust of the craft-oriented FLT-AFL by bringing a CIO type of industrial union orientation from the countryside to the cities and towns.

The new confederation, bolstered by staff leadership from the minuscule but militant Communist Party of Puerto Rico (which had been founded in 1934), was also encouraged by Muñoz Marín and by Governor Rexford Guy Tugwell. The latter was openly contemptuous of the "totally corrupt" FLT-AFL, and a strong supporter of the CIO (with whom the CGT eventually affiliated), and a thorn in the side of the sugar corporations and the Puerto Rican property-owning and professional class.

During the 1940s the CGT, in Angel G. Quintero Rivera's phrase, "spread like cane fire" across the island. More than three hundred unions were founded and dozens of strikes carried out, most leading to contracts. Its working-class leadership personified by the legendary Juan Sáez Corales, left a record of honesty, dedicated militance, class consciousness, and political awareness.

At the time, the diversification of industry was barely beginning, the economic situation was in a state of flux, and the labor force and labor movement were in transformation. In 1940 somewhere between fifty thousand and one hundred thousand workers were union members[10] (the unions claimed more than three hundred thousand at the time),[11] with the strongest unions operating in sugar, docks, transportation, breweries and distilleries, tobacco, electric power, and hotels and restaurants. The skilled trades were reported as unorganized or deficiently organized,[12] the exact reverse of the situation a quarter of a century earlier in the peak years of FLT influence. By 1949 the configuration of union strength was approximately the same, with the addition of cement workers, construction workers, and the employees of a few manufacturing firms.[13] No government employees had as yet formed unions.

Rexford Guy Tugwell, part of Roosevelt's "Brain Trust" during the New Deal, had been appointed governor in 1941, and for the first time ever, executive and legislative power began to function in complementary fashion and, also for the first time, a Puerto Rican political entity exercised at least a degree of effective power. As a result, the sterile protective labor legislation that the Socialist Party had enacted began to be implemented vigorously and, in addition, the new federal labor legislation governing wages, hours, and collective bargaining also began to apply. This administrative development added a new and important dimension to the employment relationship. It was at this time that the working-class leaders who had spontaneously emerged during the dissolution of the FLT—CGT General Secretary Juan Sáez Corales was the prototype—began to see themselves supplanted by a corps of technocrats—lawyers, administrators, legislators, teachers—who were adept in representing workers before the new governmental bureaucracies.

Labor union official addressing sugar workers, 1946. *Courtesy of Office of Information, Puerto Rico; Charles Rotkin, photographer.*

The CGT, for example, gave in 1942 an impressive demonstration of its militance and organizational ability in a strike of sugar workers which probably could have been maintained, but a continued confrontation and a direct settlement (and the credit that might have accrued to the union and its officers) were circumvented when the government (that is to say, Senator Muñoz Marín and Governor Tugwell) intervened with the promise of the activation of a minimum wage committee, whose recommendation would be implemented retroactively

One of the most proficient practitioners of the art of achieving gains for labor unions administratively was Popular Party lawyer Ernesto Ramos Antonini, who successfully prosecuted delinquent wage claims totaling tens of thousands of dollars during this period. The most artful of all, however, was the peerless Muñoz Marín, who very soon consolidated his power within the Popular

Party and, in the role of benevolent *caudillo*, became arbiter of virtually *all* conflict. An anecdote from the sugar workers' strike of 1943 is illustrative: the employees of the Roig Sugar Corporation had struck the grinding mill without warning, thereby causing considerable damage to the employer's property; an injunction was granted that included an order freezing the union's funds (which were deposited in a bank owned by the employer); the union's leaders (including local school teacher and politician Ernesto Carrasquillo, who began as the union's "adviser" and eventually dominated the organization for the next thirty years) fled to San Juan to avoid service of the court order. Arriving in the capital after midnight, they found the legislature in session, explained their problems to Senate President Muñoz Marín, who rushed a law through prohibiting the seizure of union funds.[14] The image of Muñoz Marín, who is 1948 became Puerto Rico's first elected governor, as champion of the underdog and ultimate authority in all controversies, grew rapidly and eventually became pervasive as all other leadership and institutions became tacitly subordinate.

A frequently noted characteristic of late developing countries is the tendency of neophyte labor organizations to be heavily influenced by ideologically motivated intellectuals bent on expanding workers' protests beyond the confines of the employment relationship for the radical transformation of society.[15] It is worth pausing at this point in the narrative to examine the reasons why Puerto Rico has been a case that deviates from the norm in this regard.

As noted, Puerto Rico has been no exception to the general rule of "political" unionism during the early stages of industrialization and modernization, but is clearly unusual as regards the domination of the labor movement by intellectuals and as regards the nonideological orientation of the movement. Manuel Maldonado Denis, a leading contemporary analyst of Puerto Rico's sociopolitical development, had noted that one of the principal failings of the organizations supporting independence for the island—organizations traditionally led by intellectuals—has been the inability of left-of-center groups (such as the Nationalist Party and the Puerto Rico Independence Party) to enlist working-class support.[16]

Maldonado Denis offers no explanation for the lack of left-of-center political alliances with the labor movement, limiting himself to observing in 1969, that "whatever the reason may be, the fact is that the independence movement has achieved very little acceptance among the farmer and labor sectors of Puerto Rico."[17]

An explanation for this exception to the rule of labor movements elsewhere in the developing world may be found in the alliance of Puerto Rican labor with the AFL. Ideologically inclined intellectuals establish links with workers' organizations in developing countries in a variety of ways, but one of the most common is that the working-class leaders of newly formed unions, handicapped by lack of administrative skills and even illiteracy, call on educated friends for technical assistance. The outsiders, by filling the vacuum, become indispensably adept in coping with businesses and bureaucracies, both of which are often paradoxically, more intransigent and complex in developing than in more modern societies. This originally altruistic assistance, as the outsiders come to appreciate the political potential of mass movements, sometimes evolves into dominance.

This avenue of access did not exist in Puerto Rico to the same degree as elsewhere in the developing world because the AFL filled the vacuum, providing the necessary technical as well as financial assistance. The practice of representation by a full-time, fully subsidized labor organizer-administrator is almost unknown in the less developed world, at least in the early stages of industrialization. This, of course, was the professional role that AFL General Organizer Iglesias played in Puerto Rico, thereby preempting the function that those interested in the radical transformation of society might have played. Iglesias detailed his own job description in his autobiography. His "multiple activities" included functioning not only as a labor representative, but also as a propagandist, lecturer, translator, journalist, lawyer, mediator, conciliator, and lobbyist, as well as bearer of a host of civic responsibilities in representation of the organized labor movement.[18] It was virtually all-inclusive and Juan Antonio Corretjer has in this sense accurately described the nonalliance of the Puerto Rican labor and radical movements as primarily the result of the "yankeephile short circuit which corrupted the Socialist Party."[19]

As Iglesias gradually changed the focus of his activities from labor organization and administration to lobbying and legislation, the technical vacuum, which might then have been filled by more radically inclined ideologues, was again preempted, this time by a then emerging generation of pragmatic labor technocrats. Hipólito Marcano, Francisco Colón Gordiany, and Nicolás Nogueras Rivera, who in the 1970s were still presiding over what remained of the *Federación del Trabajo de Puerto Rico*, the *Confederación General de Trabajadores*, and the *Federación Libre de los Trabajadores* respectively, are prototypic. They were the new breed of labor professionals, who served their apprenticeship under Iglesias and FLT Secretary General Rafael Alonso and who subsequently parlayed their administrative indispensability into bureaucratic dominance after Iglesias's death in 1939.

To get a bit ahead of the story, this second generation in turn began to lose control at about the same time that the industrial development program gained momentum, thereby introducing a third echelon of labor bureaucrats: representatives of international unions from the United States in pursuit of runaway mainland enterprises. David Sternbach of the Congress of Industrial Organizations, Robert Gladnick of the Internation Laides' Garment Workers Union, George Treviño of the United Steelworkers, Keith Terpe of the Seafarers International Union, and Frank Chaves of the International Brotherhood of Teamsters were prototypes of the skilled union technicians from the mainland who once again preempted the influential role that insular left-of-center ideologues might have played.

This conjecture, it must be noted, assumes that the island's middle-and upper-class radical elements would have proved capable of taking advantage of opportunities to provide assistance to the working-class organizations had they not been preempted, an assumption for which there is little evidence. Corretjer, for example, recalls that during the islandwide sugar strike of 1934, the workers, who had become disillusioned with their own leadership, appealed for outside help, but the Nationalist Party was unable to produce a single *independentista* capable of organizing and technically advising workers.[20]

The *independentistas*, most of whom traditionally have been materially comfortable and personally unacquainted with manual labor, have concentrated their efforts historically on political opposition to colonialism—on the theory that none of Puerto Rico's problems can be dealt with effectively until imperialism has been defeated. The virtually exclusive dedication of so many of the island's progressives to narrowly conceived political action has affected not only the development of the labor movement, but also most other social institutions. The introverted quest for independence has attracted and consumed the energy and talent of a significant portion of the most potentially creative and productive youth of every generation in Puerto Rico for decades. The diversion from other activities that this tightly focused dedication has caused is evident in the generally deprived state of the arts and sciences in general.

The long-time Secretary general of the FLT, Rafael Alonso Torres, writing his memoirs in the late 1930s, included a bitter denunciation of the lack of assistance received by labor from Puerto Rican intellectuals. Alonso Torres accused them, with few exceptions, of having been educated at the University of Puerto Rico, but then feeling most comfortable in the service of corporate, capitalist interests, lending their eloquence to the maintenance of "industrial despotism."[21]

To get back to the narrative, the CGT, which during the late 1930s had received considerable initial organizational assistance from the PPD, included diverse political elements among its leaders, many of whom were reluctant to submit to the sometimes benevolent, sometimes punitive tutelage of Muñoz Marín. The CGT from the outset had a clearly left-of-center thrust. Its international affiliation, for example, was with the *Confederación de Trabajadores de la America Latina* (CTAL), the western hemispheric branch of the leftist World Federation of Trade Unions (WFTU), from which the AFL had split because of Communist domination. Most important, the leadership of the CGT was outspoken in its support of independence for Puerto Rico and intransigent in its refusal to knuckle under to the unilateral hegemony of the PPD. Also important was the fact the popular front strategy, which had earlier been adopted by the Communist Parties of the world, began to fall apart, as did also the CGT's alliance with the PPD.

Muñoz Marín and the PPD, once firmly in power, moved to sever the partnership with the CGT, insisting that the labor organization cooperate "responsibly" with the program of capital attraction and industrial diversification. When the leadership of the

CGT resisted, a systematic campaign of repression and harassment was instituted that resulted in a split in the CGT in 1945 and its eventual destruction. Muñoz Marín, according to César Andreu Iglesias, a CGT activist at the time, warned the CGT leadership that unless "we cooperated we would be crushed like cockroaches." "We didn't and he did," Andreu Iglesias went on to remark.[22]

The years since 1945 and the destruction of the CGT have been chaotic with regard to a centralizing focus for the Puerto Rican labor movement. The vestiges of the FLT continued to exist while the original CGT split into the *CGT-Auténtica* under *independentista* lawyer Francisco Colón Gordiany, and the CGT-CIO under PPD stalwarts Ramón Perez Barreto and Ernesto Ramos Antonini. This latter organization in turn split three ways into the *Sindicato Azucarero*, in affiliation with the United Packinghouse Workers, CIO, the *Organización Obrera Insular*, and the *Unidad General de Trabajadores* (from which the *Comite' de Organizaciones Industriales* split).[23]

A precise genealogy of the anarchy of Puerto Rico's fragmented labor movement is not essential to the analysis at hand, but the fragmentation's impact on labor's potential is. The principal effect has been to dilute the labor movement's role as an autonomous power group within society and to emphasize even further the paternalistic role of government, the genesis of which has already been traced.

A crucial development in this process of subordination of the labor movement to the Popular Democratic Party—because of Muñoz Marín's insistence on highly centralized economic growth, took place in 1949 when Ernesto Ramos Antonini, who was second-in-command in the PPD, attempted to introduce legislation that would have increased the power of organized labor within the administration. Muñoz Marín blocked Ramos Antonini's pretensions with a pronouncement that such legislation would be superfluous because the working class already had "an indubitable defender" in the highest seat of government.[24] Ramos Antonini accepted the admonition—and the possibilities of developing an independent power base that went with it—and Muñoz Marín's hegemony emerged as impervious to challenge.

A crucial event in the development of the island's labor relations occurred in the early 1950s with the reaching of an agreement bet-

Armando Sánchez and Luis Muñoz Marín in 1968. *Courtesy of Periódico "El Imparcial."*

ween the United States and Puerto Rico, "in the nature of a compact," calling for the creation of an "autonomous" commonwealth, "freely associated" with the United States.

Delegates elected from the ranks of the Popular Party overwhelmingly dominated the Constitutional Convention of 1951. The "Populares" even then, however, were an ideologically heterogeneous entity amalgamating a wide spectrum of liberal and conservative views, and the party discipline that had prevailed adminstratively and legislatively was much less cohesive in the constitutional deliberations. The presence of a vocal minority from the Socialist Party also contributed to controversy, and agreement did not come easily on a number of crucial points.

One such controversy involved the right of workers to organize, bargain collectively, and strike. The problem resolved around the desire to consecrate these rights constitutionally, but (a) without extending them to government employees, yet (b) somehow making an exception for those employees in the public corporations who, in fact, already exercised these rights, and (c) providing the government with the means of protecting the health and safety of society if said rights were "excessively" exercised.

The first objective was attained, in the drafting of Section 6, which declares it to be one of the rights in the Bill of Rights that

> persons may join with each other and organize freely for any lawful purpose, except in military or quasi-military organizations.

This clearly meant that everyone was free to form or join a union, including government employees. The next objective, that of limiting organizational purposes in the case of certain public employees, was dealt with by declaring in Section 17 of the Bill of Rights that

> persons employed by private businesses, enterprises and individual employers and by agencies or instrumentalities of the government operating as private businesses or enterprises, shall have the right to organize and to bargain collectively with their employers through representatives of their own choosing in order to promote their welfare.

Considerable debate ensued over the meaning of "agencies or instrumentalities of the government operating as private businesses or enterprises," and neither a listing nor a definition was included in the final document. The ambiguous definition that was bandied about in the debates was really no definition at all because it attempted to combine the criteria of the function of the agencies involved and of whether the employees were covered by personnel legislation or regulations. Delegate Luis Negrón López predicted that unless a single criterion were established, the government would be placed in the situation "of never knowing how to distinguish between a private and a public enterprise."[25] Jaime Benítez, who presided over the commission drafting the Bill of Rights, left the problem for future resolution by declaring it impossible to "mathematically" determine the difference between public and private employment and that the distinction would become clarified with time.[26]

It is apparent that the framers of the Constitution were stymied by the same problem that had earlier motivated the legislators to exclude "government" from the PRLRA's definition of "employer," while including employees of certain public corporations—those already bargaining collectively—in the definition of "employees" under the Act. Delegate Negrón López repeatedly, but unsuccessfully, attempted to get the convention to understand that they were simply ratifying chaotic past practice rather than establishing uniform policy for the future.

The expedient manner in which this problem was dealt with constitutionally is evident in an exchange between delegates Negrón López and Victor Gutiérrez Franqui. Negrón López used bus service to point out that the difference between public and private enterprises could not be based on *function* of the enterprise, because it is not uncommon for similar services to be provided both publicly and privately. Gutiérrez Franqui argued that a variety of criteria could be utilized and that Negrón López should not insist on a single criterion. Negrón López insisted on a definition that would cover a situation such as that existent in the Land Authority (a public agricultural enterprise), in which the office workers were considered to be classified governmental employees covered by the Personnel Law, while the field workers were covered by collective bargaining agreements under the jurisdiction of the PRLRA. Gutiérrez Franqui responded by saying that

I would define the office personnel as employees of a governmental enterprise designed to function as a private enterprise, but since they are included under the coverage of the Personnel Law, they cannot bargain collectively with their employers. And, I would define the field workers as employees of a governmental enterprise which functions like a private enterprise and since they are not covered by the Personnel Law they can bargain collectively with their employers.

Negrón López responded:

Certainly, what your honor has done is describe the situation as it presently exists. . .and that is not what should be done because there must be certainty and absolute security and contitutional clarity as concerns workers' rights and as concerns the guarantee of public services, and this should be provided for in the Constitution.[27]

No such certainty or clarity were forthcoming, however, and the discriminatory and contradictory treatment afforded by the drafters of the Constitution was further accentuated with the inclusion of Section 18, which stipulates that

> in order to assure their rights to organize and bargain collectively, persons employed by private businesses, enterprises and individual employers and by agencies or instrumentalities of the government operating as private businesses or enterprises, in their direct relations with their own employers shall have the right to strike, to picket and to engage in other legal concerted activities.

At this point it became clear to some of the delegates that they had constitutionally consecrated the absurdity already contained in the PRLRA, of prohibiting, for example, file clerks in the Bureau of Labor Statistics from bargaining and striking, while authorizing the interruption of monopolistic service by the technicians of the Light and Power Authority. But, what was done was done, and, as we shall see in the chapter discussing contemporary collective bargaining by unions in Puerto Rico's public sector, these contradictory actions were to come back to haunt successive administrations.

A series of related events of the early 1950s marked the end of this penultimate formative period and ushered in the contemporary labor scene. First, in 1953 Hipólito Marcano, a labor lawyer and PPD legislator, managed to persuade the AFL to withdraw its Puerto Rican "state" federation charter from the FLT and instead affiliate a group formed in the 1950s, the *Federación del Trabajo de Puerto Rico* (FTPR) over which Marcano presided.[28] Second, as has been indicated, in 1952 the island—at least nominally—changed its status from colony to commonwealth, with a consequent increase in local autonomy (although that autonomy was and is severly limited in labor relations).[29] Third, because the majority was composed of sugar workers, a decision was made in 1952 to affiliate the miscellany of agricultural and nonagricultural unions constituting the CGT-CIO with the United Packinghouse Workers of America-CIO. The jurisdictional problems that continue to plague the Puerto Rican labor movement date in large measure from that action.[30] Fourth, in 1954, former CGT stalwart Juan Sáez Corales was red-baited and jailed on political grounds and, although soon released, had been effectively liquidated as a labor leader. Fifth, Alberto Sánchez, one-time close comrade of Sáez Corales and also a leading CIO-oriented leader of the CGT, renounced his radicalism, joined the Popular Party, became a staff representative of the ILGWU, one of the mainland international unions then beginning to arrive on the island, and eventually, in a move that has been derided as tokenism, became the first Puerto Rican to be elected vice-president of an international union in the United States. Sixth, the National Labor Relations Board (NLRB) of the United States established an office in Puerto Rico at this time in order to implement the Taft-Hartley Law (Labor-Management Relations Act of 1947). The regional office of the Board in Puerto Rico conducts all its business in English and has administered the severly restrictive Taft-Hartley provisions with full force, while, as we shall see, the U.S. Department of Labor's administration of such protective legislation as the Fair Labor Standards Act has been carried out in diluted fashion.

The Puerto Rican labor movement, originally oriented far to the left, moved in the opposite direction between the two World Wars, was wrenched back left-of-center during an abortive rebirth of ideological militance by the CGT in the 1940's, only to settle during the decade of the 1950s, almost motionless, in dead center of the political spectrum.

With labor organizational development in abeyance, let us turn our attention to the political and economic environment in which the contemporary labor movement has developed.

8

The Development of the Labor Force in Puerto Rico: The Political and Economic Background

The greater part of the people are poor, but I believe they are more inclined to work and earn an honest living than the people of any Latin-American country that I was ever in. When the duties are entirely taken off of American products, so that American manufacturers can have branch factories in Porto Rico, thousands of these people will be educated in the factory. They will be inspired with the desire not only to make their living, but to become home owners, as many of our workmen in the United States.

—Philip C. Hanna
U.S. Consul in Puerto Rico
December 1898

The Economic Background

Before we look more closely at the contemporary labor movement it is important that the labor force and its "education in the factory" be described within the current economic and political environment.

Economic history in Puerto Rico since the takeover by the United States can be divided into three periods. The first, from 1899 to about 1927, "was marked by the extremely rapid development of the tariff-protected commercial crops, especially sugar and tobacco; the large inflow into the island of outside capital; the consolidation of sugar holdings; and the expansion of processing and

Cottage industry during the "dead" season of sugar production; hemming handkerchiefs in a rural shed, 1946. *Courtesy of Office of Information, Puerto Rico; Jack Delano, photographer.*

handicraft activities." The second, from about 1928 to 1940, "was an era of economic stagnation, of business depression, of mass unemployment, of bankruptcies, of great suffering, and of government handouts."[1] The period from about 1940 to date has been one of increased political autonomy, limited land reform, industrial diversification, and initially booming, later faltering economic growth.

The temporary alliance of an enlightened New Deal administration in Washington and resourceful leadership in San Juan was able to parlay World War II surplusses, mainly rum sales and tariff rebates, into an imaginative program of economic development known popularly as *"Operación Manos a la Obra,"* or, nonliterally, "Operation Bootstrap."[2]

Harvy Perloff, author of one of the most influential studies of Puerto Rico's economy, noted that although it is convenient to divide the island's development into chronological periods, one should not lose sight of the

> underlying stream of continuity during. . .American sovereignty in Puerto Rico. The commercialization of agriculture and the leveling-off of agricultural employment; the increasing dependence on foreign trade; the increasing importance of manufacturing, handicraft, and commerce; the continued rapid growth of population; the widespread unemployment, underemployment, and the seasonality of employment; the spread of urban slums; the decline of the upland culture and economy; the landlessness, the poverty, and the malnutrition, and the uncertainties of political status.[3]

The antecedents of Puerto Rico's attempt to increase opportunities for industrial employment through initially generating and later attracting capital can be traced back many decades, but the immediate origins were a series of federal emergency relief and reconstruction programs of the depression and postdepression New Deal era, which provided experience in problem identification and solving and in social and economic institution building. Paradoxically, the major studies of that period agreed that the emphasis in Puerto Rico's efforts to grow economically should not be in manufacturing, and recommended instead the modernization and diversification of agriculture. The most important report, an analysis by the Puerto Rico Policy Commission, known respectively as the "Chardón Plan," and the "Chardón Commission" (in recognition of University of Puerto Rico Chancellor Carlos Chardón, who played a key role in the project), resulted from a 1934 visit to the island by Eleanor Roosevelt and then Assistant Secretary of Agriculture Rexford Guy Tugwell, who were appalled by conditions and urged President Roosevelt to appoint a commission of Puerto Ricans to recommend a developmental program. There is considerable evidence indicating that the Chardón Plan was indeed foresighted and that the decision to ignore the recommendations and instead to give almost exclusive emphasis to the establishment of manufacturing was extremely unfortunate. After nearly forty years of "development," unemployment has become endemic and the island imports virtually its entire food supply, millions of dollars in foodstuffs annually, which could be produced locally had similar incentives been given to the modernization and diversification of agriculture.

It has been argued that one of the major factors contributing to Puerto Rico's painfully slow emergence from the depression of the 1930s was the long delay in extending the Roosevelt administration's economic policies to the island.[4] This is typical of the widely held view that all the developing countries of the world need is a good dose of the New Deal, ignoring both the drastically different environmental realities of the Third World and the fact that the New Deal remedies have been far from panacean in the United States. The implicit premise is that major economic and social change can be made to occur without a concomitant political upheaval, without basic institutional change, and without shifts in the relative power of the conflicting social classes.[5]

Regardless of what the optimum decision might have been for the long run, Puerto Rico's economic development program accelerated rapidly but briefly in the immediate post-World War II period. The windfall revenues to the island's coffers that had resulted from the wartime rum boom in the United States were utilized as seed capital. Initial emphasis, in a brief experiment with nationalized industry, was given to governmentally owned and operated enterprises. Five firms, for the production of glass bottles, cardboard, brick and tile, shoes, and cement were established during the 1940s. The island, however, did not escape the militant expression of the pent-up aspirations of labor following the austerity of World War II and several of the firms were plagued by a combination of labor problems and mismanagement.

The experience with governmental operation was traumatic in other ways. Technological, administrative, and marketing problems combined with the labor problems to such a degree that by 1948 only the cement plant was showing a profit. Governor Rexford Tugwell had adamantly opposed the alternative strategy of industrial incentive to private capital and accepted the public corporation's difficulties as normal and surmountable. Economic Development Administrator Teodoro Moscoso thought otherwise and was eager to divest the government of the responsibilities for productive enterprise. When Tugwell left the governorship in 1946 the road was clear for Moscoso's ultimately successful compaign for a switch in policy to one of attraction of private investment. After lengthy negotiations and related political face-saving considerations involving the "failure" of the government's administration of the plants, the entire group of enterprises was sold in 1951 to industrialist Luis A. Ferré, who subsequently became governor in 1968.

A major shift was soon made to the all-out attraction of private enterprise capital. Taking advantage of the already existent exemption from U.S. internal revenue levies, the insular legislature added the attraction of exemption from Puerto Rican taxes as well. Plant facilities were constructed by the government for lease to private entrepreneurs, managerial and investment support services were provided, and the entire package was vigorously promoted throughout the continental United States.

The advantages to investors were readily apparent: association with the common market of the United States, common currency, integration with the U.S. judicial and postal systems, implicit immunity from confiscation, relatively economical energy sources, apparent political stability, governmentally subsidized vocational training programs, availability of loan capital, air and sea transportation facilities, and a very large reserve of unemployed and underemployed labor willing to work at wages lower than those prevailing on the mainland.

Clearly, however, the possibility of rapidly amassing fabulous profits, not before taxes but totally without taxation, was the most enticing bait of all for mainland investors. As Hugh Barton, who has probably studied Puerto Rico's development program more closely and over a longer period of time than any other economist, has observed:

Why should doubling a profit which is already double the U.S. average make so much difference? The only sensible answer seems to be that many businessmen who decide to establish a plant in Puerto Rico do so because of the possibility of "unlimited" profit. . . .a 100% return—if untaxed—makes a millionaire before the end of the tax exemption period [on a typical equity investment of $100,000]. Gold rush psychology is apparently still a part of the American scene and the possibility of "making a killing" seems to be much more of an attraction to many businessmen than does rather high probability of a more moderate return.[6]

It is not surprising, given this sort of harvest from easy pickings, that scores of new enterprises were attracted by Puerto Rico's Economic Development Administration (EDA) or "*Fomento*", as it is known locally. Nineteen new plants were founded in the initial period between 1942 and 1947; by 1950 there were 89; by 1960 there were 655; by 1969 there were 1,388 new industrial plants, and the combined total of all plants, promoted and spontaneous, had reached 2,592. Total employment in manufacturing in 1969 had reached 138,527, and 107,895 persons of this total were employed in enterprises attracted by *Fomento's* industrial development effort. What is surprising, comment economists Lloyd Reynolds and Peter Gregory, is why even more investors had not joined the gold rush. The answer they give is related to the variability of profits between individual firms and the observation that "capital rarely *rushes* in a certain direction. It *oozes* in one direction or another."[7]

The vast majority of the new enterprises have been subsidiaries of mainland operations or, if independent, are operated by mainland entrepreneurs. Most have been relatively small, few employing more than a couple of hundred people with the average in 1969 being about seventy-five employees per plant. Processing industries—plants that depended almost entirely on locally produced raw materials—predominated during the initial stage of growth in the 1940s. The 1950s were characterized by labor-intensive industry: garment-making, textiles, electronics, shoes, cigars, and a miscellany of other products requiring heavy labor inputs, but with such minimal capital investment that transfer of the operation, and the jobs, elsewhere is a perpetual threat.

A turning point of sorts was achieved in the 1960s, however, for the insular government negotiated the establishment of industries involving massive capital equipment, in particular a petrochemical complex utilizing Venezuelan crude oil in an arrangement circumventing U.S. petroleum quotas, which it was hoped would generate a vast amount of employment in "satellite" establishments engaged in the manufacture of products derived from

Garment factory established by the Economic Development Administration. *Courtesy of the Economic Development Administration, Puerto Rico.*

petrochemicals (paint, plastics, etc.) As of the mid-1970s, these hopes had been only partially fulfilled, for although some new manufacturing enterprises had been attracted by the availability of the petrochemicals, there were not nearly so many as had been predicted. For example, while net income in manufacturing as a whole rose by six percent in 1969-70, petrochemical manufacturing showed only a two percent increase. When the refineries were being established in the 1960s, the predictions of their employment creation potential were invariably expressed in terms of thousands of jobs. The satellite enterprises, however, have turned out to be nearly as capital intensive as the refineries. In fiscal 1969-70, ten new petrochemical product manufacturing firms were established, but *total* new employment amounted to only 316 jobs.[8]

Insular net income increased from about 600 million dollars in 1950, to 1.3 billion in 1960, and to more than 6.0 billion by 1975.

See Table 3 for gross national product, 1950 to 1975. One startling indicator of economic growth can be seen in the fact that there was one private motor vehicle for every seventy-eight inhabitants in 1950, one for every nineteen in 1960, and one for every six inhabitants by 1969.[9] Another sure sign of "development": Puerto Rico's air and water are rapidly being polluted and contaminated—to the point that an Environmental Quality Control Board was recently established in an attempt to counter uncontrolled emissions from both motor vehicles and manufacturing establishments.

TABLE 3

GROSS PRODUCT BY MAJOR SECTOR, PUERTO RICO 1950-1975,
MILLIONS OF CONSTANT DOLLARS

Sector	1950	1960	1975
Agriculture	132.1	164.0	274.6
Manufacturing	119.7	366.3	2,115.4
Construction and Mining	30.4	101.1	486.1
Transportation and other Public Utilities	59.7	151.6	781.0
Trade	144.2	321.5	1,470.1
Finance, Insurance and Real Estate	74.5	201.3	1,084.4
Services	46.2	146.6	824.9
Government, Commonwealth and Municipal	75.1	187.1	1,317.2
Federal Government	45.7	79.2	193.6
Nonresidents	-15.1	-91.3	-1,212.1
Statistical Discrepancy	41.9	54.0	218.1
Total	754.5	1,681.3	7,116.9

SOURCE: Junta de Planificación, Oficina del Gobernador, Estado Libre Asociado de Puerto Rico, *Informe Economico al Gobernador 1971*, abril 1976, Tabla 4.

The economic advance had been so dramatic—despite the stagnation and decline of agricultural production—that scores of visitors from other developing countries flocked to the island during the 1950s and 1960s as guest of the U.S. Agency for International Development (AID) or "Point Four," as it was known at the time. The visitors soon noted, however, that Puerto Rico is unique in several respects, including common citizenship, defense, currency, communications, and commerce with the United States.

These advantages, of course, are not unmixed blessings. Participation in the U.S.defense system, for example, brings with it submission to U.S. conscription. Puerto Rico has no voting representation in the U.S. Congress and the drafting of Puerto Ricans (as has happened in every U.S. war the United States has been involved in since the Spanish-American War) into U.S. military forces has, therefore, been subject to criticism as constituting taxation—a "blood tax"—without representation.

In this respect, it will be interesting—when appropriate data are available—to compare development in Cuba with that in Puerto Rico, the two Caribbean protectorates currently engaged in a tropical version of what used to be known as cold war competition. It is too early to predict which society will ultimately be more successful, especially if "growth" is not measured exclusively in economic terms. Both have made impressive gains, both still contend with formidable problems, and both are dependent on major world powers. In making the comparison, however, it wil become even clearer that Puerto Rico's alleged advantages are not indisputable. Noted anthropologist Robert Redfield once observed that genuine autonomy is attained through much adversity, and, with this dictum in mind, one can question whether Puerto Rico or Cuba will eventually benefit the most from, respectively, excessive U.S. presence or excessive U.S. absence.

There is a growing awareness that the much-heralded social and economic transformation (from "Stricken Land" to "Showplace of the Caribbean") has not been nearly so profound or so pervasive as claimed by self-serving or uncritical observers.[10] Oscar Lewis's study of poverty-stricken Puerto Rican families in San Juan and New York, *La Vida*,[11] served to demonstrate that more success has been achieved in disguising than in eliminating hard-core poverty. There is evidence that the Puerto Rican government, under both Popular Party and Republican Party (New Progressive) administrations, has systematically suppressed or manipulated data that would reflect unfavorably on its own accomplishments. The persistence of extreme poverty makes it clear that many of the alleged accomplishments have been grossly overstated. An extra-ordinary overall rate of economic growth fails to obliterate the inequitable distribution of the fruits of that growth. It is estimated, for example, that during one period of high accelerated growth, 1953 to 1963, the 20 percent of families with the highest incomes *increased* their share of total income from 50.5 percent to 51.5 percent. At the same time, the proportion of total income distributed among the 20 percent of famililies with lowest income *decreased* from 5 to 4 percent.[12] These are obviously insigificant redistributions.

It must constantly be kept in mind that Puerto Rico, despite an extraordinary rate of economic growth, is a very small, very densely populated island still plagued by enormous developmental problems. The economy grew at average rates of close to 10 percent for nearly 15 years, but in fiscal 1975 plummeted to a rate of minus 3.5 percent.[14] Puerto Rico always has been and still is a very poor country, despite recent indications of what eventually may prove to be significant mineral and petroleum resources, despite the personal enrichment of the upper echelons of the professional and commercial classes, and despite constant propagandistic references to the island's "transformation."

Earl Parker Hanson, the leading "semi-official" chronicler of Puerto Rico's economic development, has written one book appropriately titled *Transformation* and another called *Puerto Rico, Land of Wonders*, both of which are wondrous examples of the tendency to overstate the extent of the transformation. As Gordon K. Lewis has observed, ". . .it would be difficult, even in the field of modern government propaganda, to match the rhetorically self-congratulatory note of the Puerto Rico literature."[15]

Unfortunately, for many Puerto Ricans the transformation has been from abject poverty to poverty. By 1969 Puerto Rico had reportedly achieved a higher per capita income than any other Latin American country,[16] but internally both wealth and income are still very inequitably distributed. Economically, the island is less well off than even the poorest state of the United States. It has been calculated, for example, that in 1970 the personal per capita income in Puerto Rico was only 37 percent of the U.S. average. There were 24 percent as many telephones and 44 percent as many motor vehicles per capita, but population density was a staggering 1,375 percent higher than the U.S. average, with only about 10 percent as much arable land per capita.[17]

Fiscal 1977 showed a personal disposable income of $8.1 million, a figure that exceeded the island's GNP of $7.9 billion and the net income of $6.6 billion for the same year. "The paradox of spendable income higher than net income (total of wages, salaries, profits, and other income resulting from productive activity) is made possible by federal payments for welfare, unemployment, food stamps, covered Social Security beneficiaries that did not contribute premiums such as dependent children, disabled persons, widows, etc., for a total of more than $2.1 billion."[18] By 1977 nearly half of the island's families, constituting some 70 percent of the total population, were receiving food stamps. (A van loaded with the precious "cupones" was granted special permission to be unloaded in Puerto Rico during the dock strike in 1975).[19] Garry Hoyt has calculated that the U.S. taxpayer, by the late 1970s, was providing an annual subsidy for each person in Puerto Rico of about $1,000, a total of $3 billion. Hoyt concludes that "Puerto Rico has gradually succeeded in becoming the first colony to effectively exploit the colonizer," at least in material terms, but this has left Puerto Ricans with a "kind of fateful addiction that insulates against one's awareness of his own deterioration."[20]

The problems of Puerto Ricans are not confined to the island. In New York City, where nearly a quarter of the city's school children are Puerto Rican, the position of Puerto Ricans relative to other New Yorkers deteriorated during the decade from 1960 to 1970. By 1970 the number of persons of Puerto Rican birth or parentage had reached nearly a million and a half and nearly one quarter were receiving some form of public assistance. While 11.6 percent of all Americans were below the low-income level in 1975, this was the case for 32.6 percent of mainland Puerto Ricans (compared with 24 percent of Mexican Americans and 14.3 percent of Cuban Americans). More than half of the Puerto Rican working-age population was out of the labor force or out of work in 1975 in New York City.[21]

Extraordinarily detailed statistics that illustrate virtually every conceivable aspect of Puerto Rico's economy—including numbers of eggs laid weekly and gallons of alcoholic beverages consumed, and the like—are readily available, but with one notable exception: rates of profit to private entrepreneurs. This veil of secrecy was briefly breached in 1975, however, when a prestigious committee of mainland economists, headed by James Tobin, Yale's Sterling Professor of Economics who was appointed by the governor of Puerto Rico, provided a stunning peek at just what a gold mine Puerto Rico had been for mainland investors.

The committee first clarified the complex nature of the resource and financial flows of investment, including a fascinating account of how the profits extracted from Puerto Rico are stashed away in high-interest certificates of deposit in Guam (a U.S. territory exempt from federal taxes). The committee then went on to explain that

> The rates of return to direct private investment in Puerto Rico are very high, evidently between 15% and 20% over the last fifteen years. This may not seem high for manufacturing operations, but the typical Mainland subsidiary is holding as much as 80% of its assets in financial form. If such a firm is earning a 10% interest rate on the 80% of its assets in financial instruments, and an overall 15-20% profit rate on all its assets, then the rate of return on the 20% of its assets in physical capital must be in the range of 35% to 60%.

The report then points out that probably as much as half of the $5 billion that capitalists have been induced to invest in Puerto Rico represents financial (paper such as bonds, mortgages, certificates, etc.) rather than real assets such as machinery and equipment. "It must be remembered that. . .[investors]. . .move funds in and out of the Island because it is profitable to do so. . . .It is an illusion to view Puerto Rico as having special claim to these funds. . . ." The blue ribbon, officially sanctioned committee then concluded by emphasizing the point that politically dissident groups had been trying to make for years: "Even when direct investment *does* represent real physical investment, it does not necessarily imply an increase in Puerto Rican welfare."[22]

Political scientist Gordon Lewis has, more than anyone else, raised disquieting questions about Puerto Rico's health and welfare. One of his particularly illuminating insights is his view that the Puerto Ricans opened up the island to U.S. investors with the idea that the more socially oriented latinos could slyly milk the gringo, capitalist cow, only to learn that the animal they enticed in as an innocuous bovine is, in fact, an insatiably voracious tiger.

The Political Background

Let us now move from economics to politics, in a continued sketch of the contemporary scene. The political party that forged the "partnership" with the mainland investors was the Popular Democratic Party (PPD). The PPD, led by Luis **Muñoz Marín,** squeezed narrowly into office in 1940 and proceeded to consolidate its power until, after nearly three decades of uninterrupted electoral successes, it finally fell victim in 1968, in a partial but real sense, to its own accomplishments in raising living standards. The rural population, ironically those who had proportionately least shared in the island's economic growth, by and large remained faithful to the PPD, but the new middle classes in the burgeoning urban centers—probably partially motivated by a desire to consolidate their gains with a more conservative party—switched to the New Progressive Party (PNP) in sufficient numbers to elect multimillionaire industrialist Luis A. Ferré, who is closely linked to the Rockefeller family, to the governorship in 1968. Psychologists Charlie Albizu and Norman Matlin provide insights into the voters' view of that shift in Puerto Rican politics:

> Both Ferré and Muñoz Marín present different images to the masses and to the middle class. Ferré's image is usually described as the antithesis of Muñoz's highly patriarchal figure. The reality is slightly more complicated. Ferré's image is also highly patriarchal. Like Muñoz, Ferré is seen as a person to whom you take your problems. . . .Muñoz represents the traditional figure of the *hacendado*. . . .Ferré projects the picture of a successful businessman. . . .Ferré has managed to project the image of modern paternalism.[23]

The PPD lost electoral strength as the result of an inchoate desire on the part of the electorate for a change in administration, for new management, and was also weakened as the result of an attempt to transform the party internally from personalized leadership and direct, centralized control to collective control and partially remotely controlled administrative leadership. PPD President Muñoz Marín had relinquished unilateral party and governmental control by not permitting himself to be renominated as chief executive for the 1964 elections and attempted gradually to withdraw from the center of power. The experiment aborted, however, when Roberto Sánchez Vilella, the handpicked successor to fill the governorship in 1964, rebelled when another party regular was in turn handpicked to be the Party's candidate for the 1968 elections.

The aborted experiment abounded with ironies. Muñoz Marín, popularly known as *"el vate,"* (the bard)—indeed, one of his biographies is entitled the *Poet in the Fortress*[24]—is a philosopher-king type, who led the country as the very prototype of the patriarchal, charismatic leader. In an obviously deliberate move to pave the way for more democratic decision-making, Muñoz very undemocratically picked as his successor the least charismatic member of his cabinet. This was Roberto Sánchez Vilella, his longtime, Henry Hopkins type of administrative aide. Sánchez, a pipe-smoking grandfather had been until then the antithesis of Muñoz: trained as an engineer, he had long experience in public works and a reputation as a skilled but politically invisible and innocuous technician. As so often seems to happen, however, the role became determinant of personality and the new chief executive divorced his wife of many years, married his attractive, young legislative aide, and in the process stirred up such a storm as his flamboyant mentor had never done.

A group of dissident *"Populares,"* likewise unwilling to accept only partial decentralization of the PPD, joined Sánchez Vilella in forming the Peoples' Party (*Partido del Pueblo*), thereby splitting the PPD electorate sufficiently to bring, inadvertently, the New Progressive Party to power in 1968.

The PPD, although losing the governorship and control of the house of representatives, did manage to maintain a working majority in the senate of the insular legislature. This resulted in a virtual political stalemate since 1969, for the deadlocked parties have alternated in blocking one another's attempts to legislate (or move toward either culminated commonwealth or statehood). In 1972 the PPD, this time with youthful lawyer Rafael Hernández Colón as Muñoz Marín's handpicked candidate, managed to squeeze back into tenuous power, only to be unseated in 1976 by the PNP's equally youthful Carlos Romero Barceló.

Romero Barceló promised to make no moves toward statehood (at least during his first four years of government). He also promised to increase incentives for foreign investors and to change the administration's traditional low-wage policy, moving toward the full application of mainland minimum wage levels to Puerto Rico. Romero Barcelo argues that the poor would be the biggest beneficiaries of statehood, inasmuch as the federal tax burden would fall mostly on the affluent, while the lower classes would benefit from increases in federal social programs. According to one observer

> this philosophy appeals at least to a sizable minority of Puerto Ricans who fear the radicalism of the *independentistas* and crave the security resulting from the American connection. When a mill worker explains his New Progressive *palma* flag by saying it is *más Americano*, he does not mean that he wants his children to stop speaking Spanish, the official language. Rather he wants to be able to count on his *cupones* [food stamps] now and his Social Security check later.[25]

In Puerto Rico the debate over political status is central and perpetual. The present "association" with the United States satisfies not even its principal proponents, the members of the PPD. They, the "*Autonomistas*," think of it as a forerunner of the sort of relationships that will eventually evolve beyond nationalism in the increasingly interdependent world of the future, and they push for its "culmination," by which they mean ever-increasing autonomy within permanent association with the United States. The members of the PNP—the "*Anexionista*" descendents of the former Republican Party—deride it as an impossible ambiguity, which should be tolerated only as a stepping-stone to statehood. The fragmented supporters of independence for Puerto Rico, the social democractic *Partido Independentista Puertorriqueño* (PIP) and the marxist *Partido Socialista Puertorriqueño* (PSP), an outgrowth of the *Movimiento Pro-Independencia* (MPI) that eschewed electoral politics, disagree over tactics, but are in general accord that the present status is to be resisted as a "perfumed colony." (There were four parties espousing independence in the 1972 elections. Schisms, purges, defections, and realignments are never-ending among the supporters of independence, probably caused, at least in part, by the provocations of infiltrators from the Federal Bureau of Investigation and related agencies.)

The idea of holding a plebiscite and thereby being able to notify the U.S. Congress of the preference of a majority of the Puerto Rican voters with respect to political status has been repeatedly discussed but never conclusively implemented, precisely for that reason: the results would be conclusive for the supporters of the losing factions. Nonetheless, a plebiscite was held in 1967 in which the supporters of commonwealth status led with 60.5 percent of the votes cast, followed by 38.9 percent in favor of statehood, and less than 1 percent in favor of independence.[26] The results are regarded as inconclusive, however, because (1) there was no prior formal agreement by the U.S. Congress to abide by the results; (2) no status received an overwhelming vote of approval or, stated differently, a very large minority of the voters did not favor the status favored by the majority; (3) the principal traditional parties identified with both statehood and independence officially boycotted the plebiscite, although other ad hoc groups were subsequently formed to campaign for those ideals; (4) the total vote cast was nearly 20 percent lower than the number of votes ordinarily cast in insular elections.

A somewhat clearer indication of relative popular support for each of the status alternatives can be obtained from comparison of the votes cast for opposing candidates to public office in Puerto Rico during the past thirty years. The resolution of political status has *not* been the exclusive, or even the central, issue at stake in these elections, but the parties and the candidates are clearly identified as supporting one or the other of the alternatives and therefore a vote for one of the parties is at least an approximate indication of support. See Table 4, which provides some insights as to how preferences have been shifting. A poll taken in September 1975, which was much criticized by statehood and independence supporters, showed that support for the Popular Democratic Party was down to 44 percent, against 38.7 percent for the New Progressive Party, 2.9 percent for independence, and 14.4 percent undecided.[27]

TABLE 4

ELECTION RRESULTS, PUERTO RICO, 1948-1976

Year	Percentage favoring the party associated with commonwealth	Percentage favoring the party associated with statehood	Percentage favoring the party associated with independence
1948	61.4	13.8	10.4
1952	64.9	12.9	19.0
1956	62.5	25.0	12.5
1960	58.2	32.1	3.1
1964	59.4	34.7	2.7
1968	52.1	45.1	2.8
1972	51.4	44.1	4.4
1976	45.7	48.2	6.0

SOURCE: Henry Wells, ed., *Puerto Rico Election Factbook*, p.38, and "Estadística Electoral sobre las Elecciones Generales de 1968," Junta Estatal de Elecciones, Commonwealth of Puerto Rico. Percentages do not total 100 because of votes cast for other minor parties; *San Juan Star*, November 13, 1976

The prolonged presence of internal political unity in insular government did not preclude another sort of political ambiguity, that of the separation of commonwealth and federal jurisdictions. the commonwealth Constitution in 1952 changed the relationship from clear colonial subservience to confusing ambivalence, with the federal authority predominant in some areas, the commonwealth in others, and still others in jurisdictional limbo. One of the central conclusions, for example, of a study of labor-management relations submitted to the commonwealth senate in 1971 is that considerable uncertainty exists as to whether petitions should be filed with the commonwealth's Labor Relations Board or with the National Labor Relations Board—which has a Regional Board in Puerto Rico—and that it is common for parties to labor disputes to file with both offices. Conversely, complete clarity exists as regards the jurisdiction of the commonwealth's Bureau of Conciliation and Arbitration, inasmuch as the Federal Mediation Service maintains no office in Puerto Rico as the result of administrative accords reached years ago by the respective governments.[28] Overlappings and interstices between federal and local jurisdictions are, of course, not unique to Puerto Rico. Similar situations arise in many states of the Union as well. The ambiguity has an especially vexing dimension in Puerto Rico, however, in that the island, since 1952, is neither subjugated colony nor federated state, but instead is supposedly a locally *autonomous* commonwealth *associated* with the United States. The autonomy, however, has turned out to be nonuniformly limited and the association confusingly defined. In the United States, the jurisdictional uncertainty between the National Labor Relations Board and state labor agencies, for example, is largely administrative in character. In Puerto Rico the uncertainty has political implications. The National Labor Relations Board's Regional Office in Puerto Rico, the proceedings of which are conducted in English, is increasingly criticized as a "colonial court," for example.

This frustrating uncertainty has venerable historical roots. Competing interest groups in Puerto Rico have long oscillated in appeals to the metropolis between greater intervention and insistence on less interference in internal affairs, depending on whether the specific relationship is protective or restrictive.

The federal government in spasmodic, unsystematic fashion has over the years abdicated responsibility, yet never granted unfettered autonomy. The result has been the absence of uniform policy defining the "association." Puerto Ricans are U.S. citizens, for example, and as such are subject to military conscription, but cannot vote for the congressmen who legislate the draft or the president who administers the Selective Service System. Incessant but substantially unavailing efforts have been made to clarify with the U.S. Congress the relationship as a whole, and/or to "Puerto Ricanize" federal processes through joint accords with individual federal agencies.

In piecemeal fashion—there is no office in either San Juan or Washington that coordinates federal activities in Puerto Rico—sundry federal agencies contribute about 15 percent to the

Commonwealth government's budget annually and, through the administrative procedures involved in the funding processes, are involved in varying degrees with the recipient insular agencies in public personnel administration.

The Labor Force

The central goal of all this economic and political activity—if one is to believe the campaign rhetoric—has presumably been the provision of jobs and income for Puerto Rico's burgeoning labor force. The results, however, clearly indicate that the island has had to run at a frantic pace in order to stay in the same place and, recently, to keep from falling behind.

Lloyd G. Reynolds and Peter Gregory, with Luz M. Torruellas, in 1954-55 studied Puerto Rico's economic development and the resulting volume is the best study published to date on Puerto Rico's labor force.[29] They note, for example, that agricultural production in Puerto Rico remained virtually constant for many years despite a one-third decline in the agricultural labor force, thereby providing something of a test for W. Arthur Lewis's predictions of what is likely to happen to the labor force when development is undertaken in societies with "unlimited" supplies of labor. Lewis had hypothesized that the

> main sources from which workers come as economic development proceeds are subsistence agriculture, casual labor, petty trade, domestic service, wives and daughters in the household, and the increase in population. In most but not all of these sectors, if the country is overpopulated relatively to its natural resources, the marginal productivity of labour is negligible, zero, or even negative.[30]

In 1920 Puerto Rico's population was about 20 percent urban, by 1940, 30 percent, by 1950, 40 percent, and in 1970 had reached nearly 60 percent.[31] Reynolds and Gregory also call attention to a "sharp drop in domestic service, that unfailing indicator of economic development"; on the other hand, seemingly more at variance with Lewis, they found that the picture of a population-pressured, one-step move directly from traditional agricultural to modern manufacturing is, at least in Puerto Rico, not an accurate description of the way in which the transition takes place. The authors explain that

> the workers drawn into industry were those with the least risk in either income or status. It was wage laborers rather than peasant farmers who entered the factory. These people were already at the bottom of the social hierarchy. They had nothing to lose in terms of prerequisites, obligations, or security of employment, and had a good deal to gain from the higher income and better working conditions in industry. One can say that the Puerto Rican rural proletariat has adapted to the industrial order so readily because it had no prior commitment to any other order.[32]

As can be seen in Table 5, between 1940 and 1975 the proportion of the labor force engaged in agriculture in Puerto Rico declined from nearly half the economically active, 45 percent, to less than a tenth, 6.6 percent. While studies of Puerto Rico's vaunted program of economic development have tended to emphasize creation of manufacturing jobs, in point of fact employment in manufacturing has remained proportionately relatively stable, moving from 15.1 percent of the employed labor force in 1960 to 18.6 percent in 1975. During that same period, employment in public administration nearly doubled, going from 11.6 percent of the labor force in 1960 to 20.5 percent in 1975. If those employees who are also employed by the government in public utilities are added to public administration, it becomes clear that nearly a quarter of the employed labor force was working for the government.

As can be seen in Table 6, between 1950 and 1975, even though major shifts from rural to urban occupations were taking place, the growth of employment in the services sector was minimal. The explanation probably can be found in the fact that many of the services required by an industrializing economy—insurance, for example—are imported from the mainland.

Unemployment

The unemployment or underemployment of very large numbers of the potentially productive members of the island's labor force has been Puerto Rico's most resistant problem ever since the demise of the traditional society. Living standards for the working

TABLE 5

EMPLOYED LABOR FORCE OF PUERTO RICO BY MAJOR INDUSTRIAL
SECTORS - 1940 - 1950 - 1960 - 1975
(as percentage of total employed labor force)

Sector	1940 Percent	1950 Percent	1960 Percent	1975 Percent
Agriculture, Forestry, Fishing, Mining	45.0	36.4	23.2	6.6
Manufacturing	10.9	9.2	15.1	18.6
Home Needlework	8.8	8.6	1.7	
Construction	3.1	4.5	8.3	9.4
Trade	10.4	15.1	17.9	19.2
Transportation, Communication, Public Utilities	3.9	5.0	7.2	6.6
Services	14.3	12.9	14.0	16.3
Public Administration	2.5	7.6	11.6	20.5
Other Industries, including Finance, Insurance, Real Estate	1.2	0.7	1.1	2.4
Total employed labor force	100.0	100.0	100.0	100.0

SOURCES: Reynolds and Gregory, *Wages, Productivity, and Industrialization in Puerto Rico,* p. 10, and Bureau of Labor Statistics, Department of Labor, Commonwealth of Puerto Rico, Special Labor Force Report Number 70-2E, and *Informe Economico al Gobernador,* Planning Board, 1976.

class had traditionally been almost subhuman, but each individual had some sort of function and place. With the rise of the concept of "superfluous" human beings—those persons whose skills are not

TABLE 6

CHANGES IN OCCUPATIONAL COMPOSITION OF EMPLOYED WORKERS
IN PUERTO RICO, 1950-1970

Occupational Categories	Percentages of Total		
	1950	1960	1970
Nonfarm laborers	5.8	8.2	8.4
Farmers, farm laborers	35.9	22.7	10.2
Craftsmen, foremen, operatives	25.0	26.4	32.8
Service workers	10.8	11.1	13.0
Other white collar	19.6	25.2	26.3
Professional, technical	2.9	6.4	9.3
Total	100.0	100.0	100.0

SOURCE: Puerto Rico Manufacturers Association, San Juan, Puerto Rico

marketable in an industrial system in which human effort is bought and sold as a commodity—came both the concept and the problem of unemployment.

One of the first studies of human resources conducted soon after the U.S. takeover, a study carried out in 1905, was prophetic: "Not only do the present tendencies indicate the permanency of an agricultural population without ownership of land, but it also seems probable that the oversupply of labor which now obtains, and which depresses wages to so low a point, will continue to exist. . . ."[33]

The problem is basically one of limited resources and a rapidly growing population. It took Puerto Rico four hundred years to attain a population of one million, but only fifty additional years to attain the second million, and it will need only thirty years, by 1980 or before, to count the third million.

The problem is further complicated by the absence of a serious program of birth control, increasing longevity, a low proportion of arable land, limited investment capital, low skill levels, no autonomous control of immigration to the island, and a recent tendency for new industries to arrive on the island already in a fairly advanced state of automation. All this is exacerbated by the tendency of the type of enterprise attracted to Puerto Rico to provide additional female employment, thus increasing the size of the labor force without reducing unemployment.

The labor force in 1972 had reached a high of nearly 900,000 persons. Thousands of jobs had been created and more than a million islanders had migrated to the mainland in search of jobs and a better life (more than 578,000 migrated in the period 1945-1962 alone),[34] yet unemployment has remained uniformly high over the last four decades. The official rate has never been below 10 or 11 percent of the labor force, hitting a high of 21 percent in 1977, and, in certain rural areas, being virtually universal. In the highland town of Jayuya, 96 percent of the labor force was reported as unemployed in 1977. Without the safety valve of the exodus to the mainland, it is clear that the unemployment problem would have become unmanageable by the 1970s and, as reverse migration continues, could well ultimately become literally overwhelming.

Those who support the "discouraged worker" hypothesis maintain that the application of mainland labor force participation rates to Puerto Rico would yield a more accurate picture of the problem.

The definition of "unemployed" provokes great controversy in Puerto Rico. The offical definition of unemployed persons is "those without work who are actively seeking employment." Critics of this concept maintain that unemployed persons who have become discouraged because of the lack of job opportunities and who no longer actively seek employment should also be included. For example, in 1975 the labor force participation rate in Puerto Rico was only about forty-two percent compared with some sixty percent in the United States. Critics claim that this sort of comparison indicates that at least a third, perhaps as many as much as forty percent of the labor force is in fact unemployed.[35]

Disguised unemployment; street vendor in San Juan, 1945. *Courtesy of Office of Information, Puerto Rico; Edward Rosskam, photographer.*

Lack of an occupation in the new industrializing society is by no means a phenomenon related exclusively to older workers unequipped to make the transition from the traditional society. Thousands of very young people are affected as well.[36] In 1969 it was calculated that at least sixty-five thousand persons between the ages of sixteen and twenty-five were neither employed, nor actively seeking work, nor in school.[37] Forty percent of the population as a whole are less than sixteen years old and the educational system—although attendance is now virtually universal through eight grades or so—is clearly not meeting the vocational needs of the entrants into the labor force. Acute shortages of middle-level technicians exist in the midst of an army of unemployed, unskilled labor.

Initial optimism about the number of years it would take to achieve full employment—in the early 1950s the island's Economic Development Administration had stipulated its own goal as being an unemployment rate of five percent by 1960 fell by the wayside as, first, migration to the mainland leveled off in the late 1950s and early 1960s, and, second, it was discovered that assumptions about the multiplier potential of employment created in manufacturing had been seriously overestimated. The assumption had been that two additional jobs in the distributive and service sectors of the economy would result from each job created in manufacturing. It soon became evident that the tertiary sector of the Puerto Rican economy harbored vast numbers of underemployed and that supportive services could be substantially augmented without significant increases in employment. Furthermore, it became clear that the new manufacturing enterprises were more integrated with mainland distributive and service mechanisms than with the insular infrastructure.

Income

Wages have risen rapidly in the modern sectors of the insular economy in recent years, much more rapidly than would have been theoretically expected in a situation with an "unlimited" supply of labor. According to W. Arthur Lewis, the pressure of potential job-seekers should have operated to check excessive differentials between the traditional and modern sectors, and wages in the modern sector could have been determined "by a conventional view of the minimum required for subsistence; or it may be equal to the average product per man in subsistence agriculture, plus a margin."[38] The experience of economic development in Puerto Rico, however, indicates that the Lewis model is theoretically plausible in a strictly economic sense, but impossible politically. Ilchman and Bhargave, in commenting on various models for economic growth, quote Aristotle as having advised that "in framing an ideal we may assume what we wish, but should avoid impossibilities," and then go on to point out—in an analysis applicable to Puerto Rico—that

one can scarcely expect democratically elected mid-twentieth-century government to operate in an early nineteenth-century fashion, tolerating very high profits and consoling workers with the doctrine that their grandchildren will eventually benefit.[39]

The difficulty with using the experience of Puerto Rico to test the

Lewis thesis on wage movements is that his model was predicated on societies with large numbers of persons unproductively engaged in *subsistence* agriculture. In Puerto Rico subsistence farming had been largely replaced by agribusiness long before industrial diversification and the rural-urban transition commenced. In any event, it is clear that wages in neither agricultural nor nonagricultural industries have been determined on the basis of "the average product per man in subsistence agriculture, plus a margin." See Table 7, which shows that over the period of intensive economic growth from 1952 to 1966, agricultural workers began the period making 42 percent as much as a construction worker (the occupation easiest for an agricultural laborer to move into) and ended the period with exactly the same differential.

Wages in Puerto Rico have increased relatively more rapidly than in the United States in recent years, but were so abysmally low to begin with that the differential remains large. See Table 8 for a comparison of mainland and Puerto Rican wages in manufacturing.

Average hourly earnings in manufacturing in 1950 in Puerto Rico were $.42. By 1960 manufacturing wages had risen to $.92, more than doubling in a decade, and by 1971 had reached $1.80, doubling again. This means, however, that twenty years ago a Puerto Rican worker engaged in manufacturing was earning only about a quarter as much as his counterpart on the mainland and in 1977 was still being paid only about half as much ($3.05 compared with $5.78).

The formulation of wage policy is a perpetual problem for Puerto Rican politicians.[40] The underlying justification for the entire program of economic development is that of creating employment at wage levels commensurate with a rapidly improving standard of living. Yet, the principal attraction for potential investors is the bait of relatively low wages and of keeping them low. The dilemma has thus far been partially resolved through the mechanism of a flexible, industry-by-industry system of minimum wage establishment, which by law (a special provision of the U.S. Fair Labor Standards Act) stipulates that wages in Puerto Rico should be increased as rapidly as possible to the statutory minimum applying on the mainland, but not so rapidly as to result in unemployment.

TABLE 7

MEDIAN WEEKLY EARNINGS IN SELECTED INDUSTRIES
PUERTO RICO, 1952-1966

	Agriculture	Construction	Manufacturing	Services
1952	$ 6.60	$15.60	$17.90	$15.00
1954	8.90	16.30	19.80	17.60
1956	10.20	21.70	28.10	22.50
1958	11.30	25.00	32.70	24.60
1960	11.30	31.20	38.00	29.30
1962	12.60	37.00	41.60	34.40
1966	18.90	44.60	43.80	39.40
Absolute Increase 1952-1966	$12.30	$29.00	$25.90	$24.40
Percent Increase 1952-1966	186.3%	185.9%	144.7%	162.7%

SOURCE: *Revista del Trabajo*, Departamento del Trabajo, Estado Libre Asociado de Puerto Rico, Tomo I, Núm. 2, Abril-Mayo-Junio 1968, p. 46, and Reynolds and Gregory, *Wages, Productivity, and Industrialization in Puerto Rico*, p. 66. The table has been constructed from an amalgamation of both sources and it should be noted that discrepancies existed in certain instances, an indication that data for the earlier years are approximations at best.

The U.S. Secretary of Labor is directed periodically to appoint special tripartite committees representing the public, labor, and employers from the industry affected, with both mainland and insular representation, to study the employment in and the profitability of a given industry and to recommend the minimum wage that shall prevail until the following revision. The minimum

TABLE 8

AVERAGE HOURLY EARNINGS OF PRODUCTION WORKERS IN ALL MANUFACTURING
INDUSTRIES, PUERTO RICO AND UNITED STATES, 1950-1977, SELECTED YEARS

Year	All Manufacturing Puerto Rico	All Manufacturing United States	Ratio of Earnings in Puerto Rico to those in the U.S.
1950	$ 0.42	$ 1.44	.292
1955	0.56	1.86	.301
1960	0.92	2.26	.407
1965	1.24	2.61	.475
1970	1.76	3.36	.524
1977	3.05	5.78	.527
Absolute Increase 1950-1977	$ 2.63	$ 4.34	
Percentage Increase 1950-1977	726%	401%	

SOURCE: The U.S. data is from the *Handbook of Labor Statistics*, Bureau of
Labor Statistics, U.S. Department of Labor. The Puerto Rican data is
from the Bureau of Labor Statistics, Department of Labor, Commonwealth of Puerto Rico (averages for calendar years).

wages established in Puerto Rico have, however, unlike those on
the mainland, tended historically to become the prevailing wage
(see Table 9), because unions are generally incapable of negotiating
more than a relatively small amount in excess of the wage rate
decreed (and only in the small proportion of most industries subject
to collective bargaining). In 1958 the average hourly earnings of
manufacturing workers in Puerto Rico amounted to about 85
percent of the minimum wage in the United States. Twenty years
later, it had climbed to 133 percent, but the average earnings of
workers in the United States was 251 percent above the minimum
wage level.

This special treatment for Puerto Rico has been in effect for
nearly forty years and for most of that period all of the elements in-

TABLE 9

RELATION OF AVERAGE HOURLY EARNINGS IN MANUFACTURING IN PUERTO RICO
AND THE UNITED STATES TO THE FEDERAL MINIMUM WAGE, 1958-1977
(federal minimum wage equals 100%)

Years	Puerto Rico	United States
1958	85	211
1959	87	220
1960	90	227
1961	98	230
1962	93	210
1963	98	213
1964	96	205
1965	99	210
1966	103	220
1967	99	202
1968	98	190
1969	105	200
1977	133	251

SOURCE: Adapted from a graph prepared by the *Asociación de Industriales de Puerto Rico*, 1970, and from Bureau of Labor Statitics Reports, U.S. Department of Labor.

volved—the Puerto Rican government, industry, and organized labor, both Puerto Rican and mainland-based unions—have joined in the consensus[41]that unemployment is the problem with the highest priority and, should wages rise too rapidly, that opportunities for increased employment would be jeopardized.

Former Governor Luis A. Ferre', a lifelong supporter of statehood for Puerto Rico, was relentlessly reminded by his political opposition that when campaigning for office he frequently insisted that Puerto Ricans should not be discriminated against and that federal minima should apply to the island, but, once elected to office had abandoned this position and adopted the traditional policy of exemption for Puerto Rico. Present Governor Carlos Romero Barcelo', faced with the inevitable, has been the first chief executive to break with this tradition.

Elder statesman Muñoz Marín is credited (or discredited, depending on one's bias) with popularizing austerity among the wage-earning populace, who passively accepted the inevitability of relatively low wages on the strength of his oft-repeated dictum that "the worst wage of all is no wage."

Hipolito Marcano, the President of the Federation of Labor of Puerto Rico, AFL-CIO, testified in 1959 before a congressional committee studying the political status of Puerto Rico. His reference to wage-fixing makes it clear that labor's position was then indistinguishable from the employers' or that of the government. "We are striving for the highest possible wages at every level of our progress, but we want to keep our workers employed. . . 17,252 workers [in the clothing industry make a substandard hourly wage of $.77]. If the average hourly wages of those people were raised overnight to $l or maybe $1.25 an hour for 17,500 people we would add those same people to the unemployment figures."[42]

The consensus is tested every time the Fair Labor Standards Act of 1938 is amended by the U.S. Congress, for the provision exempting Puerto Rico each time becomes subject to reexamination. This has occurred in 1949, 1955,1961,1965,1971-72, and 1977. In each of these episodes the consensus of employers, organized labor, and government, remained intact until the 1971-72 hearings when government, employers, and some segments of organized labor remained faithful to the previous policy, but a faction representing a significant number of the island's labor unions refused to go along. The group was led by the outspoken representative of the Amalgamated Meat Cutters Union, Peter Huegel, who insisted that the mainland minimum should be made applicable to Puerto Rico, including government employees. This very significant breakdown of the traditional alliances will be described in the next chapter.

The cost of living has been rising steadily over the years and then abruptly in recent years in Puerto Rico, to the point that real hourly earnings in manufacturing were only $1.72 in 1977. See Table 10 for a comparison of annual changes in the consumer price index for wage earners in Puerto Rico, with changes in nominal and real hourly earnings in manufacturing, over the period from 1960 to 1977. The interpretation of these data and the legitmacy of comparisons with the cost of living on the mainland are hotly debated in Puerto Rico by spokesmen for labor, management, and the government, with the various points of view depending on the standards of living taken into account and how the accounting is performed.

It is difficult to be precise about comparative costs of living in Puerto Rico. The Department of Labor of Puerto Rico calculates a cost of living index only for "wage earners' families" and uses the period 1957-59 as the base years (1957-59 equals l00). The United States Bureau of Labor Statistics, in a special survey for federal employees in Washington, D.C., and San Juan, Puerto Rico, reported that in Puerto Rico living costs were 22.1 percent higher in February 1971. Amadeo Francis, in representation of Puerto Rico's employers, was quick to claim, however, that "much depends on the standard of living they maintain," and that "because of differences in diet, culture, climate, and other factors, minimum requirements in Puerto Rico are probably less than half of those in the States." Resident Commissioner Jorge L. Córdova Díaz, in official representation of Puerto Rico, stated that the cost of living "is a little higher if you choose to live in Puerto Rico according to stateside standards."[43] What the spokespersons for the employers and government were implying, of course, is that the fact that workers on the mainland have a diet of meat and potatoes whereas workers in Puerto Rico have a diet of rice and beans has resulted purely from personal choice.

It is clear that consumption patterns are changing (see Table 11) and that a policy of savings and delayed consumption for the working class had, by the 1970s, become more and more difficult to impose on that class.[44] By 1975 families were devoting a quarter of their income to food consumption. This means, of course, that the upward pressure on wage levels has become increasingly persistent

TABLE 10

CHANGES IN EARNINGS AND COST OF LIVING, MANUFACTURING WORKERS
PUERTO RICO, 1960-1977, SELECTED YEARS

Calendar Years	Consumer Price Index for Wage Earners' Families (1957-59 = 100)	Hourly Earnings in Manufacturing	Real Hourly Earnings in Manufacturing
1960	105.2	0.92	0.88
1970	138.2	1.76	1.27
1977	201.2	3.05	1.72
Absolute Increase, 1960-1977		$2.13	$0.84
Percentage Increase, 1960-1977		331%	195%

SOURCE: Bureau of Labor Statistics, Department of Labor, Commonwealth of Puerto Rico.

as wage earners become ever less persuaded that their share of in-creased productivity gains should be sacrificed in behalf of job creation for the unemployed.[45] This is especially so as the public became more aware of just how inequitably income is distributed in Puerto Rico and just how slowly the inequities are being eliminated.

Revolutionary spirit—which is essential to delayed consumption on the part of the working class—has been difficult to institu-tionalize virtually everywhere in the developing world. Puerto Rico has been no exception. The enthusiasm that accompanied the first two decades in power of the Popular Democratic Party and that facilitated the sacrifice of individual and group aspirations for the common good gradually declined as it became increasingly ap-parent that the imposition of austerity was far from uniform.

TABLE 11

CONSUMPTION PATTERNS IN PUERTO RICO, 1950-1975

Items of Personal Consumption	Percentage of Total		
	1950	1960	1975
Durable goods	8.2	12.7	13.1
Nondurable goods	63.0	57.2	51.1
Services	28.8	30.1	35.8

SOURCE: Junta de Planificacion, Oficina del Gobernador, *Informe Economico al Gobernador*, 1969, p. 214; 1975, p. 166.

Slum dwelling in tidewater flats of San Juan. *Courtesy of Office of Information, Puerto Rico; Charles Rotkin, photographer.*

The attraction of investment through the lure of exemption from taxes and the accompanying economic boom helped to create new social classes capable of very conspicuous consumption. The gap also begin to widen between the upper and lower echelons of public service. Many of the early architects of the policy of sacrificial, dedicated public service had by the early 1960s found their way into extremely lucrative private business. Jaime Benítez, who had helped set the tone in the 1940s by accepting only half the university chancellor's stipulated salary and who had consecrated the concept of "public employment being incidental to service" in the drafting of the Constitution in 1951, startled the public in 1972 by accepting a pension of $26,487.50 annually, nearly $4,000.00 more than his salary. In 1970 the governor's Advisory Council called for salary increases for top public executives ranging from 40 to 60 percent annually (while continuing to insist on austerity for their subordinates).

Average income per family, a fair indicator of national economic growth but a notoriously poor indicator of the distribution of the fruits of that growth, was calculated at $116 in 1929 and still at $117 in 1941, [46] but it rose to $2,145 in 1959 and to $4,381 in 1967. However, as is indicated in Table 12, one of the most significant *shifts* in income redistribution occurred as the number of families with incomes under $2,000—well below the arbitrarily established "poverty" level of $2,500[47]—was reduced by twenty-six percent. Even so, the vast majority of families still have income less than the revised amount, $5,702, which the insular Department of Health in 1970 was estimating that an average family of five would require to meet "basic needs." About seventy percent of the island's families were probably still subsisting at levels below that level in 1970.[48]

Personality, Productivity of the labor force

The central characteristic of the contemporary labor force in Puerto Rico is a pervasive ambiguity arising from cultural conflict and lack of social identity. Association with the United States has undeniably resulted in material advances but has also brought "an increasing dependency and more emulation of the worst aspects of the American culture," as a former secretary of Public Education in Puerto Rico has observed. This insider's explanation of how economic growth eclipsed social development is based on the view that

TABLE 12
DISTRIBUTION OF FAMILIES BY MONEY INCOME LEVELS,
PUERTO RICO, 1959-1967

	Families			
	1959		1967	
Income Levels	Number (Thousands)	Percent	Number (Thousands)	Percent
Under $2,000	297	66.3	170	40.0
Under $4,000	89	20.0	179	32.6
Under $5,000	20	4.4	56	10.2
Over $5,000	42	9.3	144	26.2

SOURCE: Herman Miller, *Poverty in Puerto Rico* (San Juan, Puerto Rico: Puerto Rico Planning Board, Office of the Governor, Commonwealth of Puerto Rico, April 1964), p. 16 (for 1959 data), and Jorge Morales Yordán, "Desarrollo Político y Pobreza," *Revista de Administración Pública* 4, no. 2 (September 1971) (Escuela de Administracion Publica, Universidad de Puerto Rico) :125 (for 1967 data).

there was the mistaken tendency to separate the quantitative from the qualitative aspects of development. It is easier for the planners and policy makers, as well as for the political leaders, to consider problems in terms of more jobs, schools, hospitals or parks. This leads to a second mistake: the material aspects of development are emphasized, while the psychological and social needs are given secondary attention. There is always the rationalization of regarding the material aspects as means for social improvement, but due to the rapidity of change, and to delusions of this view of development, the deeper and more fundamental problems are constantly postponed.[49]

Muñoz Marín, the principal proponent of a policy of concentrated economic growth, in 1955—in the midstream of accelerated development—became obviously concerned about the uses of increased material wealth and proposed "Operation Serenity" as a counterbalance to "Operation Bootstrap." He called on the community to "use its economic power increasingly for the extension of freedom, of knowledge, and of the understanding imagination rather than for a rapid multiplication of goods, in hot pursuit of a still more vertiginous multiplication of wants.''[50] His call for redefinition of the goals of growth came too late. Puerto Ricans were already solidly, and probably irrevocably, addicted to infinite consumption. About the same time that Muñoz Marín was advocating less emphasis on material values, the survey instruments of labor economists Reynolds and Gregory were ascertaining that whatever the potential ceiling to workers' income aspirations may be, it is well above their present income levels.

Economic growth and diversification has changed Puerto Rico from a traditional, agrarian, two-class society to one in which those two classes—the very well-to-do and the very poor—have maintained their relative positions while a middle sector has grown rapidly from virtual nonexistence just a generation ago to a position as the most dynamic, and potentially the most substantial sector of insular society.

An entire array of traditional values and resultant customs, however, has remained largely impervious to changes in economic and social structures. The ties of extended families remain relatively strong as does traditional tolerance for behavior that in the United States would be regarded as incompatible with "efficient" allocation of resources.

Henry Wells, a longtime observer of Puerto Rican society, has attempted an analysis of what has happened to the value structure in the transition from a traditional to a modern community. He lists the predominant values in the conflicting cultures—such traditional values as fatalism, ascription, and personalism in conflict with such modern values as self-determination, perfectibility, equality, and industry—and describes the ambiguity of present-day Puerto Rico as essentially resulting from the difficulty of cultural amalgamation. Wells concludes that Americanization will never succeed in totally obliterating Puerto Rican culture, but that "the course of Puerto Rican development cannot be understood except in terms of the impact of the predominantly modern American culture upon the traditional Hispanic culture of the island.''[51]

With regard to the transitional characteristics of the labor force (from traditional to modern), the research of Reynolds and Gregory indicates that the supposed symptoms of inadequate industrial commitment—absenteeism, turnover, low productivity—often existed in Puerto Rico simply because management never bothered to calculate the comparative costs of taking positive steps to motivate commitment. They arrived at the conclusion that "management is important in any economy but it is crucial in the context of industrial development," and go on to supply sundry examples of "employer myopia," "managerial incompetence," and "managerial deficiencies."[52] These adjectives, of course, could well be unconscious proxies for North American impatience with traditional, "nonrational," behavior.

The authors maintain that production rose, economic development took off, and efficiency increased, not because of preoccupation with capital allocative decisions, but rather simply because management finally began to manage the labor force. They point out that "in a labor-surplus economy development is often conceived of as occurring through simple addition of capital," but that "the main explanation lies" instead "in tighter and more experienced supervision, improved work organization, and higher output standards." These findings represent substantiation of Theodore Schultz's insistence on the importance of the "neglected variables"—investment in human capital and the raising of the level of the productive arts—(Schultz, incidentally, specifically points to Puerto Rico, with its heavy emphasis on education and training, as one of the principal substantiations of his theories of "human capital").[53]

With regard to adaptation to industrial discipline, Reynolds and Gregory note that although the pull of tradition is by no means inconsequential, for paternalism, attitudes toward women, family responsibility, and similar social factors *do* interfere with economic progress, but argue that the attraction of modernism is so irresistible that the old order does not really stand a chance. Conditioning for commitment is seen as a problem of developing a managerial force capable of channeling the workers' headlong plunge into the modern world. The given is worker potential for commitment; the variable is managerial competence.

It is difficult to discuss productivity in Puerto Rico with any degree of precision because no reliable, comprehensive data on industrial productivity are published. As is the case with information about profits, as indicated earlier, the government rarely mentions productivity internally, even though grandiose claims about the industriousness of the Puerto Rican labor force are routinely made in the promotional literature.

An assessment of human resources carried out in the late 1960s, however, after having noted that "there are better methods," did describe a technique that permits approximate productivity comparisons, the results of which are summarized in Table 13.

TABLE 13

RATES OF ANNUAL GROWTH IN PRODUCTIVITY BY INDUSTRIAL SECTOR, PUERTO RICO, 1960-1967

Industrial Sector	Rate of Annual Growth 1960-1967
Agriculture	2.5
Manufacturing	13.3
Construction and Mining	9.4
Commerce	6.1
Commercial Services	2.0
Public Services	10.7
Transportation	5.6
Real Estate	13.0
Other Services	10.0
Government, Insular and Municipal	−4.5

SOURCE: Bureau of Social and Economic Analysis, Puerto Rico Planning Board, Office of the Governor, Commonwealth of Puerto Rico, *Manpower Report to the Governor: A Report on a Society in Transition* (n.d., ca. 1968), p. 42.

The rates of growth, approximate as they may be, are instructive. Productivity in the "public services" sector, which includes those oft-mentioned public corporations providing water, electricity, and transportation, showed one of the highest annual rates of productivity increases, 10.7 percent. This is attributed to "the tremendous technological improvements and economies of scale resulting from the expansion of services rendered to keep up with population growth," and to the fact that services were vastly augmented with an increase in employment of less than 1 percent during the seven-year period. The situation is quite the contrary in the conventional public sector, the only sector to register a *decrease* in productivity, 4.5 percent, as employment grew faster than service.

The Economic Development Administration, which regularly attempts to attract investors with advertisements in *The New York Times* and the *Wall Street Journal* (on April 28,1976, for example), computes worker productivity on the basis of output per wage dollar. On that basis, in 1972 the U.S. national average was alleged to be $3.36 of output per dollar invested in wages and the average in Puerto Rico $4.03. In other words, no matter how efficient the operation is or how industrious the workers, if the wage if low enough the "productivity" will be high.

The labor force's adaptability, trainability, rationality, productivity, and sophistication provide a perpetual source of wonder and admiration for Reynolds and Gregory. They sum up by writing that "for the most part one is struck not by the oddities of workers' reactions buy by the extent to which they parallel those of seasoned factory workers in the United States." They go on to say, "All in all, these workers' adaptation to the industrial way of life impressed us as surprisingly complete and rapid, a matter of a year or two rather than 10 or 20 years."

They characterize the individual Puerto Rican factory workers as emerging from the transitional process "as composites of the traditional and the modern industrial man," and note that considerable success has been achieved by those enterprises which ameliorate the drive for increased efficiency with retention of many of the elements of the tradititional society—personalized relationships and a certain amount of paternalism, for example.

The representative sample of Puerto Rican industrial workers, interviewed by Reynolds and Gregory some twenty years ago indicated a "surprisingly high" level of overall job satisfaction, and there were few workers who expressed objections to the "necessary routines of factory life."[54]

More recent evidence, however, strongly suggests that the degree of satisfaction with employment has lessened significantly during the decade of the 1970s. Increasing job dissatisfaction is manifested if one accepts the thesis that uninhibited, undisciplined, destructive behavior on picket lines is at least partly a catharsis from the frustrations of industrial discipline, and the evidence is bolstered impressionistically by the extraordinary degree of sabotage that has taken place in Puerto Rico during the current decade. To such events in the contemporary history of organized labor in Puerto Rico we now turn.

9

The Coming of the U. S. Based International Unions: The Pursuit of Runaway Industry and the Problems of "Union Colonialism"

Asoka Mehta, for many years India's chief economic planner (until jailed by Indira Gandhi) achieved an unsought degree of notoriety when comparative labor scholar Everett Kassalow singled him out as proponent of the "classic" formulation of the strictures that governmental planners throughout the Third World would impose on labor organizations. Mehta reasoned that consumption-oriented unions were acceptable in more modern societies, but in developing countries " 'the chief problem is economic growth, and therefore the major question for unions is subordination of immediate wage gains and similar considerations to the development of the country.' "[1]

Mehta's restrictive prescription is typical, but not novel. The working class in Puerto Rico has been unabatingly urged to subordinate consumption to production since the beginning of the century. In 1900, for example, when the FLT threatened a general strike because of the forty percent decrease in the purchasing power of wages resulting from the abrupt switch to U.S. currency, Luis Muñoz Rivera penned a precautionary editorial, the central point of which has been reiterated countless times over the years. His advice was simple: (l) the political party he represented had the best interests of the workers at heart and was profoundly concerned about the inadequacy of wages; (2) capital, however, must be *guaranteed* a profit and, if profits are threatened by insensate demands, investment will not be forthcoming; (3) the overriding *patriotic* duty of every working man should be self-sacrifice in the interest of economic growth through creation of employment.[2] In essence, these points have down to the present day continued to constitute the guiding rationale for governmental labor policy, regardless of the party in power. The modern expression of what the "patriotic" duty of the labor movement should be in Puerto Rico was formulated in 1957 by David F. Ross, an employee of Puerto Rico's Economic Development Administration, and, as synthesized by Gordon Lewis, made the following points. "(1) that trade unions belong fully only to advanced industrial societies; (2) that they generally stand in the way of economic progress since they are invariably opposed to technological innovation; and (3) that in any case so long as government adequately safeguards the workers' interests through minimum wage and other legislation little need for trade union activity arises."[3]

In modern times, once the rationale was professionally[4] buttressed, politicians and editorialists[5] have hammered away at getting across the message. Muñoz Marín during the 1940s and 1950s pushed his party's line that "the worst wage of all is no wage," which advice is essentially no different from that which his father had propagated sixty years earlier. The Popular Party's principal economic architect, Teodoro Moscoso has been warning workers for years that it would be tantamount to treason should their demands force a single enterprise to shut down.[6]

The most recent professional buttressing of the doctrine of austerity came in the form of the "Tobin Report" (referred to in chapter 8). The mainland economists reiterated in 1975 that "what the island faces is not a conventional labor-management dispute over the division of an ample pie, but a difficult struggle to keep the pie itself large and growing." Notwithstanding their having found—and for the first time having revealed—that investors in manufacturing operations in Puerto Rico were probably netting a return "in the range of 35 percent to 60 percent," these economists recommended a "freeze of pay scales" for government employees, a "policy of wage and salary restraint" for workers in the private sector, "deferment of the application of Mainland minimum wage standards to the Island," the "freezing of all wage standards" under Commonwealth control, the "suspension or reduction of minimum wages for youth," and a "thorough review of all legislation which raises labor costs...."

As so often before, the Tobin committee also recommended tax reform and that "the same standards of restraint, or even more severe ones, must apply to executive and managerial salaries, as to the wages of production workers."[7] The administration, given essentially the same advice decade after decade, strives diligently to impose austerity on the working class, but founders when it comes to reforming the tax structure or freezing executive and professional compensation.

Once committed to the strategy that a docile, austere, cooperative labor force was essential to investment, it became necessary for successive political parties, once in power, to eliminate those elements in the labor movement identified as rejecting the sacrificial rationale, to encourage and co-opt those seen as potentially acquiescent, and to substitute governmentally controlled labor administration for untrammeled trade unionism.

The motives of the PPD in subverting and controlling the labor movement are debated in retrospect, with one school condoning the policy as benevolent paternalism while another school condemns it as malevolent collaboration with economic imperialism.

Were all the evidence available, an objective analysis would probably conclude that at the outset both motives were almost equally present. There can be no doubt that Muñoz Marín and many of his early collaborators were liberals with a genuine concern for social justice and that their dominance of the labor movement was possible only because the workers perceived the Popular Party as the most viable champion of their security. In the mid-1950s, for example, a large sample of workers was asked to rank the institutions they perceived as helping them the most:

> On the whole, sentiment was rather evenly divided in the sample as to the relative virtues of employers and unions as promoters of worker welfare. Women clearly favored employers while men tended to favor the unions slightly. More important than either, however, was the insular government or its personification in the charismatic leadership of Governor Muñoz Marín.[8]

Whether the unions, left to their own devices, could have achieved more for the workers is impossible to know, but given the competition in the labor market it is doubtful, at least in the short run, that they could have. The Association of Sugar Producers, for example, in 1945 flaunted their disdain for the bargaining power of the militant CGT by offering a wage increase of one-eighth of a cent per hour.[9] In 1949 the CGT-CIO considered an island-wide strike in the sugar industry as successful when wage gains averaging only two and three cents per hour were negotiated,[10] another indication of labor's capability on its own.

Nonetheless, it is also clear that the conservative faction in the party, notably the three principal economic planners, Teodoro Moscoso, Rafael Picó, and Rafael Durand, later became so closely identified with vested interests that their commitment to social justice can retrospectively be legitimately questioned. It is also clear that the strategies pushed by those individuals within the Popular Party who were more opportunistic and less committed to social justice ultimately prevailed over those who were less opportunistic and more committed to social justice.

In any event, it is difficult not to perceive a large degree of manipulative cynicism in Muñoz Marín's official pronouncement on labor's role when—after his party has been instrumental in crushing the CGT and fragmenting the labor movement—he explained blandly that the government, because of the labor movement's lack of unity, had no alternative but to take the lead in providing security for the working class.

It was ironic that the government's dominance of labor's defensive function should come at that moment in history when organized labor in Puerto Rico, after four decades of struggle for recognition and the right to bargain collectively, had in fact received recognition and was preparing to bargain. Prior to the early 1930s there is no record of any but the most rudimentary written agreements,[12] and collective bargaining did not become feasible until after the effective application of the Labor-Management Relations Act and the passage of the insular Labor Relations Act in the mid-1940s.

Despite governmental paternalism, despite the depressed state of the economy, despite the surplus labor market, despite fragmentation of the labor movement, despite inexperience of most of the labor leadership,[13] and despite the witch-hunting political persecution that the most dynamic of the World War II era labor leadership was subjected to,[14] the unions in the 1940s were clearly beginning to develop a remarkable degree of organizational and bargaining expertise.

Part of the increase in expertise can be traced to the creation of the Labor Relations Institute at the University of Puerto Rico in 1950 by legislative fiat, in implementation of a recommendation made by Harvey S. Perloff in his prescriptive book *Puerto Rico's Economic Future.* Despite the fact that the Institute has never been adequately financed and despite the fact that an absurdly disproportionate share of its efforts was devoted to training programs for visiting trade unionists from other Latin American countries, hundreds of neophyte Puerto Rican trade unionists have benefited from its extension offerings over the past quarter of a century. Their opportunities for demonstrating their proficiency were abruptly and severely limited, however, thereby perpetuating a frustrating Puerto Rican tradition—that of encouraging workers to organize but discouraging them from pressing their demands effectively and autonomously.

The government's preemption of the role as labor's defender grew rapidly. An International Labor Office study of labor policies in the West Indies conducted in the 1940s reported that the "insular Department of Labor plays a prominent part in labour relations work," and exercises "responsibilities in regard to questions which are often elsewhere left for settlement by collective bargaining without governmental intervention."[15] The government's role, already extensive, had by the 1970s grown even further and eventually came to include virtually every phase of labor relations, even that of the arbitration of grievances, a function rarely assumed by public agencies in the United States.[16]

Governmental intervention has even included sponsoring organizing drives of favored unions, beginning with support for the CGT over the FLT in the early 1940s, and continuing with notoriously active support in the 1960s for the Seafarers International Union (SIU) over the International Brotherhood of Teamsters (IBT).

Once the unions were organized, the government's presence in the negotiation process also became highly pervasive and, in one case, that of the migratory agricultural workers, the insular Department of Labor directly assumed the negotiation of the contract, thereby wholly supplanting rather than merely supplementing the workers' efforts.[17]

The most fundamental contract demand of all, of course, is that involving wages, and Puerto Rico's flexible, industry-by-industry wage-fixing process represents a substantial preemption of the unions' role in bargaining.[18] David Ross, the Economic Development Administration's semiofficial chronicler, describes the process succintly: "The industry [minimum wage] committees appointed by the [U.S.] Secretary of Labor became in effect compulsory arbitration boards, and their operation *took the place of collective bargaining..*" Ross goes on to explain that

> although it was galling to the Puerto Rican pride to have this function performed by Federal agency under a Federal law, the Secretary of Labor generally executed his stewardship in a benevolent manner, and the only apparent concern of the committees was to do as much as they could for the unfortunate Puerto Rican worker.[19]

Ross was only partially correct. The minimum wage-fixing process drastically limited the role of unions in bargaining with their employers, but did not entirely take "the place of collective bargaining." With both wages and hours regulated by law, the unions preserved a modicum of bargaining autonomy by negotiating minor gains above the stipulated minima, and also have been relatively successful in negotiating fringe benefits.[20]

Once the terms of employment are agreed upon, the contract must be enforced and administered and in the United States this process has traditionally involved only limited governmental intervention. Alleged contractual violations are processed in multistep grievance procedures and, if no accord is reached, are settled arbitrarily by a private neutral who is paid by the parties to the dispute. In an approximate way, the inverse has held true in Puerto Rico. Labor agreements include pro forma procedures for the processing of grievances but, in fact, grievances involving discipline and discharge are very commonly immediately elevated to the next to last step and forthwith almost automatically taken to the Bureau of Conciliation and Arbitration of the insular Department of Labor where final and binding arbitration is provided free of charge. In addition, wage grievances have in like manner traditionally been filed directly with the Wage and Hour Bureau of the insular Department of Labor for the adjudication of employee claims. This circumvention of the grievance procedure continues informally despite an insular Supreme Court ruling—the *Ceferino Pérez* doctrine, as it is referred to locally—requiring labor and management to exhaust the procedures stipulated in their contracts.[21]

Given the inadequacy of finances of Puerto Rican labor organizations generally, and given the tendency of management in Puerto Rico to exploit any weakness adroitly, one would hesitate to recommend private arbitration, which must be paid for by the parties to the dispute at rates that could prove prohibitive for labor organizations in Puerto Rico. At the same time, it appears that the ready availability of governmentally provided arbitration has hindered development of grievance settlement procedures at the enterprise level. Consequently, the resultant lack of involvement for grievance representatives has limited the development of secondary labor leadership. The influence of shop stewards, so important in England and in the United States, is almost totally lacking in Puerto Rico.

Another debilitating consequence of the bureaucratization of labor relations, combined with low literacy levels and technically inexperienced leadership, has been the already noted tendency of labor organizations to defer to and depend on labor lawyers. Simon Rottenberg, who studied the labor relationship in Puerto Rico in the late 1940s, noted a "high degree of participation in union policy-making by a group of attorneys... with influence...far beyond what has come to be considered standard or normal in the United States."[22] If anything, despite rising literacy levels and increasing leadership expertise, the dependency of Puerto Rican labor organizations on legal counsel had become more pronounced in the 1970s than it had been thirty years earlier as a result of the continually increasing complexity of the labor relationship[23] as well as the presence of much opportunism and some altruism on the part of the attorneys involved.

A final area in which the Puerto Rican labor movement has seen trade union involvement replaced by governmental action has been in political involvement in the larger community. The working-class strategy of remaining aloof from party alliances and instead mobilizing labor support or opposition for legislative friends or enemies, known as "voluntarism," has never functioned in Puerto Rico. This was true in the FLT era because the labor movement could find no dependable friends in any of the parties and decided it had no alternative but to elect working-class representatives directly. It has also been true in the modern era from the formation of the Popular Party on. The various political parties have traditionally been careful to cultivate, in token fashion, the support of influential labor leaders and to nominate a few for the legislature, thereby supposedly obviating the need for unions to involve themselves in political action.

In this fashion a certain number of chosen labor leaders have been granted their turn in the legislature over the years, for as long a time as they were able to demonstrate significant working-class support or became successful in acquiring a political base independent of the labor movement. This classic modern examples have been Popular Party labor leaders Ernesto Carrasquillo, longtime president of the Senate Labor Committee Armando Sánchez, at one time the president of the House Labor Committee, and Hipólito Marcano, for many years a fixture in the Senate. Sánchez was one of the most powerful labor leaders on the island when first elected to the legislature, but he gradually lost partial control of his organization, the "*Sindicato Azucarero Packinghouse*," while distracted with legislative responsibilities and was eventually eliminated from the Popular Party ticket in the mid-1960s. Carrasquillo has retained firm control of his organization, the *Unión de Trabajadores de Yabucoa*, and remained entrenched in the legislature until voluntarily retiring in 1972. Marcano, President of the *Federación del Trabajo de Puerto Rico*, managed to develop sufficient personal leverage within the Popular Party to permit him to remain in the legislature, although his influence in the labor movement is now a shadow of what it was in the 1950s. Marcano himself has admitted that he no longer devotes any time whatever to trade union activities, that his presidency of the state federation is "an honorary thing" that consumed none of this time.

Marcano's leverage—and longevity—within the PPD, even

without his labor connections, has resulted from his multifarious activities, the variety of which is extraordinary even for a developing county in which skilled individuals commonly perform many roles. An articulate, spellbinding orator and brilliant tactician, the gifted Marcano permitted his talent to be diffused in too many directions. At one point, in the 1960s, Marcano was president of the state Federation of Labor in Puerto Rico, the Regional Director of the AFL-CIO for Puerto Rico, a senator in the insular legislature, a director of the Workers' Bank, the Grand Master of the Masonic Lodge, the Dean of the Law School of the Inter-American University, the president of the Evangelical Council, a practicing labor lawyer, a lecturer at the Labor Relations Institute of the University òf Puerto Rico, and Puerto Rico's peripatetic delegate to the ORIT and the ICFTU.

A strong case could be made in support of the argument that the working class has benefited from the presence of labor leaders in the legislature. The list of protective labor laws approved at their behest is impressive. A perhaps equally strong case could be made, however, that the delegation of legislative authority to a chosen few has seriously inhibited the rank-and-file and lower-level union leadership from democratic participation in the search for political solutions to their own problems. It is also germane to note that some forty years after the passage of the Wagner Act and an open invitation to organize unions and bargain collectively, less than a quarter of the labor force in the United States is covered by collective agreements. Would greater good for a greater number have been achieved via protective labor legislation applicabfe to all workers, rather than legislation enabling a minority to bargain for themselves?

The question of governmental presence in labor relations is a perplexing phenomenon also in that it is difficult to determine what degree of legal protection is most conducive both to the prevention of abusive advantage by those employers making use of an imbalance in bargaining power, and to the development of a democratically autonomous labor movement. Some comparative questions might illuminate the dilemma. For example, would the United Auto Workers' Union in the United States have become as autonomously vigorous as it has, had General Motors and the Ford Company been congenial rather than hostile and not forced the

autoworkers, as it were, to "attain autonomy through adversity?"
Yet, could labor in the United States have attained its autonomy
without the enabling legislation of the New Deal, legislation for
which the labor movement never lobbied? Or, in Central America
one can note the two very different labor movements in Honduras
and Costa Rica. The Honduran labor movement is relatively militant, solvent, and autonomous, while the Costa Rican unions are
lethargic and dependent. Can the conclusion be drawn that Honduran workers developed vigorous organizations in spite of governmental opposition (and that of the United Fruit Company) while
the Costa Rican workers have been stunted in their efforts to
achieve autonomy because of a government that spoiled them with
benevolence?

These are speculative matters, however. In Puerto Rico,
whatever the short-run benefits of governmental benevolence for
the working-class as a whole, it was clear by the mid-1950s that
organized labor, with most of its leadership either neutralized or
compromised, has been seriously weakened as an autonomous
vehicle for worker protest. It is noteworthy, for example, that the
painstaking study of Puerto Rico's labor economics, carried out by
Reynolds and Gregory in the 1950s, contained only four fleeting
references to labor unions in its three hundred pages. The labor
movement, still recuperating from the fragmentation of the CGT
and the dissolution of the FLT, had become largely superfluous to
the working class.

Another factor of fundamental importance in an analysis of the
dilution of class consciousness is the extraordinary mobility of the
Puerto Rican labor force. An ebbing and flowing but never-ending
stream of workers from Puerto Rico to the mainland, back and
forth, has taken place for decades, in an individualized search for a
better life and an escape from misery and exploitation. This uneasy
transience (Gordon Lewis has observed that Puerto Rico imports
its products and exports its workers) and the shifting working-class
base it has engendered have functioned as an escape valve for Puerto Rico, have provided the mainland with a cheap labor supply for
menial employment, and have also vitiated attempts to develop a
cohesive, politically conscious labor movement in Puerto Rico.

Also of importance has been the influence of the fact that
thousands of Puerto Ricans have served in the U.S. military and

those who survived, have been the beneficiaries of aid from the Veterans Administration, which in turn has subsidized a multitude of individualized small businesses and artisanry which, again, have contributed to a weakening of class cohesion.[23] The situation was changing, however, and, as almost always in the colonies, the change came from outside.

The impetus came with the arrival in force of the "international" unions from the mainland ("international" because of locals in the United States and in Canada). "Minimum wage plus a nickel is not for us,"[24] was the way the Secretary Treasurer of the International Union of Electrical Workers summed up the disruptive new approach to collective bargaining that the U.S.-based unions brought to the island beginning in the mid-1950s. With them came an entirely new dimension for the island's labor relations.

North American labor organizers were to prove disruptive not only to collective bargaining, but to the entire fabric of industrial relations. By 1965 the AFL-CIO's most outspoken spokesman in Puerto Rico, Keith Terpe of the Seafarers International Union (SIU), was claiming that the international unions had done more for the island's workers "in one week" than Senator Hipólito Marcano (as a symbol of Popular Party paternalism) had done "in a life time," and was calling for a general strike to protest "anti-labor legislation" promulgated by the Popular Party.[25]

A number of Puerto Rican labor unions had been associated with the U.S. labor movement since the turn of the century, but the relationship had been fraternal, mutually supportive, and, most important, noncompetitive in either labor or product markets. With industrial diversification and economic growth, all this changed. Developing Puerto Rico, increasingly dependent on the U.S. for investment and markets, found that the association brought unanticipated complications as well as dividends when it became clear that the mainland entrepreneurs brought aggressive union organizers on their coattails.

For nearly four decades General Organizer Iglesias had been the all-encompassing representative of the AFL as well as of those international unions with locals on the island in the role of liaison and foreign correspondent. The harbinger of change was the CIO's David Sternbach, who came to the island in the late 1940s, not as a briefly visiting technical adviser, but instead to take up permanent residence and to take the lead in aiding the incipient CGT in its struggle with the AFL-affiliated FLT. From this point on, the influence of U.S. labor organizations became not only one of general policy formulation from a discreet distance, but also one of intensive, personal administrative involvement.

The next development of importance was the decision in 1955 by International Ladies' Garment Workers' Union President David Dubinsky not to oppose efforts to exempt the island from federal minimum wage legislation, even though the exemption provided mainland employers of his union's members with an incentive to flee to Puerto Rico. Instead, rather than pushing for wage parity, Dubinsky lobbied in an attempt to narrow the gap between the wage rates in Puerto Rico and in New York City. The ILGWU also sent organizers to Puerto Rico as a means of neutralizing the competitive advantage through collective bargaining. As insider David Ross has explained, the tendency became, "under Dubinsky's tremendous influence on the minimum wage committees, to have the minima set a little below what he thought the union could achieve by bargaining. . . ."[26]

Also crucial in the influx of mainland intervention was the impact of a jurisdictional dispute between dock workers' unions in the Port of New York. A lengthy strike, which "had disastrous effects on the island's economy,"[27] took place on San Juan's waterfront in 1954 and resulted from negotiations that stalled because the settlement reached in Puerto Rico would affect the accord reached in New York. Insular governmental control of labor relations was fast slipping away.

By the mid-1950s the island's industrial development program was going through what Ross termed its "exuberant years," a time in which scores of new industrial firms began production in Puerto Rico, but also a time of reduced employment opportunities on the mainland. In 1957 the AFL-CIO Convention formally denounced Puerto Rico as a haven for runaway industry. After this, the deluge. By 1958 the lone organizer from the ILGWU had been joined by such a flood of representatives of other mainland unions as to justify the creation of a "state" federation of the newly merged AFL-CIO, the *Federación del Trabajo de Puerto Rico*, with Hipólito Marcano as president and an impressive list of twenty-two vice-presidents, mostly from the United States.[27] By 1963 there were twenty-six international unions operating on the island and, in 1972, after some had left and others arrived, the total stood at thirty.

David Dubinsky, speaking, flanked by Hipólito Marcano. Robert Gladnick, one of the first representatives of an international union in Puerto Rico, is seated at the table far right. *Courtesy of Foto Medina, Puerto Rico.*

Prior to 1958, although plainly disconcerted by the AFL-CIO's invasion, the Popular Party felt that the situation was still under a reasonable degree of control and the program of economic development not in serious danger. Apprehension was moderated by the fact that Popular Party stalwart Marcano presided over the labor federation itself while equally dependable partisans were strategically ensconced in three of the most crucial sectors of the insular economy: Armando Sańchez in the principle union representing sugar workers, and Juan Pérez Roa riding herd over the dock workers for the Popular Party. Furthermore, master politician and diplomat Muñoz Marín had established very influential, personal contact with the presidents of those international unions most personally interested in Puerto Rico: Dubinsky of the ILGWU, Ralph Helstein of the Packinghouse Workers, and Paul Hall of the SIU. Muñoz Marín, as always in that period, was successful in getting across his philosophy that "a low wage is better than no wage." There is also evidence suggesting that the PPD offered the AFL-CIO unions a relatively free hand in organizing the island's workers in exchange for the commitment from the AFL-CIO's support in Washington for commonwealth status (as opposed to statehood or independence).

The North American Congress on Latin America has also pointed out, in this regard, that

> the AFL's traditional and unquestioning acceptance of the capitalist system as best for both workers and capitalists logically led to its unqualified support for the Bootstrap ideology. Clearly there was room for debate and even struggle over wage levels—but the fundamental agreement between business, government and labor on the need for foreign investment in Puerto Rico as the only avenue to development created a firm basis for mutual cooperation.[29]

Complacency with the new partners turned to panic, however, in 1958, when the International Brotherhood of Teamsters, recently expelled from AFL-CIO, arrived on the scene in vigorous fashion and with no jurisdictional restraints. The Puerto Rican government, convinced that it would be futile to petition the Teamsters for wage moderation turned to the AFL-CIO for help. The SIU, which had initially cooperated with the teamsters in Puerto Rico, was assigned the responsibility and given support to oppose the teamsters wherever they appeared. Leo Suslow, an industrial relations expert and highly placed official of the Economic Development Administration, coordinated the government's assistance to the SIU, at one point reportedly even occupying a desk at SIU headquarters.[30] The insular confrontation became a symbolically important microcosm of the Teamsters' struggle with the AFL-CIO on the mainland. Teamster President James Hoffa visited the island to bolster the efforts of Frank Chávez, the Teamster organizer in Puerto Rico whose exploits in challenging both employers and SIU as well as the government fast became legendary (he was shot to death by one of his own body guards in an apparently unrelated incident in 1967).

The jurisdictional scene in Puerto Rico, already somewhat chaotic, became utterly so as raiding and counterraiding became the order of the day. The Teamsters survived despite the opposition and were still active in the 1970s eventually coming to be accepted by the government, at least for a time, as fundamentally non-threatening. Ironically enough, not so with the government's one-time ally, the SIU. Seafarers' Union chief Terpe in the early 1960s turned against the Popular Party, coming out in support of Agustín Benítez, a Puerto Rican International Brotherhood of Electrical Workers' member who became a "neorrican" (a "New York Puerto Rican") and who replaced Marcano in 1961 when the latter was abruptly dismissed by George Meany as regional director of the AFL-CIO. In 1963 Terpe joined with Benítez in securing an AFL-CIO charter for a Central Labor Council for San Juan, over which organization Terpe presided for the next decade, in effect undercutting Marcano's state federation. For the Popular Party, however, the most distressing blow of all came in 1965 when Terpe characterized the Sánchez Vilella administration as "anti-labor" and, as mentioned above, attempted with much fanfare to mobilize support for a general strike.

The contemporary phase of the development of organized labor in Puerto Rico has been characterized by the gradual domestication of the internationals. The North American organizers had brought with them a higher level of bargaining expertise, but this alien proficiency was soon forced to come to terms with the realities of Puerto Rico's economy. The specter of the abrupt closing of a firm (many firms are housed in buildings leased from the Economic Development Administration and have minimal ties binding them to the island) is an ever-present threat at the bargaining table that cannot be ignored. Relatively few firms have made good their constantly reiterated threat to move elsewhere unless wage demands are restrained, but those who do shut down have a markedly inhibiting influence on labor militance in an economy where alternative employment is severly limited.

Traditional values change slowly and most of the organizers from the United States have either partially adapted to those values or have gradually been replaced by bicultural Puerto Ricans. Reynolds and Gregory noted in the mid-1950s that "Puerto Rican factory workers appear to court paternalism instead of resenting it,"[31] and the imported leadership was able to do very little to change this norm. North American attempts to institutionalize grievance procedures, to cite one example, have foundered on the traditional reluctance—referred to locally as the "*ay bendito*" complex—to apply rules impersonally.

An at least equally important factor in the domestication process of the mainland labor unions has been the fall from power in 1968 of the Popular Party and the rise to tenuously shared power of the statehood-oriented New Progressive Party. A significant number of the labor professionals who direct the activities of the internationals—and especially those still identified with the Central Labor Council and most specifically Terpe and Benítez—came to be identified as pro-statehood, and tend to react to any move toward either autonomy or independence in either the government or the labor movement as subversive. Terpe, for example, who in 1965 had been characterizing the Popular Party as "anti-labor," joined with the New Progressive Party administration and the Manufacturers' Association in 1971-72 to take the lead in denouncing the previously mentioned destruction of the consensus of employers, government, and organized labor with respect to the application of federal minimum wage levels to Puerto Rico.

The break in the ranks, after thirty years of consensus, that finally destroyed the traditional united front on the alleged need to give special wage treatment to Puerto Rico in order to be able to use the bait of lower wages to attract capital investment, resulted from several factors. Of crucial importance is the fact that organized labor's position on wage policy in Puerto Rico for many years was unofficially, but rigidly, delegated by both Muñoz Marín and George Meany to David Dubinsky, President of the ILGWU. The garment firms had been among the first to establish in Puerto Rico in large numbers, and Meany deferred to Dubinsky as the leader of the union most heavily and directly affected. Muñoz Marín was anxious to cater to Dubinsky and to work out the best arrangement possible for Puerto Rican development with the knowledge that the ILGWU's strategy was oriented toward protecting jobs and standards on the mainland, where the vast majority of its membership is employed. Shifts in ILGWU policy, therefore, are not primarily attributable to any objective change in the needs of Puerto Rican workers, but rather to the situation prevailing in the United States. With the retirement of both Dubinsky and Muñoz Marín in the 1960s, easier opportunity to speak out was given to the leaders of other AFL-CIO unions, who had been growing dissident on the issue but had not previously been heard from. Republican Governor Luis A. Ferré attempted to rebuild the alliance with the AFL-CIO unions through Seafarers' International Union (SIU) representative in Puerto Rico, Keith Terpe, but neither Terpe nor SIU President Paul Hall nor Governor Ferré was able to dominate the situation in the manner of Muñoz Marin and Dubinsky.

There is little doubt also that some labor leaders in Puerto Rico genuinely feared that rapid increases in minimum wage levels would hinder union organizational efforts. These fears began to decline only after organizational enclaves had been successfully established. Coupled with this individualistic outlook was the fact that there existed no single, adequately staffed, central labor organization capable of developing a wage policy independently of government. Labor's top leadership had, by and large, been absorbed into the governing establishment and followed the Popular Democratic Party line faithfully. This alliance began to fall apart in the mid-1960s, however, and, by the mid-1970s, former labor supporters of the PPD policy were openly criticizing the low-wage strategy.

Beyond partisan political obligations and considerations, however, was the unavoidable evidence that unemployment continued to be a problem *despite* the attraction of low wages. The Economic Development Administration had predicted an unemployment rate of four percent by 1960, but both 1960 and 1970 came and went and unemployment refused to drop below eleven percent and finally climbed to more than twenty percent and stayed there. The impression grew that it was futile, as well as inequitable, to expect employed workers to perpetually subsidize employment creation efforts, which never seemed to bear dividends anyway—other than dividends on capital investment.

The dissident labor leaders no longer subscribed to the proposition that rapidly rising wages will automatically check increases in employment opportunities. This excerpt from their testimony before a committee of the United States Senate gives the flavor of the new labor position:

We call upon the Congress of the United States to reject a myth which has been perpetuated for 30 years in Puerto Rico

- that low wages will create more jobs. The constant cries that a high minimum wage will cause loss of jobs and an economic crisis must be put to rest once and for all. Fact contradicts the argument. The only thing that low wages produce is misery for the large majority of workers who barely make ends meet and create a burden for the tax paying community both in Puerto Rico and the United States while enabling considerable profits.[33]

The spokesman for the ILGWU also made a statement at variance with the historical consensus in which, for the first time, the Garment Workers' representative testified that "substantial increases in minimum wages in prior years have in no way hurt economic development in Puerto Rico. Present levels of unemployment are not the result of past minimum wage action and the proposed increases will not curtail employment opportunities.[34]

Once the long-prevalent unanimity of government, management, and labor has been breached—with important leadership in the United States from vice president Leon Schacter of the Amalgamated Meat Cutters Union and with expert counsel from

A Delegation from MOU, the United Labor Movement, at a recess during minimum-wage hearings in 1971. *Left to right:* Pedro Grant, Eugenio Cuevas, Robert Alpert, Peter Huegel, José Caraballo, Osvaldino Rojas, Miles Galvin. *Courtesy of the Merkle Press.*

that union's Washington representative, Arnold Mayer—most other union leaders abandoned the traditional strategy (of low pay being better than no pay). The tireless Peter Huegel had more than anyone else finally got across the realization that unemployment had continued to rise, rather than declining or even remaining stable, despite thirty years of holding the line, and that it was futile to expect the Americanized workers of Puerto Rico to compete with such low-wage havens as the Dominican Republic and Korea. Also, with or without insular unanimity on the issue, it had become increasingly difficult to find a majority of United States congresspersons who would go along with the discriminatory treatment of Puerto Rico ad infinitum. Finally, in 1977, the Fair Labor Standards Act was amended, increasing the minimum wage in the United States in four annual steps:

> January 1, 1978—to $2.65 an hour
> January 1, 1979—to $2.90 an hour
> January 1, 1980—to $3.10 an hour
> January 1, 1981—to $3.35 an hour

In Puerto Rico all workers currently covered by industry wage orders setting minima of less than $2.30 an hour will receive automatic annual increases until parity with the mainland rate is achieved. The industry wage boards were authorized to provide larger annual increases, but not smaller raises.

To return to labor's organizational efforts, the international unions had arrived in Puerto Rico at a time when the indigenous labor movement was in a state of disarray and the newcomers were quickly able to dominate the scene, but the imported hegemony was short-lived. The state federation of the AFL-CIO which had been founded in 1958 in a spirit of renaissance and labor unity and which attempted to amalgamate the newly arrived leadership with the established insular leadership, soon became the "completely helpless victim,"[35] to use Knowles's phrase, of the jurisdictional jungle that Puerto Rico fast became.

The internationals also lost allure as the result of practices that were abrasive to insular sensibilities[36] and that eventually brought persistent accusations of "union colonialism"[37] on the part of disenchanted local leadership. In early 1961 a former SIU organizer and one of the most tireless trade unionists and political activists on the island, Pedro Grant, took the lead in coordinating the efforts of the *Central Unica de Trabajadores* (CUT), which issued a historic *"Manifiesto"* denouncing the internationals, not without justification, among other things for having come to Puerto Rico with the deliberate purpose of discouraging the further movement of factories from the United States to Puerto Rico. The internationals' strategy, it was charged, was that of intimidating the employers with threats of imposing mainland wage levels.[38] This approach, of course, placed Grant and CUT in the embarrassing position of appearing to favor a low-wage economy. This countermovement to the mainland organizations gradually disintegrated. Grant became the principal organizer of the International Brotherhood of Boilermakers in an arrangement providing considerable autonomy, but the essential grievances remained unresolved.

To these most recent events in the development of organized labor, the uneasy relationship between the international unions and the independent unions and the upsurge in militance of the public sector unions, we now turn in the final chapter.

10

Current Events in the Labor Scene in Puerto Rico

A survey conducted by the Department of Labor of Puerto Rico in 1970 indicated that some 116,000 workers, or 20 percent of all wage and salary workers, belonged to labor organizations. The proportion organized in Puerto Rico might be compared with the mainland, where 22.6 percent of the total labor force was organized in 1970, taking into accout that 29 percent of the agricultural workers in Puerto Rico were organized (and 55 percent of those employed in the sugar industry), compared with an infinitesimal percentage of the agricultural labor force in the United States. It should also be noted that 47 percent of the manufacturing labor force was unionized in the United States in 1970 compared with only 30 percent in Puerto Rico. Barely 7 percent of government employees was organized in Puerto Rico in 1970 compared with 18 percent in the United States. See Table 14.

The referred-to survey included a question for those respondents who reported that no union existed in their place of employment asking whether they would be interested in joining a union in the event one were organized. Forty-two percent of these unorganized workers answered affirmatively and twenty percent were uncertain—a total of about 240,000 workers, indicating that far more workers were interested in becoming union members than had yet been organized.[1]

Numerous factors have contributed to the low incidence of unionization—the relatively small size of many of the units, the high incidence of female employment, the high rate of unemploy-

TABLE 14

PERCENTAGE OF EMPLOYED WORKERS WHO ARE UNION MEMBERS
BY MAJOR INDUSTRIAL GROUPS
PUERTO RICO, 1970

Industry	Percentage
All industries	20
Agricultural industries	29
Sugarcane	55
Others	7
Nonagricultural industries	20
Construction	17
Manufacturing	30
Trade	6
Transportation, communication & public utilities	61
Services	20
Public administration	7
Other	(a)

SOURCE: Ruben A. Vilches, "Union Membership in Puerto Rico in June 1970," Bureau of Labor Statistics, Department of Labor of Puerto Rico, mimeographed, p. 4.

(a) Less than 5%.

ment, governmental paternalism, and employer opposition. Two factors in particular should be singled out, however. The first is the extraordinary degree of interunion competition and the tendency to concentrate organizing resources on the affiliation of the already organized (it is not uncommon for a given bargaining unit to have been affiliated with two or three unions during a single decade) rather than the organization of the unorganized. The second is the much greater sophistication of management relative to labor, which has been quick to meet the challenge of professional organizers from the international unions with technically proficient industrial strategists of their own. Several insular law and management consulting firms cater to employers desirous of avoiding dealing with unions. The usually recommended combination of superficially enlightened personnel policies and dilatory legal tactics has proved to be a highly effective deterrent.

By the 1970s, however, the emphasis had long since switched from the organizing of the unorganized to the affiliation, or "pirating," of the already organized. The advent of the internationals had spawned a new type of labor leader. These leaders were ambitious individuals who had received technical apprenticeship as international union staff members, but who then often resigned, taking members with them in a free-lance combination of labor representation and entrepreneurship. This phenomenon added considerably to the already confusing disintegration of the contemporary labor movement, which had long been characterized by the tendency to found dual unions and new central bodies rather than attempting to reorient existing organizations.

The pattern initiated by Iglesias and his followers, who in 1898 had organized the *Federación Regional de los Trabajadores* only to abandon it a year later and found the dual *Federación Libre de los Trabajadores* when political differences became manifest, is followed faithfully to the present. Attempts are rarely made to exert majority control from within at the central federation level, and are unusual even at the local level where disaffiliction, decertification, and other interfactional disputes over administration of existing contracts and ownership of union physical property lead to debilitating litigation. The result has been structural chaos that surpasses the disarray of the aftermath of the disintergrating FLT-CGT struggle of the 1940s. In 1972 some 550 local unions and/or bargaining units existed, at least 100 of which were independent and wholly unaffiliated, and the remainder loosely affiliated with at least 17 "central" bodies. Each of these organizations implicitly claimed all-inclusive, insular jurisdiction, but none could legitimately speak for organized labor in Puerto Rico in any substantive sense. These would-be federations, some of them themselves mutually interlocking, included:

Federación del Trabajo de Puerto Rico (Federation of Labor of Puerto Rico)
Central Labor Council of San Juan
Seafarers International Union
International Brotherhood of Boilermakers
International Brotherhood of Teamsters
United Steelworkers of America
Amalgamated Meat Cutters and Butcher Workmen
Congreso Central de Trabajadores (Central Congress of Workers)
Sindicato Puertorriqueño de Trabajadores (Puerto Rican Workers Union)

Unidad General de Trabajadores (General Union of Workers)

Federación Libre de los Trabajadores (Free Federation of Workers)

Unión de Trabajadores Industriales (Union of Industrial Workers)

Congreso de Uniones Industriales (Congress of Industrial Unions)

Confederación General de Trabajadores (General Confederation of Workers)

Confederación Obrera Puertorriqueña (Puerto Rican Labor Confederation)

Confederación Laborista (Laborite Confederation)

Movimiento Obrero Unido (United Labor Movement)

In addition, one regional central body existed, the *Sindicato Obreros Unidos del Sur* (Union of Workers of the South), and some of the other international unions, the International Association of Machinists, the United Auto Workers, and the Brotherhood of Railway Clerks were not reluctant to organize outside their normal jurisdictions (to cite only two examples, the Auto Workers had managed to affiliate a local union of credit union employees and the Railway Clerks had taken in the helicopter pilots of Puerto Rico's Water Resources Authority). One individual in the 1960s went so far as to file petitions for union representation elections under his own name, "Waldemiro Arroyo Insular Labor Association," rather than that of the organization alone.

Bargaining units of under a dozen individuals, local unions with fewer than one hundred members, and "central" bodies federating only two or three local unions had become common by the early 1970s. Few union officials were willing to be lieutenants, virtually all striving to be generals in the labor struggles, which had become internal rather than external. When a legislator sympathetic to the labor movement, such as Luis Ramos Yordán (the nephew of the legendary Ernesto Ramos Antonini), extended invitations to labor leadership for consultation about upcoming bills, between thirty or forty individuals would crowd into his office. Any leader not included, no matter how minuscule his or her following, would become deeply offended, a result of what longtime reporter of the Puerto Rican scene Harold Lidin has described as the "fragile ego world of the labor leader."[2]

A spirited attempt to stem the disintegrating tide was made in

1972 with the founding of yet another central body, the *Movimiento Obrero Unido* (MOU) (United Labor Movement),[3] which showed great early promise before it too fell victim to the prevailing, schismatic sectarianism. The new, loosely knit federation was the brainchild of Peter Huegel, with the organizing impetus coming from Pedro Grant. Huegel had been assigned to Puerto Rico in 1969 with the mission of salvaging the Packinghouse Workers' Affiliate, following the merger of that international union with the Amalgamated Meat Cutters Union. He rapidly demonstrated himself to be the most thoughtful and innovative labor representative on the island, tacitly usurping the representation of the AFL-CIO from the retiring Agustín Benítez and simultaneously building bridges to the nonaffiliated, independent union leaders who found his honest and tireless dedication appealing. Grant, a zealous supporter of independence and a leading figure in the Puerto Rican Socialist Party (PSP), was a veteran labor organizer who had once worked for the SIU before attempting unsuccessfully to go it alone as an independent organizer and eventually becoming the secretary treasurer of the International Brotherhood of Boilermakers.

MOU managed to get off the ground by emphasizing that (1) Grant would act as "coordinator," rather than permitting any one individual to usurp the leadership; (2) unions, both AFL-CIO and independent, would be fraternally associated rather than formally affiliated; (3) the organization would be nonpartisan politically, and (4) would attempt to rally support only for those issues for which virtually general consensus existed.

The first such issue was that of opposition to the policy of discriminatory application of minimum-wage legislation to Puerto Rico, the doctrine of "low pay being better than no pay." This effort, which gained the support of a significant number of important unions, was followed by a successful appeal to the Nixon administration for exemption from the wage freeze, and by impressive shows of strength protesting the rising cost of living (largely the work of Grant's aide, Guillermo Bobonis). Also important in MOU's development was the coordination of aggressively effective support for a number of strikes, notably those of the employees of *El Mundo* newspaper and the Water Resources Authority. Perhaps most important of all in MOU's rapid rise to prominence was its effective use of the news media, with perpetual insistence on the needs of the working class being taken into account in social and economic planning. The barrage of publicity tended to create an exaggerated image of MOU's strength and masked the flimsiness of the ties that bound the associated unions.

MOU's decline came as rapidly as its rise to power and prominence. As had happened so many times in the past with similar organizations, the debilitating factor was that of party alliances. Grant was charged with subverting the MOU to the direction of the PSP and all possibilities for compromise fell by the wayside as bitter denunciations were exchanged. Some of Grant's closest collaborators, publicist Guillermo Bobonis among them, left the organization in 1974, and although MOU still exists, by 1978 it had become little more than an instrument of the PSP, a shadow of what it once had been.

A group of union officials who had withdrawn active support from MOU, but some of whom continued to maintain informal alliances with Grant's operation, got together in December 1975 to establish the Comité de Acción Sindical (CAS) (Trade Union Action Committee) as a means of maintaining at least a semblance of a unified voice for organized labor in island politics. Headed by Luis Enrique Pagán and José Gil de La Madrid of the Teamsters, Ernesto Díaz and Mike Arias of the Hotel and Restaurant Workers, Peter Huegel of the Meatcutters, and Osvaldino Rojas Lugo of the State Insurance Fund Employees' Union,[4] CAS has limited itself to sporadic pronouncements and refrained from getting involved in organizational affairs.

An additional incipient labor central point—in reality little more than a rallying point—the *Frente Unido de Trabajadores* (FUT) (United Labor Front) was also founded in the 1970s. This organization had ties to the *Confederación Latinoamericana de Trabajadores* (CLAT) (Latin American Confederation of Workers), an international labor organization of Christian socialist orientation that has traditionally denounced both U.S. and Soviet imperialism. This effort, if successful, would mark one of the few times that Puerto Rico's working-class organizations have looked to other than the United States for support and guidance (the CGT in the early 1940s was briefly affiliated with CTAL, a Latin American confederation with leftist orientation based in Mexico, and the CGT-*Auténtica*, under Francisco Colón Gordiany, established links, during the regime of Juan Domingo Perón in the late 1940s, with the Argentine based *Agrupación de Trabajadores Latinoamericanos* (ATLAS).

The addition of the Christian socialist presence in Puerto Rico—which was reported to be amply funded (including subsidization of study trips to Venezuela and Costa Rica for Puerto Rican labor leaders), but short on members—placed Puerto Rico closer to the mainstream of Latin American political currents. Most labor movements in Latin America tend to be trifurcated, with one group receiving aid and guidance from the United States, another from the Communist bloc, and another from European Socialist parties. It was much too early to predict whether similar efforts in Puerto Rico would provide centralizing influences or simply contribute to even greater Balkanization of the labor movement.

The mid-1970s also witnessed the emergence of what has since become known as the "New Unionism" in Puerto Rico. Much in the way in which the "new left" has distinguished itself from the "old left" in politics, the phrase is used to describe a marked increase in militance within both international and independent unions, but especially the latter as they attempt to remove themselves from the tutelage of some of the more colonialist internationals. The editors of the North American Congress on Latin America's reports have described the new tendency—probably in somewhat overly idealized fashion—as the actions of a new leadership that is

> challenging the premises of business unionism in Puerto Rico by restoring internal union democracy to their organizations, building labor unity, combatting collaboration with the capitalists and actively carving out a role in the political struggles of their nation. And, more than at any other time in Puerto Rico's history, growing sectors of this new union movement accept the tasks of the independence and socialist struggles as their own.[5]

At this point it is essential that the distinction between *"independentista"* unions and "independent" unions be clarified. In Puerto Rico the former are understood to be those labor organizations known to be led by individuals who espouse the political goal of independence for Puerto Rico. The latter are those not affiliated with the AFL-CIO or with any U.S.-based international union (such as the Teamsters or the UAW, which although not affiliated with the AFL-CIO, are not in the Puerto Rican context considered to be "independent" unions). There are any number of independent unions led by individuals who vigorously oppose *political* independence (supporting either commonwealth or statehood) but jealously maintain organizational autonomy. José Caraballo of the *Sindicato Obreros Unidos del Sur* was typical of this type. Conversely, there are a number of individual labor leaders who are prominently identified with the cause of political independence for Puerto Rico, but who function as representatives of U.S. international unions. Pedro Grant of the International Brotherhood of Boilermakers, a militant *independentista*, is typical of this type. The nomenclature of "independence" also tends to suggest independence from the traditional dominance over the past quarter century of the Popular Party. It is also important to understand that the party affiliations or political preferences of individual union officials, be they supportive of commonwealth, statehood, or independence, have little discernible effect on the membership of their organizations, at least on their voting behavior.

Certainly many of the unions generally understood to constitute the "New Unionism" are, however, both organizationally independent of U.S. internationals and led by individuals identified with political independence. The editors of the Puerto Rico Legal Project—probably somewhat idealistically—have described this new tendency as

(1) break-away unionism, whereby Puerto Rican locals have disaffiliated themselves from the internationals; (2) dual unionism, whereby independent democratically-run unions have arisen to challenge the internationals for the representation of the workers; (3) the achievement of a modicum of liberalization and local democracy under the umbrella of the international.[6]

This renewed militance has been manifested by bitterly contested representation elections, strikebreaking tactics on the part of employers (sometimes in combination with incumbent unions), lengthy strikes (conflicts of nearly a year's duration or more have occurred during the 1970s at *El Mundo* newspaper, Ponce Cement Corporation, and Crown Cork, a can manufacturing firm), and picket-line violence and industrial sabotage.

Another manifestation has been the increased involvement of the PSP in labor affairs. It will be recalled that the political parties espousing independence had rarely established links with Puerto Rico's working class. As Manuel Maldonado Denis has noted,

> the really endemic problem of *all* the independence movements of this century. . .was precisely that of their relative isolation from the working class. . . .if we analyze the process through which the PPD was created we will note that their original success resulted in achieving the convergence of the ideal of independence with that of social and economic achievements for the people of Puerto Rico.[7]

Both the PIP and the PSP, in their rush to emulate the PPD and achieve working-class support, made up for lost time in the 1970s. The MPI (later to become the PSP) became directly involved for the first time in 1969 during a bitterly contested strike of eight month's duration at the General Electric Plant in Palmer, Puerto Rico, and has been prominent in any number of labor conflicts since that time. The PIP has been less active in this regard, although the PIP leadership played an important role in the strikes at the University of Puerto Rico and in the public school strikes. Both PIP and PSP, during those periods when they managed to achieve minority representation in the legislature, have been outspoken champions of the labor movement and the working class generally. Both the PIP and the PSP have also frequently supplied legal counsel for working-class groups involved in litigation. In 1971 the PIP began to subsidize *La Hora*, a newspaper that consistently emphasized social and economic issues of interest to working people, in contrast with the politically doctrinaire *independentista* publications of prior decades. The most labor-oriented publication of all is *Claridad*, the PSP's periodical, which attempts to appeal directly to the working class.[8]

The increase in the length of strikes, in picket-line violence, and in industrial sabotage, although impossible to ascertain its causes, is probably related to a move on the part of employers to break strikes by taking advantage of the availability of the huge reserve army of the unemployed. Several law firms have specialized in providing counsel on ways of keeping unions out, and on hard-nosed negotiations should a union get in. In a 1977 strike at the

Gulf Oil Refining Company, the union accused the company of bringing strikebreakers into Puerto Rico from the mainland. Similar charges had been made during the strike at *El Mundo* and at Prinair, an airline. At least one company, Security Associates, an industrial security firm with headquarters in Houston, Texas, has been under fire in Puerto Rico for several years as a "professional strike-breaking outfit."[9] The number of private security guards had reached fourteen thousand, an increase of at least 100 percent during the five-year period prior to 1978.

The change in behavior has been sufficiently marked in recent years to inspire in all of the island's daily newspapers repeated editorials condemning the violence. Typical was *El Mundo*, which on January 23, 1972, editorialized that the labor situation had come to constitute "the most urgent problem faced by the country." The paper's concern was not altogether exaggerated. When the twenty-two hundred employees of the Puerto Rico Telephone Company walked out in January, 1972, telephone service was effectively curtailed within a matter of hours—despite automatic equipment—when cables were severed throughout the island. Literally dozens of incidents of heavy damage to productive facilities took place in other strikes during the 1970s.

In fact, the chickens were coming home to roost. During the late 1950s and early 1960s, as commented on earlier, the SIU and the Teamsters had carried on a running battle in dozens of representation campaigns, introducing a level of violence never before witnessed in Puerto Rico, even during the height of the industrial wars in the cane fields decades earlier. There is also little doubt that the PPD administration had encouraged or at least countenanced, the SIU's using any means necessary in the ultimately futile attempt to keep the Teamsters out of Puerto Rico.

In the forefront of the wave of violence (either as an aggressor or a victim, depending on conflicting versions of the various incidents) has been the *Unión Nacional de Trabajadores* (UNT) (National Workers Unión, a protégé of the International Brotherhood of Boilermakers and headed by Radames Acosta and Arturo Grant, Pedro Grant's son. Founded in 1970, the UNT launched an aggressive organizing campaign, mainly in the construction industry, and simultaneously (either through ineptitude or design) became embroiled in a direct confrontation with the Regional Of-

San Juan tabloid devoted entire front page to labor unrest on July 1, 1976. *Courtesy of "El Nuevo Dia," San Juan Puerto Rico.*

fice of the National Labor Relations Board in the latter's implementation of the Taft-Hartley Act. In 1971 the UNT was invovled in four organizing campaigns, and all four companies brought charges against the union for allegedly engaging in violence.In 1973 a worker was shot and killed duirng a strike in which the UNT was involved. Acosta and Grant were enjoined from continuing the strike and, although Grant was acquitted, Acosta was found guilty of criminal contempt in December 1976 and was sentenced to ninety days imprisonment and fined five hundred dollars for having disobeyed the injunction. In 1975 the NLRB issued an order to decertify the UNT as the bargaining agent at Carborundum and Jacobs Construction because the employer "could not be expected. . .to bargain with a union engaging in violent misconduct infecting and even destroying any possible harmonious bargaining relationship."[10]

More was to come. In 1975 Federico Cintrón, Executive Secretary of MOU, was arrested by agents of the Federal Bureau of Investigation and accused of having robbed a branch of the *Banco Popular* in suburban San Juan. The case took on mysterious complications when a federal judge accused Cintrón, probably because of known sympathies for the Cuban revolutionary government, of being an "urban guerrilla with international connections," and set bail at half a million dollars (ultimately reduced to two hundred thousand dollars and then to twenty thousand dollars on appeal).

In September 1977 attorney Alan Randall, who had long specialized in the representation of management in labor cases and who had a reputation for fairness, was shot and killed in terrorist fashion. An anonymous leaflet (signed "A.B.") was later circulated to the press and claimed that Randall was executed because he had

participated in repressive anti-labor actions during the historic period in which the labor and political struggles. . .had achieved great vigor. The strike movement, the continuous triumphs of the unions over the bosses, the increasingly successful use of revolutionary violence by our working people during the first half of the present decade, had broken the sepulchral silence which had characterized the Puerto Rican labor movement for decades.

The coldly analytical and articulate communication accused Randall of having been an agent of the Central Intelligence Agency and went on to argue at length in favor of increasingly violent levels of class struggle.[11]

The case, already mysteriously ugly because of anti-Semitic, terrorist overtones, was further complicated the following month when the body of a minor Teamster official, Juan Rafael Caballero, who had been reported missing ten days earlier, was found in a remote area of the island. The Teamsters accused the police of having tortured and killed Caballero during a vigilante type of interrogation, and they staged a demonstration to protest the alleged harassment. The police denied the accusations, but a source close to the investigation said that the inquiry had thus far led "to the same group of 12 or 15 people, many of whom are former members of the Puerto Rican Socialist Party and many of whom are involved with the Teamsters union. . . ."[12]

These developments, turbulent as they were, paled in comparison with the frenzied activity in the public sector during this same decade. Part of the problem, and there were many, was the structure of the government itself. Public administration had undergone a profound revamping under the prodding of Muñoz Marín and Rexford Guy Tugwell in the 1940s and had been further modified with the ratification of commonwealth status in 1952. The structure that emerged is similar to that of a state government with an executive branch presided over by a governor and composed of the traditional agencies and departments plus a burgeoning number of public corporations, bicameral legislature, judicial branch, and municipalities that combine the features of counties and cities in the mainland. The entire structure is ambiguously "associated" with the United States.

More than a quarter of all government workers by 1972 were employed by the public corporations, which were threatening to become a fourth branch of government. The virtually uncontrolled growth of these highly autonomous entities had by the 1970s come to pose the most critical structural problem in government in Puerto Rico.

Public administration in Puerto Rico has come to be characterized by two divergent tendencies: the centralization of the provision of services on an insular rather than municipal basis, and the decentralization of administrative control. One result has been the atrophy of municipal government; another, mounting chaos in intragovernmental employment standards.

In recent years, as population grew, urbanization increased, zeal in public service faltered, expectations mounted, finances become strained, and as the intertia of the legistative and judicial branches became increasingly obstructionist, the consolidation that accelerated action in the creative phase of the 1940s and 1950s took a lethargic turn and government became decreasingly efficient from the 1960s on. Furthermore, management in the public sector—given salary differentials that made recruitment difficult— was probably less competent than in the private sector.

Throughout most of the post-World War II period the commonwealth government had in effect functioned as a parliamentary system in which no significant ambiguity existed concerning the locus of decision-making power. The structural problems in government, therefore, did not become apparent until the dispersion of Muñoz Marín's monolithic political power, which began to occur in the mid-1960s. Added to growing internal disunity was uncertainty growing out of the haphazard relationship of commonwealth and federal governments, the result principally of what Gordon Lewis described as the contradictions inherent in "the management of an empire by a democracy."

The largest employer in Puerto Rico is government. In 1940 those employed in public administration comprised barely 2.5 percent of the employed labor force. By 1950, after the initial transition from laissez-faire orientation to governmental direction, the proportion on the public payroll had tripled to 7.6 percent, in 1964 jumped to 19 percent, and by 1974 had reached 28.6 percent.[13] In terms of the proportion of the total population employed by state and local government, Puerto Rico, with 533 government employees per 10,000 inhabitants, in 1970 ranked well ahead of every state in the Union with the exception of Wyoming.[14]

Employment in government is administered through a variety of personnel systems established as part of a difficult and still not altogether successful transition from political patronage to the merit principle. By 1975 only about a third of the approximately two hundred thousand public workers were included in the commonwealth government's central system of classified, competitive employment, the balance being either exempted from both the protections and restrictions of that system, or covered by an analogous system within an individual public corporation or municipality. The most debilitating deficiency in public personnel administration is the lack of all-inclusive uniformity in classification and compensation standards and in employment conditions.

The wages of government workers in Puerto Rico, low by U.S. standards, likewise failed to keep pace with increases in other sectors of the insular economy. See Table 15. In the years between 1952 and 1971, median weekly earnings in the economy as a whole increased by 261 percent, while median weekly earnings in public administration have increased by 166 percent—the lowest proportionate sectorial increase in the entire economy with the exception of finance, insurance, and real estate. In 1952 employees in public administration were earning 67 percent more than the average of median earnings in all sectors; by 1971 their advantage had been reduced to 22 percent. The comparative orbit for government employees, however, is more occupational than sectorial. Extremely wide differentials for similar occupations exist between the classified public sector and the public corporations and the private sector. For example, building maintenance foremen in the classified public service were in 1968 being paid 125 percent less than their counterparts in the public corporations while classified service typists were getting 79 percent less, stenographers 53 percent less, and welders 64 percent less. The disparities between the classified public service and the private sector for the same occupations were similarly diverse. Carpenters working for the government were paid 38 percent less than in private employment, office clerks 55 percent less, heavy equipment operators 75 percent less, welders 91 percent less, to cite only a few of the disparities. The principle of equal pay for equal work is difficult to achieve in practice anywhere, but disparities of these magnitudes led to especially invidious comparisons in Puerto Rico, where the equality of remuneration for similar work is supposedly constitutionally guaranteed.

It is generally recognized that the substandard wages paid to public sector employees have for many years in effect subsidized the expansion of the services these same employees provide.[15] The tacit recognition of this fact is so deeply ingrained that any move to

TABLE 15

MEDIAN WEEKLY EARNINGS OF WAGE AND SALARY WORKERS BY INDUSTRY
GROUP IN PUERTO RICO, OCTOBER 1952 THROUGH OCTOBER 1971

Industry Groups	1952	October 1960	1971	Percent Change 1952-71
Agriculture	$ 6.50	$ 9.40	$24.20	272%
Construction	15.60	31.30	63.50	307
Manufacturing	13.60	32.10	63.80	369
Trade	15.50	29.90	64.80	318
Finance, Insurance, Real Estate	38.20	51.30	94.30	147
Transportation, Communication, Public Utilities	20.20	38.20	81.40	303
Services	8.60	22.30	64.90	655
Public Administration	21.10	42.30	82.60	166
All Industries				261

SOURCE: Bureau of Labor Statistics, Department of Labor, Commonwealth of
Puerto Rico.

improve salaries is automatically opposed as inevitably detrimental
to governmental programs.[16] The "Methian formula" (which was
described in chapter 9 as prescribing arrested consumption and
increased production for the working class in developing countries)
had been applied in Puerto Rico in its purest form to employees in
the classified public sector. The alternative of increasing
governmental salaries *and* governmental services through the device
of increased taxation is perpetually studied, but it never approaches
the point of serious implementation, regardless of the party in
power (Puerto Rico collects less than 12 percent annually of the net
national product because of a regressive tax structure and

widespread tax evasion). Over the years, the government of Puerto Rico has been seen as both a provider of an ever-increasing level of services and as the employer of last resort, but with inadequate subsidization of either.

Unilateral determination of working conditions in the public sector in Puerto Rico was bolstered by application of the National Labor Relations Act with its provision that subdivisions of government not be considered as employers. The first legal breakthrough came in 1945, with the passage of the Puerto Rico Labor Relations Act (PRLRA),[17] which also attempted to exclude government, but which nevertheless included within its coverage certain of the recently created public corporations. This discrimination resulted from the fact that various public utilities had been established through expropriation of private firms where collective bargaining existed and the legislature found itself incapable of depriving those employees newly inducted into public service of privileges previously obtained. The Puerto Rican legislature, faced with a situation in which existing labor organizations with considerable bargaining power in such crucial industries as electric power were adamant in retaining their right to bargain collectively,[18] "resolved" the situation by accommodating within the definition of *employer* in the PRLRA those "corporate instrumentalities" already established (except for the University of Puerto Rico) "as well as such other government agencies as are engaged or may hereafter engage in lucrative businesses or activities for pecuniary profit."

At the same time, however, the Act excluded from the definition of *employer* the government of Puerto Rico or any political subdivision other than the aforementioned corporate instrumentalities. The legislature thereby created for the regular employees of the commonwealth and municipal governments, and for government itself, a situation that has become increasingly untenable over the years. It is apparent in retrospect that the employees of the governmental agency monopolistically providing electric power, for example, were granted the right to bargain collectively—including the right to strike— while the same rights were withheld from, for example, the employees of the Park and Recreation Commission, clearly not because the services of the former are less essential, but principally because the employees of the traditional agencies were not yet organized and were thus incapable of exerting pressure on the legislature.

The legislature had also established an insular civil service system (Act 345 of May 12, 1947), and certain of its provisions, drafted at a time when collective bargaining in the public sector was virtually unheard of, also contributed to the ultimate confusion and discrimination within the public sector. A series of interpretations left the employees of certain public instrumentalities in an employment relations limbo, neither covered by the provisions of the Personnel Act, nor protected by the Labor Relations Act. In addition, special legislation created a separate personnel system for the police force. The public school teachers, after an intensive lobbying effort, succeeded in having themselves exempted from the Personnel Law also. It was clear by the end of the decade of the 1940s that policy in public employment was anything but uniform and an opportunity for clarification and standardization should have been welcome. Such an opportunity arose in 1951, with the drafting of the commonwealth Constitution, but the framers chose to ratify chaotic past practice rather than establish uniform policy for the future.[19] Policy concerning participation of public employees in the determination of their working conditions, vitiated by the special treatment afforded employees of certain public utilities, remained that of permitting workers to organize but selectively prohibiting organizational action. Jaime Benítez, one of the principal constitutional architects, referring to the right of public employees to bargain and strike, insisted that "a constitutional regime cannot institute the contradiction of guaranteeing to an infinitesimal minority the right to suspend the execution of laws," ignoring the fact that the drafters of the Constitution had already consecrated just such a "contradiction."[20]

Legislative and constitutional provisions were, of course, based on developmental strategy that held that if it was necessary to control labor organizations in the private sector, it was absolutely intolerable that autonomous pressure groups be recognized within government itself. All attempts at bilateralism by public employees during the 1940s and 1950s were resisted by the administration on grounds, in an expression of the legislature, that "serving the People means rising above the demands of a group."[21] Or, in the words of the commonwealth's director of personnel, "the true motive of a strike is not to obtain better wages or working conditions, but rather is designed to provide a demonstration of strength and power. A strike against government is a strike against sovereignty.''[22] This was the recurrent theme developed by the Popular Party administration: the real danger of public employee organization lies not solely in the threat to a tightly budgeted and precariously developing economy, but in the possibility of usurpation of the concentrated political power necessary to rapid and reasonably equitable growth.

Pressure was building within the ranks of government employees, however, and after some initially easily squelched efforts to demand equity with other sectors of the economy, the suppressed groups burst forth in the 1970s with a vengeance. A number of factors combined to both push and pull the long-acquiescent public servants into militance. The rapid growth of public sector employment increased anonymity and alienation. Government workers became more aware that they had been inequitably subsidizing the services they rendered and this led to a decline in the messianic zeal that had characterized the early years of the PPD administration. The inadequacy of the grievance resolution mechanisms of the civil service system triggered an insistence on apolitical procedures. As the economy grew and diversified, employment alternatives increased. Public employers could no longer afford a take-it-or-leave-it attitude with discontented subordinates. The relative decline in remuneration plus steady increases in the cost of living were also important in bringing about decreased conformity. The relative freedom from fear brought about by the civil service system, which had been primarily designed to protect employees from the political patronage system, served to create an atmosphere of permissiveness conducive to union organization. Public sector union organizing was burgeoning in the United States, beginning in the 1960s, and this metropolitan example served as an additional legitimating influence. Coveted modernization had come to imply collective bargaining in government. Finally, the demands for organizational recognition began to gain momentum at that point in history when Muñoz Marín withdrew from the center of power and began to encourage participatory rather than acclamatory democracy.[23]

One of the earliest attempts to achieve union representation in public employment occurred during the insular government's brief experiment with public entrepreneurship in the 1940s. The employees of Puerto Rico's glass factory confronted the public administrators with a strike a month after it opened in 1945 and operations were not resumed until nearly six months later. Similar problems plagued the other enterprises[24] and the union leaders were accused of the "crime" of having caused trouble for the industrialization program. Félix Morales, one of those involved and one who has been active in the labor movement ever since, pointed out at the time that the "socialist" program was pointless if it could not provide social justice even for the workers employed in the nationalized industries.[25]

A rank-and-file protest movement within the normally staid Puerto Rico Teachers' Association—an affiliate of the U.S.-based National Education Association (NEA)—succeeded in pulling out some 90 percent of the island's public school teachers just before the Thanksgiving weekend in 1946. Muñoz Marín, then still insecure in power, "fraternally" advised the teachers that they could without losing face return to work on Monday in the knowledge that the PPD administration would deal with their problems. The teachers went back to work, but their problems were only partially resolved. Ten years later the Teachers' Association expressed a very mild threat of collective action should the legislature fail to act on their salary proposals. By then Muñoz Marín was at the zenith of his prestige and power, and fraternalism turned to paternalism. The threat of lobbying pressure was summarily squashed and the chastened leadership obliged to make abject apologies.[26]

About this same time, however, two of the unions of employees in the public corporations, which had inadvertently been granted the right to organize—and even to strike—were beginning to demonstrate freedom from the prevailing paternalism and lead the way for others. These exemplars were the *Unión de Trabajadores de la Industria Eléctrica y Riego* (UTIER) of the workers of the Electric Power Authority, and the *Unión de Trabajadores de la Autoridad Metropolitana de Autobuses* (UTAMA) of the workers of the Transit Authority. Their bargaining history dated back prior to the creation of the public authorities that came to employ them during World War II. Both continued to negotiate militantly in the post-World War II period, including frequent strike threats and, in the case of the bus workers, the carrying out of stoppages. Both also continued to build on the differential in wages and benefits that increasingly separated them from the classified government workers.

As always, however, the ultimate arbiter of legitimacy was Muñoz Marín who, apparently sensing the inevitability of bilateralism in government employment, moved in 1960 to transact the transition on the best possible terms. The result, in effect, was the issuance of a franchise for the organization of government employees to the American Federation of State, County and Municipal Employees, (AFSCME) an AFL-CIO affiliate. The implicit arrangement was that the Puerto Rican government's recognition of AFSCME, including checkoff of union dues, was contingent on the union's functioning as a mutual aid and defensive organization, renouncing the strike and leaving collective bargaining vague.

A government-dominated Federation of Government Employees had been organized in the early 1940s but soon dissolved. An Association of tax collectors had unsuccessfully attempted to negotiate with the Treasury Department in 1956. A number of other public employee organizations also existed in the 1950s, including associations of prison guards, police, internal revenue agents, sanitation inspectors, and welfare workers. None had managed to achieve recognition for purposes of determining working conditions, however, and all these became fair game for AFSCME. The organizing campaign, with the PPD's obvious approval, generated initial enthusiasm and more than three thousand employees were reported as having joined during the first sixteen months. In December 1960 the Federation of Public Employees of Puerto Rico was formally constituted as an affiliate of AFSCME.[27]

From this point on, the transition to bilateralism gained momentum and by the late 1960s it had become difficult to find a political figure in Puerto Rico—in any party—who still publicly opposed recognition of government employee unions. One group in particular, however, chafed at a situation that permitted the organization of unions and the checkoff of dues, but precluded collective bargaining or the right to strike. This was the

Brotherhood of the Employees of the Commonwealth's workmens' accident compensation agency which, under the tenacious leadership of the ambitious Osvaldino Rojas Lugo, in 1969 managed to achieve special legislation permitting the Brotherhood's members to become the first public employees outside the public corporations to bargain collectively. They were to use this right very frequently and very aggressively—including the exercise of a right they had not been granted, that of the strike—throughout the early 1970s and thus to set the tone for the turmoil that followed.[28]

The administrative and legislative history since 1969, including the passage of the special legislation for the employees of the workmen's compensation fund, has been one of delay and procrastination. Governor Rafael Hernández Colón in 1973 named a high-level commission, headed by former dean of the University of Puerto Rico's Law School, David Helfeld, to study the problem of collective bargaining in the public sector. The commission released its exhaustive report in 1975, complete with proposed legislation that was similar in many respects to Hawaii's law. But by January 1978 no action other than the establishment of an ineffectual Office of Labor Affairs in the Governor's Office in 1976 had been taken. Any chances that the government had of achieving orderly employment relations in the public sector had long since been swept away as one group after another forced de facto recognition in the most haphazard fashion conceivable. The PPD-favored Federation of Public Employees, AFSCME's affiliate, with its insular leadership not pushing for collective bargaining and clinging anachronistically to a no-strike policy,[29] gradually crumbled as its jurisdiction was challenged from all sides by independent unions, often with two and three organizations attempting to achieve exclusive recognition in the same agencies.

Significantly, those public employees who had been legally authorized to strike since the 1940s, tended to exercise that right sparingly until the decade of 1960s, while those employees prohibited from striking have made increasing, almost promiscuous use of that weapon. See Table 16. In 1968 only 2.4 percent of public employees in Puerto Rico engaged in strikes. By 1973 the proportion had risen to 11.2 percent (compared with 1.7 percent in the United States that same year).[30] Teachers, employees of the University of Puerto Rico, firefighters, and the personnel of the light and power company were among those striking that year and at one point Governor Hernández Colón found it advisable to call out the National Guard.

For the insular administration, the decade of the 1970s must have seemed endless as the harried government attempted to cope with one labor conflict after another in the island's most esential sectors and as the economy sank deeper into a "stagflation" that far surpassed that of the mainland. The year 1978 opened with a major conflict between UTIER and the light and power corporation, replete with charges and countercharges of sabotage and provocation. The bus drivers were also on strike and the firefighters were threatening to go out also. The administration, anxious to link the strikers with radical political groups, took advantage of the independence movement's increased visibility in virtually all labor conflicts and concentrated a barrage of public announcements condemning the involvement of the PSP in the strike. The accusations, largely based on innuendo, echoed similar outcries in earlier strikes when Secretary of Labor Julia Rivera de Vincenti, the daughter of Prudencio Rivera Martínez, a founder of the Socialist Party in Puerto Rico and a contemporary of Santiago Iglesias, repeatedly warned the public that "persons foreign to the labor movement and who have never helped the workers in any way are involving themselves in labor matters in pursuit of their own goals which have nothing to do with labor interests.[31]

The government's countercampaign and that of the press had a discernible impact on public opinion. An editorialist for *El Mundo* referred to one of the several stoppages in the Medical Center as an "inhuman strike."[32] In January 1972 the *San Juan Star* gave its first annual "The Greater Love Hath No Man Award" to the "Medical Center employees who walked off their jobs and abandoned their patients because of unconfirmed rumors that there might be some unspecified changes at the center."[33]

The more important cause of the decline in public support for strikes in government, however, has been the resulting inconvenience. The clearest indication of this change could be seen in the public reaction to the May 1972 strike of construction workers employed by the light and power corporation. These workers, who form a unit separate from the main body of corporation employees

TABLE 16

STRIKES IN THE PUBLIC SECTOR IN PUERTO RICO, BY GOVERNMENTAL DIVISIONS, 1964-1974

Years	Municipalities (strikes illegal) Number of:			Medical-Hospital (strikes illegal) Number of:			Departments and Agencies (strikes illegal) Number of:			Public Corporations (strikes legal) Number of:		
	Strikes	Workers Involved	Person Days Lost	Strikes	Workers Involved	Person Days Lost	Strikes	Workers Involved	Person Days Lost	Strikes	Workers Involved	Person Days Lost
1964										1	24	264
1965										1	1,045	14,550
1966												
1967							2	320	320	3	1,221[1]	2,082[2]
1968	4	685	1,270	5[1]	1,040	3,480	2	315	615	3	2,369	4,318
1969	3	1,631	1,756	1	375	1,500				7	2,916	6,234
1970	3	2,440	6,800							8	1,232	11,903
1971	5	962	4,402	4	1,004	4,349	2	1,860	3,720	10	3,559	27,723
1972	5[1]	236	1,348	1	200	800	6	3,477	7,957	15	14,957	129,107
1973	30[2]	8,054	61,057	4	1,820	3,310	7	2,211	12,687	12[1]	10,000	64,742
1974	6	3,405	5,532	7	3,800	11,335	2	1,429	17,245[3]	3	268	2,954

1. Data lacking on one strike.
2. Data lacking on two strikes.
3. Data lacking on strike in public school system.
4. First four months of 1974, only.

SOURCE: David M. Helfeld, Report of the Governor's Commission for the Study of Labor Relations in the Public Sector in Puerto Rico, San Juan, Puerto Rico, 3:89.

affiliated with UTIER, struck in support of contract demands. The stoppage resulted in almost immediate power failures, apparently attributable to sabotage.[34] After several days of no electric light, refrigeration, cooking facilities, or television, bands of irate citizens throughout the island forced picketing strikers to flee power substations, while repairs were carried out by nonstriking employees.[35]

The fragmentation and disunity that had long characterized labor organization in the private sector also prevailed in public sector unionism. In 1974, 30 separate unions represented the employees in the public corporations, and the proliferation of associations in the commonwealth departments and agencies and in the municipalities defied accounting. In 45 municipalities, 81 associations of municipal employees had been certified for dues checkoff. A total of 116 groups had received similar certifications in 36 commonwealth departments and agencies. In the Department of Health alone, there was a total of 31 associations, in Public Instruction there were 10, in the Treasury Department there were 9, with 8 in the University of Puerto Rico.[36] The vast majority were in independent, nonaffiliated unions.

This organizational chaos began to change, very tentatively, in 1977, with the founding of a loosely knit Confederation of Government Workers (Confederación Unida de Trabajadores Estatales, CUTE). The new organization which loosely linked seven unions, both AFL-CIO affiliates and independent organizations, had close ties with the already-mentioned FUT and with the Confederación Latinoamericana de Trabajadores (CLAT), an international labor organization of Christian socialist orientation. The founding of CUTE was probably at least partly inspired by a desire to counterbalance the *Bloque Laboral*, another loose federation of public sector unions, which had been sponsored earlier by MOU, presumably with support from the PSP.

In 1978, eighty years after the U.S. invasion and after a century of struggle and compromise by the organized labor movement in Puerto Rico, it was difficult to find more than a few encouraging signs for the future. A survey conducted by the insular Bureau of Labor Statistics claimed that at the end of fiscal 1975 only 14 percent of the labor force was organized, down from 16 percent only a year before, and down from 20 percent in 1970.[37] A major part of the decline could be attributed to shrinkage in the labor force itself. The rate of participation in the labor force had steadily declined as creation of jobs lost ground to increases in population and reverse migration from the mainland. In 1950, 53 percent of those who could be working were in the labor force. By 1975, the rate was down to 42.3 percent.[38]

Equally important, however, was the fact that the labor movement had been taking a pounding, partly because of its own disunity and even corruption (the 1970s, to cite only one example, saw a major, sordid scandal involving several prominent labor leaders at the Workers' Bank). The several long, violent strikes ended with no clear winners and many losers. Most AFL-CIO unions had virtually ceased organizing and were attempting to hold on to what they had. The International Longshoremen's Association, once in the forefront of labor activism but now depleted by automation and internal strife, had come to exist organizationally as well as occupationally on the margin of society. The widely esteemed Osiris Sanchez, the dock workers' ubiquitous adviser, was virtually their only link to the world beyond the waterfront. The Hotel and Restaurant Workers' Union, which for a time, behind the leadership of the astute Robert Alpert, had provided an example of how a union could be simultaneously honest, democratic, progressive, and effective, had been riddled by the decline in tourism. The leading forces in the influx of the U.S.-based internationals, such as the formerly flamboyant Keith Terpe of the SIU (as well as Clifford Depin of the ILGWU and George Treviño of the Steelworkers) were rarely heard from and Alpert had left the island. The Federation of Labor, AFL-CIO had become a paper organization, revived from its somnolence only at convention times. The Central Labor Council, AFL-CIO, was keeping such a low profile as to have become almost invisible.[39] The Teamsters continued to be aggressive, but were heavily embroiled in debilitating controversy.

MOU was still outspokenly active, but was having difficulty maintaining support because of its identification with the PSP. The once prestigious leaders of the FLT, personified by Santiago Iglesias and Nicolás Nogueras, who had risen to prominence in league with the Socialist and Republican Parties, had long since disappeared from the scene or were in semiretirement. Those who had risen with PPD and the CGT, such as Hipólito Marcano, Francisco Colón Gordiany, and Armando Sánchez, were on the verge of retirement. Many of the once vigorously independent offshoots of international unions who had gone into business for themselves, as it were, such as business unionist par excellance Arturo Figueroa and the once-imposing Juan B. Emmanuelli and Frank Ruiz, were reduced to resisting raids from the newer breed of independent organizers. The leaders of the "New Unionism" were in a state of disarray, spent by confrontations with the NLRB, wracked by fratricidal infighting within the political factions favoring independence, and reeling from counterattacks by hard-line employers in government and industry.

Most of the early leadership in the public sector union movement—such as Evaristo Toledo, Algimiro Díaz, Rafael Angel Valle, and Jose' Ramón Morales—were no longer in the mainstream. They had been replaced by a newer generation of leaders, such as Andre's Miranda, Jaime Cruz, Luis Lausell, Hector Rene' Lugo, Osvaldino Rojas Lugo, Graciela Martínez, and Filiberto Bonilla. Unions in the public sector were in constant turmoil; they lacked cohesion, were losing public support, and appeared to be losing ground to an increasingly adamant administration.

The prospects of no labor organization looked bright. The Labor Relations Institute of the University of Puerto Rico was providing little in the way of guidance out of the morass into which the labor movement was becoming mired. The Meatcutters' Peter Huegel and MOU's Pedro Grant, both scarred by countless frustrations, were among the few individuals in the labor movement in whom one could see hope for the future. Both had been unsuccessful in their efforts to create a labor central body that could provide an integrating rallying point for fulfillment of needs: for training potential leadership, pooling resources for organizing drives, ameliorating jurisdictional conflict, giving mutual assistance in collective bargaining and strikes, producing research data, procuring legal aid, conducting political action, and speaking with one voice for organized labor.

Might it have been different? It is impossible to know, but it is clear that the Puerto Rican government's paternalistic posture—nurtured in a colonial framework—reduced the participation of labor to a minimum even in those job-related, purely defensive areas usually permitted unions in other developing countries (which are not all that crucial to development anyway). Nor has organized labor been significantly involved in the formulation of social economic policy in Puerto Rico.

The exclusion has resulted, according to Gordon Lewis, in part because of the attitudes of the technocrats, who have been highly influential in shaping Puerto Rico's steadily retrogressive developmental program and who see "the union only as an unwelcome intruder in ...the sphere of economic engineering."[40] Given these attitudes, the labor movement—one of the few institutions that could have given at least partial voice to the aspirations of the working class—has been treated as an entity to be manipulated. In the process, the opportunity for enlisting labor's collaboration in social and economic planning has been lost.[41]

More than thirty years ago Rexford Guy Tugwell lamented the fact that those liberal administrators in Puerto Rico who were anxious to achieve social justice had been unable to achieve effective alliances with the "potential but unused allies" among the "vast mass of farmers and workers who hated the same upper classes" as Tugwell.[42] The golden opportunity for such an alliance came and went with the rise and fall of the PPD and the CGT. The populist effort turned sour, perhaps inevitably, as the policy of attracting capital to the island with the initial bait of low wages became a policy of perpetual low wages (at the same time that infinite, unbridled consumption of American goods was encouraged on all sides).

The sense of powerlessness has been heightened by the awareness that the labor representatives most proficient in influencing labor policy are those U.S.-based representatives who can utilize their mainland connections as powerful resources in the always-vulnerable colony. In this regard a noted Puerto Rican educator and historian has defined colonialism as:

> among other things...a condition in which basic policies involving a people's economic existence...are dictated from afar, by a power remote and different, and implemented by local representatives of that power, not directly responsible to the people. Colonialism can also be a willingness to accept a psychological inferiority in exchange for a modicum of local power or economic gain, an acquiescense in surrendering to a distant government or social or economic group, the basic

responsibility of shaping a country's destiny without properly consulting the popular will.[43]

The New Deal came to Puerto Rico and with it undeniable material gains as well as the creation of a monstrous middle class (with Muñoz Marín and others in the PPD probably now seeing themselves in retrospect as reluctant Dr. Frankensteins). The transformation also left a society wracked by social disorganization and ambivalance. Ten years ago Eldon Kenworthy, in a prescient analysis of Puerto Rico, had this to say:

The New Deal metaphor generates, first, the false impression that we understand what is happening in the Third World and therefore are entitled to shape events there. Then, it biases the way in which we intervene. Believing that economic growth requires uninterrupted political stability and that revolutionaries are heretics and outsiders, we place our power at the disposal of counterrevolutionaries. The reformist element usually remains stillborn, while the repressive element comes to life. The result is increased polarization-hence violence-within these societies.[44]

The one optimistic note emerging from this narrative, which has essentially been a chronicle of institutional development and labor leadership, is that the Puerto Rican working class itself has somehow managed to survive with more vitality and with a greater self-awareness and sense of purpose than any other segment of an ambivalent society. This is a triumph in and of itself, given the enormous problems. In a fundamental sense, it augurs well for the future.

Notes

Introduction

1. For example, Victor Alba, *Historia del movimiento obrero en America Latina*, pp. 417-433, includes a chapter on "El movimiento sindical en las Antillas," which discusses Haiti (which has never had a significant labor movement), but ignores Puerto Rico (which has); Robert J. Alexander, *Organized Labor in Latin America*, pp. 233-34, treats Puerto Rico in two brief paragraphs; Moises Poblete Troncoso and Ben G. Burnett, *The Rise of the Latin American Labor Movement*, pp.131,135,157n., mention the island only with passing reference to the Puerto Rican labor movement's panamerican participation; Juan Arcos, *El Sindicalismo en America Latina*, ignores Puerto Rican labor entirely. This situation is on the verge of change, however. Two researchers at the University of Puerto Rico Gervasio García and Angel G. Quintero Rivera, were completing dissertations on the history of the labor movement in Puerto Rico in the mid-1970s and Puerto Rican historian Lidio Cruz Monclova was preparing a volume on *El Proletariado Puertorriqueño en el Siglo XIX*.

2. The exact population of Puerto Rico according to the 1970 census was 2,712,033, with a population density of 792.8 per square miles. The population density in the capital city of San Juan was 9,856.2 per square mile. *Number of Inhabitants*, Final Report, Puerto Rico, U.S. Bureau of the Census, U.S. Census of Population, 1970 (Washington, D.C.: U.S. Government Printing Office, 1971), Table 7.

3. For a concise and very readable survey in English of information, past and present, on Puerto Rico, an excellent source is Kal Wagenheim, *Puerto Rico*, (New York: Praeger, 1970).

4. A predatory English expeditionary force managed to gain control of San Juan, Puerto Rico's capital city, in 1598, but the control was temporary because the occupiers were reportedly unable to withstand the rigors of the tropics and abandoned their prize before the year was out. Later on in the same century a Dutch force also failed to wrest the island from Spanish control.

5. The island as a whole was originally called San Juan Bautista by Columbus, and the city that was to become the capital was initially called Puerto Rico. After a time the names were interchanged; the capital was referred to as San Juan and the island as a whole as Puerto Rico.

6. Robert W. Anderson, *Party Politics in Puerto Rico* (Stanford, Calif.: Stanford Universtiy Press, 1965), p.3.

195

7. An account written in 1582 reported that *all* the Indians previously inhabiting the island had been exterminated, principally as the result of forced labor in the mines. Jhoan Melgarejo, in *Cronicas de Puerto Rico (1493-1797)*, Eugenio Fernández Méndez, ed. (San Juan, Puerto Rico: Ediciones del Gobierno del Estado Libre Asociado de Puerto Rico, 1957), pp. 114-16. Other accounts make it seem more likely that not all the indigenous population was exterminated, but rather that some were able to flee to the mountains or to other islands.

8. The *encomienda* ("commission") was the device utilized by the Spanish crown to legalize the forced labor of Indians while simultaneously attempting to control exploitation. The *encomienda* was originally "a temporary grant by the crown of jurisdiction and manorial rights over lands conquered from the infidels, made to knights as a reward for services in the Moorish wars. The peasants on these lands presumably were crown tenants, and life rights to their services were given to the *encomenderos*. As developed in the Indies, the *encomienda* was the patronage conferred by royal favor over a portion of the natives concentrated in settlements near those of the Spaniards; the obligation to instruct them in the Christian religion and the elements of civilized life, and to defend them in their persons and property; coupled with the right to demand tribute or labor in return for these privileges... It was an attempt to reconcile the crown's determination to deal kindly with the natives and the need for a stable and continuous labor supply, and it became the basis for Spanish-Indian relations over a period of two and a half centuries" (C.H.Haring, *The Spanish Empire in America* [New York: Harcourt, Brace & World, 1963 (first published 1947)], p. 40.

9. R. A. Van Middeldyk, *The History of Puerto Rico From The Spanish Discovery to the American Occupation* (New York: D. Appleton & Co., 1903), pp. 147-48.

10. Wagenheim, *Puerto Rico*, p. 49.

11. Angel G. Quintero Alfaro, "Educational Innovation and Change in Societies with Less Advanced Technology," (unpublished manuscript, 1971), p. 12.

12. Four valuable sources of information about this period are: Lidio Cruz Monclova, *Historia de Puerto Rico*, 3 vols., (Río Piedras, Puerto Rico: Editorial Universidad de Puerto Rico, 1957-1962); Harvey S. Perloff, *Puerto Rico's Economic Future*, (Chicago: University of Chicago Press, 1950); Gordon K. Lewis, *Puerto Rico, Freedom and Power in the Caribbean*, (New York: Monthly Review Press, 1963); Manuel Maldonado Denis, *Puerto Rico, una Interpretación Histórico-Social* (México: Siglo XXI, 1969).

13. Robert J. Hunter, *A Survey of Historial, Economic, and Political Affairs of Puerto Rico* (Washington, D.C.: Government Printing Office, 1959), p. l; Bailey W. and Justine Diffie, *Porto Rico: A Broken Pledge* (New York: The Vanguard Press, 1949) pp. 11 and 17-18. Edward J. Berbusse, *The United States in Puerto Rico, 1898-1900* (Chapel Hill, N.C.: University of North Carolina Press, 1966), p. 9-10; Berbusse, a Jesuit, is the only author I have found (citing Monclova and de la Fuente) who maintains that a significant number of the post-1810 immigrants were not conservative: "Among the heterodox were those who ridiculed the dogmas and authority of the Catholic Church... [and] in the secrecy of the Masonic lodges, new politial and philosophical ideas were discussed." If this is so, the new ideas took little root in the Puerto Rican environment. For example, Santiago Iglesias, *Luchas*

Emancipadoras (San Juan, Puerto Rico: Imprenta Venezuela, 1958), 1:40, notes that in February 1897, when the news of the death of the Cuban revolutionary Antonio Maceo reached the island, this Spanish victory was celebrated by the people in the streets of San Juan.

CHAPTER I

1. The most conscienscious research in the early history of the working class in Puerto Rico thus far published is *Lucha Obrera en Puerto Rico*, Angel G. Quintero Rivera, ed., (San Juan, Puerto Rico: Centro de Estudios de la Realidad Puertorriqueña, 1971, an anthology of significant documents together with introductory commentary and an extensive, annotated bibliography. See also, Gervasio García Rodriguez, "Primeros fermentos de organización obrera en Puerto Rico: 1873-1898," paper presented at the XLI Congreso Internacional de Americanistas, Mexico City, September 2-7, 1974. Mimeographed, Centro de Estudios de la Realidad Puertorriqueña.

2. Charles Meyers, "India," in *Labor and Economic Development*, Walter Galenson, ed., (New York: John Wiley & Sons, 1959), p. 26. (Emphasis added).

3. By political modernization I mean the growth of a complex of dynamic institutions that break with the static, status-oriented traditional society, including industrialization, but also including economic and social planning, expansion of trade and finance and other tertiary service functions, provision of public utilities and welfare services, development of a communications and transportation infrastructure, education related to development, and urbanization.

4. Melvin M. Tumin, with Arnold S. Feldman, *Social Class and Social Change in Puerto Rico*, (Princeton, N.J.: Princeton University Press, 1961), p. 457.

5. Earl Parker Hanson, *Puerto Rico: Ally for Progress* (New York: D. Van Nostrand, 1962), pp. 18-19.

6. José C. Rosario, who carried out a painstaking study of agricultural workers in Puerto Rico in the 1920s, estimates that prior to 1815 (when trade in agricultural products began to develop) 86 percent of the population was engaged in subsistence agriculture. "The Porto Rican Peasant and his Historical Antecedents," in Victor S. Clark and Associates, *Porto Rico and Its Problems*, (Washington, D.C.: The Brookings Institution, 1930), p. 555.

7. Angel G. Quintero Rivera, "Background to the Emergence of Imperialist Capitalism in Puerto Rico," *Caribbean Studies* V. 13,no. 3,(October 1973). In this carefully researched study, Quintero concluded that the "economy of nineteenth century Puerto Rico corresponds perfectly to Dobb's description of feudalism," p.41. In an earlier work, "El desarrollo de las clases sociales y los conflictos políticos en Puerto Rico," Quintero, however, found the social system of that period difficult to precisely categorize other than as "a semi-feudal, hacienda economy." (p.3).

8. Ibid., p. 47.

9. Eugenio Fernández Méndez, "Introducción: El Siglo XIX o la forja de una nacionalidad," in Salvador Brau, *Disquisiciones Sociológicas y otros Ensayos*, (Puerto Rico: Universidad de Puerto Rico, Ediciones del Instituto de la Literatura, 1956), p.10.

10. Quintero Rivera, "Background," pp. 39-40.

11. Fernández Méndez, "Introducción," p. 20. Quintero Rivera, it should be noted,argues that it is erroneous to describe the industrial development that took place in Puerto Rico in the nineteenth century as truly capitalist or even as giving rise to capitalism.

12. Victor S. Clark and Associates, *Porto Rico and Its Problems*, (Washington, D.C.: The Brookings Institution, 1930), p. 499.

13. García Rodríguez, "Primeros fermentos," p. 557.

14. Rosario, "The Porto Rican Peasant," p. 557.

15. Quintero, Rivera, "Background," pp. 44-45.

16. Azel Ames, *Labor Conditions in Porto Rico*, (Washington, D.C.: Government Printing Office, Department of Labor, Bulletin no. 34, vol. 6, May 1901), p. 377; Leo S. Rowe, *The United States and Porto Rico*,(New York: Longmans, Green and Company, 1904), p. 103.

17. Quintero Rivera, in "Background," p. 47, referring to nineteenth century developments, maintains that "we cannot speak...of capitalism in this century, nor of a bourgeoisie, nor of a proletariat. García Rodríguez, examining essentially the same evidence, makes a diametrically opposed interpretation, maintaining that the transformation of the hacienda in commercial plantation did indeed result in the proletarization of the Puerto Rican worker. "Primeros fermentos de organización obrera en Puerto Rico: 1873-1898," p. 7.

18. Quintero Rivera, "Background," p. 48.

19. Labor Gómez Acevedo, *Organización y Reglamentación del Trabajo en el Puerto Rico del Siglo XIX*, (San Juan, Puerto Rico: Instituto de Cultura Puertorriqueña, 1970).

20. Rafael Alonso Torres, *Cuarenta Años de Lucha Proletaria*,(San Juan, Puerto Rico: Imprenta Baldrich, 1939).

21. Fernando Sierra-Berdecía, former Secretary of Labor of Puerto Rico, for example, wrote that "the Samuel Gompers of the Puerto Rican labor movement was Santiago Iglesias, who in 1896 began labor organization and education on the island." "Puerto Rico, Labor Unions and Labor Relations," *The Status of Labor in Puerto Rico, Alaska, Hawaii*, Reprint from the *Monthly Labor Review*, December 1955, Bulletin no. 1191, (Washington, D.C.: U.S. Department of Labor), p.13. William H. Knowles wrote that Iglesias arrived in Puerto Rico "and found that the island was without unions...." "The Puerto Rican Labor Movement," *Proceedings of the Industrial Relations Research Association*, May 8-9, 1962. For similar attributions to Iglesias of the role of initiator of organized labor in Puerto Rico, see Gordon Lewis, *Puerto Rico*, p. 223; Julio Rivera Rivera, "Orígenes de la Organización Obrera en Puerto Rico, 1838—1898," *La Revista Historia*, 5, no. 1 (April 1955): ll (mimeographed version); Juan S. Bravo, "Apuntes Sobre el Desarrollo del Movimiento Obrero en Puerto Rico" (San Juan, Puerto Rico: Department of Labor of Puerto Rico, 1965), mimeographed, p. 2; Manuel O. Díaz, "Puerto Rican Labor Movement—A Historical Development" (Master's thesis, Clark University, 1934), pp. 27-29; Antonio J. González, "Apuntes para la Historia del Movimiento Sindical de Puerto Rico," *Revista de Ciencias Sociales*, Universidad de Puerto Rico, September 1957, pp. 1-3 (mimeographed version).

22. For a discussion of the two schools of though on the origins of organized

labor in Puerto Rico, see Carlos Roca Rosselli, "Historia de las Relaciones Obrero-Patronales en la Industria Azucarera de Puerto Rico" (Master's thesis, School of Public Administration, University of Puerto Rico, 1967), pp. 53-60. Those authors who have questioned Iglesias's role as the founder of organized labor in Puerto Rico include Lidio Cruz Monclova, quoted in an interview in *Noticias del Trabajo*, publication of the Department of Labor of Puerto Rico, Year XXVII, nos. 362-63, (July-August 1967), p. 7; Andrés Rodríguez Vera, *El Triunfo de la Apostasía*, (San Juan, Puerto Rico: Tipografía La Democracia, 1930), pp. 7, 46, and 50; and César Andreu Iglesias, "Luchas Iniciales de la Clase Obrera," *Album de la Asociación de Choferes de Puerto Rico*, (San Juan, Puerto Rico: Confederación General de Trabajadores, 1941).

23. Quintero Rivera, in *Lucha Obrera en Puerto Rico*, p. 139, refers to a statement by Lidio Cruz-Monclova indicating that at least forty strikes took place during the last third of the nineteenth century.

24. Rafael Alonso Torres, *Cuarenta Años de Lucha Proletaria* (San Juan, Puerto Rico: Imprenta Baldrich, 1939), chapter 6,, "Ideas Modernas Penetran en la Conciencia Popular," pp. 91-121. Alonso Torres on p. 98 records, for example, that Eduardo Conde, a Puerto Rican artisan who was one of the founders of the organized labor movement, had for several years been a merchant seaman on a shipping line between Spain and the Caribbean and that this had permitted him to visit Spain and to assimilate "some of their strange socialist-radical ideas." (Alonso Torres, who became one of the principal leaders of the Puerto Rican labor movement in the 1920s and 1930s, had long since been co-opted from labor radical to labor "statesman" at the time he wrote his memoirs.

25. The most trenchant analysis of which I am aware of the "great man theory" of historical development in Puerto Rico is that of Gervasio García in a review of the book by Manuel Maldonado Denis, *Puerto Rico, una Interpretación Histórico Social* (México: Siglo Veintiuno Editores, 1969). García tellingly criticizes the tendency to exaggerate the role of the individual personality in general and specifically draws attention to the tendency to view the working class "como parte interte del paisaje social y no como actores del drama histórico. Es decir los trabajadores aparecen como seres sin historia propia." And, in effect, the history of the working class in Puerto Rico eventually came to be synonymous with the autobiography of Santiago Iglesias. "Apuntes Sobre Una Interpretación de la Realidad Puertorriqueña," *La Escalera* no. 4 (June 1970); p. 24.

26. Santiago Iglesias-Pantín, *Luchas Emancipadoras*, 2 vols. (San Juan, Puerto Rico: Imprenta Venezuela, 1958 and 1962), an autobiography on which most of the secondary sources of information about the development of the Puerto Rican labor movement are based. Also see Juan Carreras, *Santiago Iglesias Pantín* (San Juan, Puerto Rico: Club de la Prensa, 1965).

27. Quintero Rivera *Lucha Obrera*, 139, has located copies of publications of Puerto Rican artisan groups dating as far back as 1873.

28. Rafael Alonso Torres, *Cuarenta Años de Lucha Proletaria*, pp. 161-62. It is noteworthy that the short-lived organization was "regional" rather than "national," thus indicating it was intended as an integral part of the workers' international movement.

29. Santiago Iglesias Pantín, *Luchas Emancipadoras*, 1: 47-55.

30. Julio Rivera-Rivera, "Orígenes de la Organización Obrera en Puerto Rico (1838-1898)," mimeographed version, p. 22.

CHAPTER 2

1. Wagenheim, "Educational Innovation," p. 62.

2. Quintero Alfaro, "Educational Innovation," pp. 12-13.

3. Brigadier General George W. Davis, *Report on Civil Affairs of Porto Rico, 1899* (Washington: Government Printing Office, 1900), pp. 493-94.

4. Gordon Lewis traces the absurdities and inefficiencies of the U.S. colonial regime in detailed fashion and attributes them to the contradiction in terms involved in "the management of an empire by a democracy" (p. 122). Lewis quotes Puerto Rican constitutional scholar Pedro Muñoz Amato as attributing the ambiguity in administration to "trying to reconcile the considerations of expediency involved in the imperialistic venture with the fundamental postulates of American constitutional democracy. As usual, the conclusions were reached on political and economic grounds but clothed with the precarious respectability of legal phraseology that betrays its rationalizing function" (p. 109).

5. Quoted by Bailey W. and Justine W. Diffie, *Porto Rico: A broken Pledge* (New York: The Vanguard Press, 1949), p. 3.

6. U.S. Commissioner Henry K. Carroll, reporting testimony of U.S. Consul General Hanna, *Report on the Island of Porto Rico; its Population, Civil Government, Commerce, Industries, Production, Roads, Tariff, and Currency, with Recommendations* (U.S. Treasury Department Document 2118) (Washignton, D.C.: Government Printing Office, 1899), p. 794.

7. Leo S. Rowe, *The United States and Porto Rico* (New York: Longmans, Green and Co., 1904), p. 11.

8. Quoted by Lewis, p. 87.

9. The model has undergone several revisions: see Henry A. Landsberger. "An Approach to the Study of Peasant Organizations in the Course of Socio-Political Development," (Ithaca, N.Y.: School of Industrial and Labor Relations, Cornell University, 1966), mimeographed 59 pp.; "The Role of Peasant Movements and Revolts in Development" (Ithaca, N.Y.: School of Industrial and Labor Relations, Cornell University, October 1967),mimeographed 100 pp.; "The Role of Peasant Movements and Revolts in Development: An Analysis Framework," *Bulletin* of the International Institute for Labour Studies, International Labour Office, Geneva, Switzerland, no. 4, February 1968, pp. 8-85.

10. Henry K. Carroll, *Report on the Island of Porto Rico* (U.S.Treasury Department Document no. 2118 (Washington, D.C.: Government Printing Office, 1899). For Carroll's eye-witness account of conditions at the turn of the century, see "Conditions of the Laboring Classes," pp. 48-52. See also Lido Cruz Monclova, *Historia de Puerto Rico* (Siglo XIX), l: 658. "Las condiciones de la gran masa proletaria eran harto lamentables...."

11. Victor S. Clark and associates, *Porto Rico and Its Problems*, (Washington, D.C.: The Brookings Institution, 1930), p. 39.

12. Ralph Hancock, *Puerto Rico: A Success Story* (New York: Van Nostrand, 1960), p.45; see also Berbusse, *The United States in Puerto Rico* p. 157; Roca-Rosselli, p. 15.

13. Gordon Lewis, *Puerto Rico, Freedom and Power in the Caribbean*,(New York: Monthly Review Press, 1963), pp. 93-94.

14. For a comprehensive analysis of political development in Puerto Rico, see vol. 285 of *The Annals of the American Academy of Political and Social Science* (January 1953); the entire issue, edited by Millard Hansen and Henry Wells, is devoted to Puerto Rico. See especially "From Colony to Commonwealth" by Antonio Fernós Isern, pp. 16-22. Isern observes that "not only did the people of Puerto Rico expect to retain, under the United States sovereignty, all political authority that Spain had relinquished to them as an autonomous state in 1897, but they looked forward to added freedom, if for no other reason than that the change of political allegiance meant a change from a monarchial system to a republican democratic regime" (p. 18). He goes on to describe the disappointment when the United States in its first legislative act assumed, "without consultation with the people of Puerto Rico," absolute sovereignty for the United States.

15. See Rowe, especially chapter 2, "The Political and Legal Aspects of Change of Sovereignty," pp. 20-38. Santiago Iglesias Pantin *Luchas Emancipadoras*, p. 152, gives credit to the military government for several important legal advances, but laments the fact that the local reactionaries were soon successful in watering down the edicts. Walter Weyl reports that in his first message to the new legislature, Governor Hunt, the first civil governor, took pains to explain that "the full benefits of the American system can only be realized through legislation sweeping away un-American principles and substituting American." The governor went on to explain to the new legislators that for example, "there is no room for lawlessness in Porto Rico, but the right to organize to secure better wages by peaceable measures is perfectly lawful...(pp. 808-9).

16. Walter E. Weyl, "Labor Conditons in Porto Rico," *Bulletin No. 61*, U.S. Department of Labor, Washington, D.C., November 1905, p. 806.

17. Azel Ames, "Labor Conditions in Porto Rico," *Bulletin No. 34*, Department of Labor, Washington, D.C., May 1901, p. 398.

18. Iglesias, pp. 171-96. Weyl, "Labor Conditions," p. 726. "The net result of the changes in wages and in the currency in the coffee district was to leave the worker worse off than before."

19. Rowe, "Policial and Legal Aspects," p. 144.

20. Iglesias recounts that only weeks after the change in sovereignty he was threatened with expulsion from the island, as an "undesirable alien" (and one who was not yet a U.S. citizen and who certainly could not have safely returned to Spain) by Muñoz Rivera, who headed the local government in cooperation with the occupying U.S. forces. Iglesias recalls that he hoped to obtain either U.S. citizenship or become a "citizen of Puerto Rico." Iglesias, *Luchas Emancipadoras* l:98-99.

21. Iglesias, *Luchas Emancipadoras*, pp. 83-85.

22. Henry K. Carroll, *Report on the Island of Porto Rico*,(1899), p. 795.

23. Berbusse, p. 119.

24. Iglesias, l:90.

25. Ibid., p. 94.

26. Ibid., p. 98

27. Ibid., p. 198.

28. Bernard Mandel, *Samuel Gompers* (Yellow Springs, Ohio: Antioch Press, 1963), p. 323.

29. Samuel Gompers, *Seventy Years of Life and Labor* (New York: E. P. Dutton and Company, 1925), 2:69-70.

30. Igualdad Iglesias de Pagán, *El obrerismo en Puerto Rico*, (Palencia de Castilla: Ediciones Juan Ponce de León, 1973), pp. 158-60.

CHAPTER 3

1. U.S. Congress, *An Act Temporarily to Provide Revenues and Civil Government for Porto Rico, and for Other Purposes*, 56th Cong., 2d Sess., April 12, 1900, 31 Stat. 77 (Foraker Act).

2. Statement by Senator Joseph B. Foraker, Chairman of the Committee that heard testimony pursuant to legislation for Puerto Rico, U.S. Congress, *Congressional Record*, 56th Cong., lst Sess. vol. 33, pt. 3, p. 2478.

3. The incident is remarkably similar to the classic case in U.S. labor jurisprudence of the Philadelphia Cordwainers who, more than twenty years after the constitution of the American Republic, were convicted of having criminally conspired to raise wages in violation of then-still-binding, English Common law.

4. William G. Whittaker, "The Santiago Iglesias Case: Origins of American Trade Union Involvement in Puerto Rico," *The Americas* 25, no. 4 (April 1968): 385-86. (The FLT had begun to receive assistance from the AFL as early as December 1900, but was apparently not accepted as a formal affiliate of the AFL until 1905. See Iglesias, *Luchas Emancipadoras*, 1:202, 216, and Alonso Torres, *Cuarenta Años de Lucha Proletaria*, pp. 258-59, 277.)

5. Whittaker, "The Santiago Iglesias Case," p. 391.

6. Ibid., pp. 378-93.

7. Félix Mejías, *Condiciones de Vida de las Clases Jornaleras de Puerto Rico* (San Juan, Puerto Rico: Junta Editora de la Universidad de Puerto Rico, 1946), pp. 82-83.

8. "Many labor matters are studied and decided in Washington, "For example, on labor's side, Santiago Iglesias was once released from prison (October 5, 1898) while the Spanish authorities were still in control, "on petition of the government in Washington," *Luchas Emancipadoras*, 1:77, and, on the entrepreneurial side, it is clear that for several years prior to the Spanish-American War that island's commercial interests were eagerly anticipating annexation within the U.S. market. See Gervasio Garcia, "Primeros Fermentos," p. 26.

9. Iglesias, *Luchas Emancipadoras*, 1:152..

10. U.S. Congress, *Joint Resolution to Provide for the Administration of Civil Affairs in Porto Rico*, 56th Congress, lst Sess., May 1,1900, 31 Stat. 715, sec. 3.

11. Iglesias, *Luchas Emancipadoras*, 1:339.

12. Personal interview, Angel G. Quintero Rivera, January 25, 1972. For a modern manifestation of the linkage between mainland labor interests and mainland labor's assistance to Puerto Rican labor, see David K. Ross's description of David Dubinsky's decision to organize the garment industry in Puerto Rico solely to protect the standards of the International Ladies Garment Workers' Union in the United States, pp. 146-51.

13. For an early example of AFL problems in explaining the nuances of the differences between racism and the maintenance of standards, see "President Gompers

in Puerto Rico," *American Federationist*, (April 1904), p. 305.

14. Mandel, *Samuel Gompers*, p. 211.

15. González, "Apuntes para la historia," p. 12.

16. Victor S. Clark and Associates, *Porto Rico and Its Problems* (Washington, D.C.: The Brookings Institution, 1930), p. 499.

17. For a summary description of the industrialization of sugar production by U.S. capital, see Carlos Roca Rosselli, "Historia de las relaciones obrero-patronales en la industria azucarera de Puerto Rico" (Master's thesis, School of Public Administration, University of Puerto Rico, 1967), chap. 1, pp. 1-46.

18. "...any freeman who did not own or cultivate as a tenant land enough to support himself and his family was required to be registered and to carry a libreta, or certificate, issued by a local magistrate, containing besides the unual data for identification, the name of his employer and the conditions under which he was employed. Any laborer found without a libreta was subject to arrest and punishment as a vagrant." Rosario, "The Porto Rican Peasant," p. 545.

19. Lewis, *Puerto Rico*, p. 93.

20. Ibid., p. 100.

21. Weyl, "Labor Conditions in Porto Rico," *Bulletin No. 61*, U.S. Bureau of Labor, Washington, D.D., November 1905,pp. 750, 814.

22. Quoted by Sidney Mintz in "Cañalmar: the Subculture of a Rural Sugar Plantation," p. 315, in Julian H. Steward and others, *The People of Puerto Rico, A study in Social Anthropology*. A Social Science Research Center Study, College of Social Sciences, University of Puerto Rico (Urbana: University of Illinois Press, 1956).

23. Carroll, *Report on the Island of Porto Rico*, pp. 50-51 and 721.

24. The FLT had no individual presiding officer for the first five years of its existence, being led by an executive committee. General Organizer Iglesias was elected "permanent president" at the fifth convention in 1908. Alonso Torres, *Cuarenta Años de Lucha Proletaria*, p. 235.

25. See González, p. 7, and Santiago Iglesias, *Luchas Emancipadoras, l:359, 376*.

26. Alonso Torres, *Cuarenta Años de Lucha Proletaria*, Appendix, pp. xii and xiii.

CHAPTER 4

1. For the best compilation of documents expressing the labor ideology of that time, see Angel G. Quintero Rivera, ed., *Lucha Obrera en Puerto Rico*, bibliography and pp. 14-42.

2. Iglesias, *Luchas Emancipadoras*, 1: 136-38.

3. Rosendo Matienzo Cintrón, quoted by Iglesias, *Luchas Emancipadoras*, 1: 386-87.

4. Santiago Iglesias Pantín, *Gobierno Propio Para Quien?*(San Juan, Puerto Rico: Federación Libre de los Trabajadores, 1907), pp. 24-29, my translation.

5. For an expression of the opposition to the politics of dependency, written in retrospect, see Andrés Rodríguez Vera, *Federación Obrera Panamericana?* (San Juan, Puerto Rico: Imprenta La Democracia, 1924).

6. Mandel, *Samuel Gompers*, p. 208.

7. Iglesias, *Luchas Emancipadoras*, 1: 276.

8. Charles W. Anderson *Politics and Economic Change in Latin America*, (Princeton, N.J.: D. Van Nostrand Co., 1967), p. 105.

9. Adolf Sturmthal, "Economic Development and the Labour Movement," chap. 8 in *Industrial Relations and Economic Development*, Arthur M. Ross, ed. (New York: St. Martin's Press, 1966), pp. 165-81, esp. pp. 174, 179.

10. Ramón Lebrón Rodríguez, *El Problem Obrero de Puerto Rico* (San Juan, Puerto Rico: Tipografía El Compás, 1924), p. 103, my translation.

11. Willian H. Knowles, "Unionism and Politics in Puerto Rico," a study done for the United States-Puerto Rico Commission on the Status of Puerto Rico, Washington, D.C., 1966

12. Federación Libre de los Trabajadores, *Procedimientos del Sexto Congreso Obrero de la Federación Libre de los Trabajadores* (San Juan, Puerto Rico: Tipografía M. Burillo, 1910), p. 11.

13. William H. Knowles, "The Puerto Rican Labor Movement," *Proceedings of the International Industrial Relations Research Association*, Spring Meeting, May 8-9, 1962, pp. 536-41.

14. In 1910 the FLT's committee on labor legislation went on record complaining that the legislators had year after year, shown almost total indifference for labor's legislative proposals. It noted that "if in the legislature we could count on only three or four conscientious labor represnetatives...the success of our efforts would have been more practical and more beneficial for working people" (*Procedimientos del Sexto Congreso Obrero*), [San Juan, Puerto Rico, FLT, 1910], p. 12. My translation.

15. Bolivar Pagán, *Historia de los Partidos Políticos Puertorriqueños 1898-1956*, (San Juan, Puerto Rico: Librería Campos, l: 169. My translation.

16. Ibid., pp. 168-69.

17. Robert W. Anderson, *Party Politics in Puerto Rico* (Stanford, Calif.: Stanford University Press, 1965), p. 35.

18. Alonso Torres. *Cuarenta Años de Lucha Proletaria*, p. 349.

19. Moises Poblete Toncoso and Ben G. Burnett, *The Rise of the Latin American Labor Movement* (New York: Bookman Associates, 1960), pp. 129-32. Alonso Torres, *Cuarenta Años de Lucha Proletaria*, pp. 349-51. Santiago Iglesias was both a delegate to AFL conventions and an officer of the Pan-American Federation of Labor, just as Hipólito Marcano, present-day president of the Puerto Rican Federation of Labor, is a delegate to AFL-CIO conventions and is an officer of the Inter-American Regional Organization of Workers.

20. Lewis, *Puerto Rico*, p. 235.

21. Knowles, "Unionism and Politics in Puerto Rico," p. 5.

22. Iglesias, *Luchas Emancipadoras*, l:126.

23. Ibid., 1:263.

24. Ibid., 1:28-30.

25. Samuel Gompers, *Seventy Years of Life and Labor*, (New York: E.P. Dutton & Co., 1925), l:97-98.

26. See, for example R.del Romeral (Ramón Romero Rosa), "La Cuestión Social y Puerto Rico," pp. 16-32, and Juan S. Marcano, "Páginas Rojas," pp. 59-70, in Angel G. Quintero Rivera, ed., *Lucha Obrera en Puerto Rico*, my translation of passage from p. 72.

CHAPTER 5

1. The *Proceedings* of the AFL for 1902, p. 15, reports that "Mr. Iglesias has been continued as organizer in Porto Rico for nearly fourteen months. His work has been fraught with considerable success, many unions having been organized by him, and placed in affiliation with their respective international organizations, while other unions having no international head, have been directly chartered by the American Federation of Labor." For a list of the unions chartered during Samuel Gompers's first visit to the island in 1904, see Torres, *Cuarenta Años de Lucha Proletaria*, p. 332.

2. Ames, *Labor Conditions in Porto Rico*, p. 411.

3. Ibid., p. 412.

4. Estimates compiled by Manual O. Díaz, "Puerto Rico Labor Movement—A Historical Development" (Master's thesis, Clark University, 1943), p. 15. Also, see Bailey W. Diffie and Justine W. Diffie, *Porto Rico: A Broken Pledge* (New York: Vanguard Press, 1931), p. 166.

5. Weyl, "Labor Conditions in Porto Rico," p. 811.

6. Juan Carreras, *Santiago Iglesias Pantín* (San Juan, Puerto Rico: Editorial Club de la Prensa, 1965), p. 117. Membership figures of labor organizations in Puerto Rico are almost invariably wildly exaggerated, it not being unusual for individual labor leaders to claim to have organized more workers than exist in the entire employed labor force.

7. These are the same factories and the same industry, incidentally, that received considerable notoriety many years later when the management of Consolidated Cigar Corporation attempted to have a union representation election set aside on the ground that some of the employees had been induced to vote for the union because of witchcraft. Management was represented by the law firm with which Richard Nixon was once associated.

8. Alonso Torres, *Cuarenta Años de Lucha Proletaria*, p. 332.

9. Iglesias, *Luchas Emancipadoras*, 1:333-39.

10. *Unión Obrera* (periodical of the FLT) (March 26, 1905), p.1.

11. Joseph Marcus, *Labor Conditions in Porto Rico* (Washington, D.C.: Government Printing Office, U.S. Employment Service, Office of the Secretary, U.S. Department of Labor, 1919), pp. 19-20. Also, see "Strikes in Porto Rico," Special Bulletin, Bureau of Labor of Puerto Rico, June 1, 1918.

12. Quintero Rivera, ed., *Lucha Obrera en Puerto Rico*, p. 45.

13. For discussion of this period, see Antonio J. González, "Apuntes para la Historia del Movimiento Sindical de Puerto Rico: 1896-1941," pp. 9-11. González sums up the period as one of "guerra abierta," rather than of negotiations.

14. Quoted by Félix Mejías in *Condiciones de Vida de las Clases Jornaleras de Puerto Rico*, p. 89.

15. *Annual Report of the Governor of Porto Rico*, 1915.

16. Ibid., 1916, p. 31.

17. Iglesias, *Luchas Emancipadoras*, 2:168, 200, 218-19.

18. *Procedimientos del Sexto Congreso Obrero de la FLT*, (San Juan, Puerto Rico: Tip. M. Burillo, 1910), p. 7 and prefatory pages.

19. See Weyl, *Labor Conditions in Porto Rico*, p. 807 and Marcus, *Labor Condi-*

tions in Porto Rico, p. 19.

20. Roca Roselli, "Historia de las Relaciones," p. 95.

21. The political adversaries of the FLT, in fact, accuse it of not having undertaken the organization of agricultural workers, but instead of moving in and taking over the leadership of spontaneous strikes. Juan Antonio Corretjer, "Albizu Campos y las Huelgas en los Años 30," p. 12. This may have been true to some extent after the FLT had begun its decline in the 1930s, but there is no doubt that the impetus to organization in the pre World War I period came simultaneously both from the urban centers— the "*Cruzada del Ideal*" of the FLT—and as a result of spontaneous elements in the plantations.

22. To cite only one typical example, although strike activity in sugar had been sporadic in the Yabucoa area (Central Roig) for three decades, no permanent organization of sugar workers was achieved until 1939. See Irving Monclova, "Una Unión Obrera Independiente en Puerto Rico: la Unión de Trabajadores Industriales y Agrícolas de Yabucoa, 1960" (Master's thesis, University of Puerto Rico, 1961) pp. 39-43.

CHAPTER 6

1. Victor S. Clark and Associates, *Porto Rico and Its Problems* (Washington, D.C.: The Brookings Institution, 1930), p. 52.

2. See, for example, the U.S. Department of Labor Report of 1919 by Joseph Marcus, p. 19.

3. Dudley Smith, *Puerto Rico's Income* (Washington, D.C.: Association of Sugar Producers of Puerto Rico, 1943), p. 10, cited by Félix Mejías, *Condiciones de Vida de las Clases Jornaleras de Puerto Rico*, Rio Piedras, Puerto Rico: Monografias de la Universidad de Puerto Rico, 1946), p. 59. The figures cited are money, not real wages.

4. Mejías, *Condiciones de Vida*, p. 103.

5. Bailey W. and Justine W. Diffie, *Porto Rico: A Broken Pledge* (New York: The Vanguard Press, 1931), pp. 45, 88.

6. Harry A. Franck, *Roaming Through the West Indies* (New York: Century, 1921), pp. 299-300.

7. For more detailed accounts of this change in tactics, see Mejías, *Condiciones de Vida*, pp. 72-75; Quintero Rivera, *Lucha Obrera*, p. 72; González, "Apuntes para la historia," pp. 15-17; Pagán, *Historia de los Partidos*, 1:168-71.

8. U.S. Congress, *An Act to Provide a Civil Government for Porto Rico, and for other Purposes*, 64th Cong., 2d Sess., March 2, 1917, 39 Stat. 951, (the Jones Act); U.S. Congress, *An Act to Provide for the Organization of a Constitutional Government by the People of Puerto Rico*, 81st Cong., 2d Sess., July 3, 1950, 64 Stat. 319 (Public Law 600).

9. Henry Wells, *The Modernization of Puerto Rico, A Political Study of Changing Values and Institutions* (Cambridge, Mass.: Harvard University Press, 1969), pp. 97-98, 103.

10. See Bolivar Pagán, *Historia de los Partidos Politicos en Puerto Rico* 2 vols. (San Juan, Puerto Rico: Librería Campos, 1959), *1*:168-69, and Angel G. Quintero-Rivera, ed., *Lucha Obrera en la Historia Obrera Puertorriqueña* (San Juan, Puerto

Rico: Centro de Estudios de la Realidad Puertorriquena, 1971), p. 72.

11. Wells, *The Modernization of Puerto Rico*, pp. 101-3.

12. Iglesias, *Luchas Emancipadoras*, 2:25-26.

13. Ibid., pp. 55-58

14. Ibid., p. 58.

15. Ibid., p. 84.

16. Bolivar Pagán, *Historia*, p. 169, explains that the AFL came to understand that party discipline was much stronger in Puerto Rico than in the United States.

17. Anderson *Party Politics in Puerto Rico*, p. 35. For the party's program, see Angel G. Quintero Rivera, ed., *Lucha Obrera en Puerto Rico*, pp. 89-94.

18. Pagán, *Historia,* pp. 170-171.

19. Anderson, *Party Politics in Puerto Rico*, p. 35.

20. Wells, *The Modernization of Puerto Rico*, p. 106 and Pagán, *Historia*, 1:185.

21. Mejías, *Condiciones de Vida*, p. 79, n. 23.

22. Ibid., pp. 75-76, n. 18.

23. Antonio J. González, mimeographed version, "Apuntes Para La Historia," p. 18.

24. Quoted by Mejías,*Condiciones de Vida*, p. 76 n. 19.

25. *Procedimientos del Sexto Congreso Obrero* (San Juan, Puerto Rico: Federación Libre de los Trabajadores, 1910), pp. 150-51 (reprinting Resolution 7 from Fifth FLT Congress in 1908).

26. Angel G. Quintero Rivera, ed., *Lucha Obrera*, p. 88 (quoting Rojas in the debates over the platform of the Socialist Party, which took place in 1919).

27. Ibid., p. 83 (also quoting Rojas). My translation.

28. For more detailed accounts of the dissension that led to the split, see Mejías, pp. 76-80, and for analysis of the dissenting points of view, see Quintero Rivera, *Lucha Obrera*, pp. 96-97 and 108-17.

29. Andrés Rodríquez Vera, *Federación Obrera Panamericana?*, pp. 30-32, my translation.

30. Lewis, *Puerto Rico*, pp. 80-81.

31. Carlos Roca Rosselli reports, for example, that in the 1932 harvest, wages were reduced from ninety cents a day to fifty and sixty cents a day, p. 96.

32. Robert W. Alexander, *Organized Labor in Latin America* (New York: The Free Press, 1965), p. 234.

33. Quintero Rivera, ed., *Lucha Obrera*, pp. 96-97.

34. Mejías, p. 72 n. 9.

35. *Proceedings of the AFL Convention of 1939*, pp. 284-289, 396, and 561-62 (cited by Manuel O. Díaz, "Puerto Rican Labor Movement—A Historical Development." (Master's thesis, Clark University, 1943), p. 91.

CHAPTER 7

1. Victor S. Clark, *Porto Rico and Its Problems* (Washington, D.C.: The Brookings Institution, 1930), chap. 2, "Workers in Country and Town, pp. 12-53, passim (this particular chapter was prepared by Frank Tannenbaum, who was a member of the survey staff),

2. David S. Ross, *The Long Uphill Path: A Historical Study of Puerto Rico's Program of Economic Development* (San Juan, Puerto Rico: Editorial Edil, 1969), p. 6.

3. Ibid., p. 4. See also Sidney W. Mintz, *Worker in the Cane: A Puerto Rican Life History* (New Haven, Conn.: Yale University Press, 1960); and, Arthur D. Gayer, Paul T. Homan, and Earl K. James, *The Sugar Economy of Puerto Rico* (New York: Columbia University Press, 1938) and Henry Wells, *The Modernization of Puerto Rico, A Political Study of Changing Values and Institutions* (Cambridge, Mass.: Harvard University Press, 1969), p. 91.

4. Quintero Alfaro, "Educational Innovation," p. 15.

5. Murray Edelman, "The Conservative Political Consequences of Labor Conflict," chap. 2 in *Essays in Industrial Relations Theory*, Gerald G. Somers, ed. (Ames, Iowa: Iowa State University Press, 1969), pp. 174-75.

6. For descriptions of the formation of the *Partido Popular Democrático*, see Robert W. Anderson, *Party Politics in Puerto Rico* (Stanford, Calif.: Stanford University Press, 1965), Gordon K. Lewis, *Puerto Rico: Freedom and Power in the Caribbean* (New York: Monthly Review Press, 1963); Rexford Guy Tugwell, *The Stricken Land* (Garden City, N.Y.: Doubleday & Co., 1947); Henry Wells, *The Modernization of Puerto Rico* (Cambridge, Mass.: Harvard University Press, 1969); Manuel Maldonado Denis, *Puerto Rico: Una Interpretación Histórico-Social* (Mexico City: Editores Siglo XXI, 1969).

7. Edelman, "Conservative Political Consequences," pp. 174-75.

8. Abraham Maslow, "A Theory of Human Motivation," *Psychological Review* 50 (1943): 370-96.

9. The impetus for the new center came from the *Asociación de Choferes de Puerto Rico*.

10. Mejías, *Condiciones de Vida*, p. 70 n. 5.

11. Díaz, "Puerto Rican Labor Movement," p. 110.

12. Mejías, *Condiciones de Vida* p. 70 n. 5.

13. Simon Rottenberg, "Labor Cost in the Puerto Rican Economy," *Revista Jurídica de la Universidad de Puerto Rico* 20, no.2 (November-December 1950),: 128.

14. Monclova, "Una Unión Obrera," pp. 74-75.

15. See, for example, Walter Galenson, who summed up the experience of the labor movements in several new countries by observing that "the leaders of the new unions are rarely drawn from the working class itself. They are almost always middle class in origin, either professional, intellectual, or clerical workers, . . . seeking to bring about a radical reformation of society through the mass organization of the workers" (Walter Galenson, ed., *Labor and Economic Development* [New York: John Wiley & Sons, 1959, p. 7). See also Arthur Ross, ed., *Industrial Relations and Economic Development* (London: Macmillan, 1966), "Sources and Functions of Union Leadership in Developing Countries," pp. xx-xxiv. Everett Kassalow, ed., *National Labor Movements in the Post War World* (Chicago, Ill.: Northwestern University Press, 1963), "Sources of Trade Union Leadership," pp. 236-43. William H. Friedland, *Unions and Industrial Relations in Underdeveloped Countries*, Bulletin 47, New York State School of Industrial Relations, Cornell University, Ithaca, N.Y., 1963, pp. 18-20.

16. Manuel Maldonado Denis, *Puerto Rico Una Interpretación Histórico-Social*

(México: Siglo Veintiuno Editores, 1969), p. 170.

17. Ibid. My translation.

18. Iglesias, 1:339.

19. Juan Antonio Corretjer, "Albizu Campos y las Huelgas en los Años 30," Conferencia dictada en el Ateneo de Puerto Rico el 11 de septiembre de 1969, impresa por la Liga Socialista Puertorriqueña, Santurce, Puerto Rico, 1969, pp. 3-4.

20. Juan Antonio Corretjer, *La Lucha por la Independencia* (San Juan, Puerto Rico: Publicaciones de Unión del Pueblo Pro Constituyente, 1950), pp. 70, 64, as quoted by Manuel Maldonado Denis, *Puerto Rico Una Interpretación Histórico-Social*, pp. 231-32.

21. Alonso Torres, *Cuarenta Años de Lucha Proletaria*, pp. 345-48.

22. César Andreu Iglesias, personal interview, May 11, 1971.

23. Jose Antonio Ortiz, "Cuadro Sinóptico del Desarrollo del Movimiento Obrero de P.R., "University of Puerto Rico, one sheet, mimeographed (covers period 1940-1957).

24. Robert W. Anderson, *Party Politics in Puerto Rico* pp. 212-15.

25. Estado Libre Asociado de Puerto Rico, *Diario de Sesiones de la Convención Constituyente de Puerto Rico* (Orford, N.H.: Equity Publishing Corporation, 4 vols. 1961), 3: 1620.

26. Ibid., p. 1618.

27. Ibid., pp. 1620-21.

28. In an occurrence that surely deserves to go down in history, the FLT's charter was withdrawn by the AFL because the FLT leadership "had become involved in politics." The FLT, of course, had been involved in politics with the explicit approval of the AFL for half a century previously. María Luisa Guerra de Colón, "Trayectoria, Acción y Desenvolvimiento del Movimiento Obrero en Puerto Rico" (Master's thesis, School of Public Administration, University of Puerto Rico, 1963), p. 86. Thus ended a half a century of FLT affiliation with the AFL, but despite the severance, the principal FLT leadership, a dynastic arrangement involving Nicolas Nogueras and Nicolás Nogueras, Jr., remains outspokenly loyal to the metropolis politically.

29. The original "organic" law establishing the relationship between the United States and Puerto Rico, which was enacted in 1900, although officially denominated as "temporary," was not revised until 1917 when U.S. citizenship was granted and provisions made for a popularly elected insular Senate. The original Act was significantly augmented by further amendments in 1950, which provided for Commonwealth status—which was inaugurated in 1952 following a referendum—and for the popular election of the governor. The Spanish *Estado Libre Asociado* literally means "Free Associated State"; detractors deride the concept from both the right and the left, claiming that Puerto Rico is neither "free" nor a "state," although clearly "associated" in a relationship of exploitation and dependency.

30. William H. Knowles, "Unionism and Politics in Puerto Rico," pp. 10-11.

CHAPTER 8

1 Perloff, *Puerto Rico's Economic Future*, pp. 25-26. Eugenio Fernández Méndez has listed the principal economic activities in the following sequence: min-

ing, sugar, cattle, smuggling, incipient trade, diversified agriculture growing out of agrarian reform, coffee, sugar again, manufacturing. Eugenio Fernández Méndez, ed., *Crónicas de Puerto Rico* (San Juan, Puerto Rico: Commonwealth of Puerto Rico, 1957), 1:xvii.

2. For accounts of this last period see Rexford Guy Tugwell, *The Stricken Land, The Story of Puerto Rico* (New York: Doubleday, 1947), and the detailed and authoritative study by David F. Ross, *The Long Uphill Path: A Historical Study of Puerto Rico's Program of Economic Development*(San Juan, Puerto Rico: Editorial Edil, 1969). Also informative is the study by Robert J. Hunter, *Puerto Rico, A Survey of Historical, Economic and Political Affairs* U.S. House of Representatives, Committee on Interior and Insular Affairs, November 25, 1959 (Washington, D.C.: U.S. Government Printing Office, 1959).

3. Perloff, *Puerto Rico's Economic Future*, pp. 25-26.

4. See, for example, Ross, *The Long Uphill Path*, pp. 19-45.

5. For a perceptive essay on this premise, see Eldon Kenworthy, "Our Image of Their Problems," *The Nation*, December 2, 1968, pp. 586-91.

6. Hugh C. Barton, Jr., "Puerto Rico's Industrial Development Program, 1942-1960," prepublication copy of a paper presented at a seminar of the Center for International Affairs of Harvard University, October 29, 1959, p. 17. (San Juan, Puerto Rico: Economic Development Administration, 1959), p. 17.

7. Lloyd G. Reynolds and Peter Gregory with Luis Torruellas, *Wages, Productivity and Industrialization in Puerto Rico*(Homewood, Ill.: Richard D. Irwin, 1965), pp. 21, 308.(A joint publication of the Social Science Research Center of the University of Puerto Rico and the Economic Growth Center at Yale University).

8. Junta de Planificación, Oficina del Gobernador, *Informe Económico al Gobernador 1970*, San Juan, Puerto Rico, 4 de febrero de 1971, pp. 27, 41.

9. Junta de Planificación, Estado Libre Asociado de Puerto Rico, Indicadores Socio-Economicós por Regiones (Años Seleccionados), San Juan, Puerto Rico, Junta de Planificación, septiembre de 1970, p. 1.

10. For a concise expression of the "nationalist" view, see Patricia Bell, *Puerto Rico—"Island Paradise" of U.S. Imperialism* (New York: New Outlook Publishers, 1967).

11. Oscar Lewis, *La Vida* (New York: Random House, 1965). Also see Lloyd H. Rogler and August B. Hollingshead, *Trapped, Families and Schizophrenia* (New York: Wiley, 1965) (a Social Science Research Center Study of the University of Puerto Rico).

12. Rolando Castañeda y José A. Marrero, "La distribución del ingreso en Puerto Rico," *Revista de Ciencias Sociales* 9, no. 4 (diciembre 1965):354.

13. A National Planning Association report on Puerto Rico by William H. Stead in 1958 assessed Puerto Rico's liabilities and assets including, respectively, no known mineral deposits of commercial significance (copper and nickel have since been discovered), no fuels except sugarcane waste called bagasse, limited forests and forest products, very limited commercial fishing potential (because of the extreme depth of surrounding waters—no banks), a fully exploited hydroelectrical potential, and, on the plus side, adequate water supply, excellent climate and natural beauty, strategic location on ocean and air routes (referred to by Robert J. Hunter, *Puerto Rico: A Survey*, pp. 26-27).

14. David Vidal, "Puerto Rico Seeks Way Out as Economic Woes Mount," *New York Times*, October 15,1975.

15. Lewis, *Puerto Rico*, p. 176.

16. In 1969, for example, the U.S. had a per capita income of $3,766, Puerto Rico had $1,281, Argentina had $730, Venezuela had $788, Mexico had $503, and Bolivia had $158. Data for Puerto Rico from Junta de Planificación, *Informe Económico al Gobernador 1971*, San Juan, Puerto Rico, Oficina del Gobernador, marzo de 1972, Tabla 1. Data for U.S. and Latin American countries, Organización de los Estados Américanos, *America en Cifras 1970*, Washington, D.C., 1971.

17. "The Need for the Selective Application to Puerto Rico of the Provisions of the Fair Labor Standards Act," statement by Amadeo I.D. Francis, Executive Director of the Puerto Rico Manufacturers' Association before the Subcommittee on Labor, U.S. Senate Labor and Public Welfare Committee, on Fair Labor Standards Amendments of 1971, July 19, 1971, p. 3.

18. *The Dorvillier News Letter*, San Juan, Puerto Rico, 25th year, no. 50, December 17, 1977, p.1.

19. *San Juan Star*, San Juan, Puerto Rico, October 9, 1975.

20. Garry Hoyt, "Puerto Rico, A Chronicle of American Carelessness," *San Juan Star*, San Juan Puerto Rico, November 20, 1977.

21. Lois S. Gray, *A Socio-Economic Profile of Puerto Rican New Yorkers*, Regional Report no. 46, Bureau of Labor Statistics, U.S. Department of Labor, Middle Atlantic Regional Office, July 1975, pp. 2-3; *Puerto Ricans in the Continental United States: An Uncertain Future*, A Report of the U.S.Commission on Civil Rights, October 1976, pp. 19-21.

22. James Tobin, et al., *Report to the Governor*, The Committee to Study Puerto Rico's Finances, San Juan, Puerto Rico, December 11, 1975, pp. 43-45.

23. Charlie Albizu and Norman Matlin, "The Death of Poetry: The '68 Puerto Rico Elections," *Caribbean Review* 1, no. 1 (Spring 1969):2-3.

24. Thomas H. Aitken, Jr., *Poet in the Fortress* (New York: New York American Library, 1964).

25. Laurence I. Barrett, "Puerto Rico, Trying to Make it Without Miracles," *Times*, February 16, 1976, p. 21.

26. Henry Wells, Gen. Ed., *Puerto Rico Election Factbook*, Washington, D.C.: Institute for the Comparative Study of Political Systems, a Division of Operations and Policy Research, Inc., November 5, 1968, p. 37.

27. David Vidal, "All Sides in Puerto Rico Agree that U.S. Tie Is a Key Problem," *New York Times*, October 16, 1975.

28. Carlos J. Lastra, Concepción Pérez Pérez, and Federico Cordero, *Informe sobre el Estado de las Relaciones Obrero-Patronales en Puerto Rico*, Informe sometido al Senado del Estado Libre Asociado de Puerto Rico por el Instituto de Estudios Administrativos y Legislativos, Inc., Santurce, Puerto Rico, February 11, 1971, pp. iv-v, 133, 227-29, 253-54. In his analysis of this jurisdictional problem, Federico Cordero notes that it is ironic that the insular Labor Relations Board had greater authority when Puerto Rico was a possession than it does now that the island is a "self-governing" commonwealth, p. 253.

29. Reynolds and Gregory, *Wages, Productivity, and Industrialization*, p. 11.

30. W. Arthur Lewis, "Economic Development with Unlimited Supplies of

Labour," *The Manchester School of Economic and Social Studies* 22, no. 2 (May 1954).

31. U.S. Department of Commerce, Bureau of the Census, *Number of Inhabitants, Puerto Rico*, 1970 Census of Population, Washington, D.C.: Government Printing Office, September 1971, Table 2, pp. 53-59.

32. Reynolds and Gregory, *Wages, Productivity, and Industrialization*, p. 291.

33. Walter E. Weyl, "Labor Conditions in Porto Rico," Bulletin no. 61, Bureau of Labor, Department of Commerce and Labor, vol. ll, November 1905, p. 816.

34. Stanley L. Friedlander, *Labor Migration and Economic Growth, A Case Study of Puerto Rico* (Cambridge, Mass.: The MIT Press, 1965). p. 49.

35. For a discussion of the controversy, see Rubén A. Vilches, "La medición del desempleo en Puerto Rico," *Revista del Trabajo* 1, no. 4 (octubre-noviembre-diciembre 1968), and the entire issue of the *Revista del Trabajo* 3, nos. 13-14 (enero-junio 1971(, Departamento del Trabajo, Estado Libre Asociado de Puerto Rico.

36. A recent study compared youth unemployment rates in seven countries with the following results: Japan, 2.3; West Germany, 3.8; Great Britain 4.4; Sweden, 5.6; Canada, 10.8; United States, 12.7; and Italy, 13.4 percent. Constance Sorrentino, "Unemployment in the United States and Seven Foreign Countries," *Monthly Labor Review*, 93, no. 9 (September 1970):19. During this same year, 1968, Puerto Rico's youth unemployment rate was 27.4 percent. Bureau of Labor Statistics, Department of Labor, Commonwealth of Puerto Rico.

37. Rubén A. Vilches, "El Problema Poblacional de Puerto Rico y el Proposito de Lograr una Civilización Superior," *Revista del Trabajo* 2, no. 7 (July-August-September 1969) (Department of Labor, Commonwealth of Puerto Rico, San Juan, Puerto Rico):6.

38. W. Arthur Lewis, "Economic Development," p. 189.

39. Warren F. Ilchman and R. C. Bhargava, "Balanced Thought and Economic Growth," *Economic Development and Cultural Change*, July 1966, pp. 385-99.

40. For a discussion of some of the implications of the dilemma, see Carlos J. Lastra, *The Impact of Minimum Wages on Labor-Oriented Economy* (San Juan, Puerto Rico: Social Science Research Center, University of Puerto Rico, 1964).

41. Luis F. Silva-Recio, *Public Wage Fixing and its Effect on Collective Bargaining and the Labor Movement in Puerto Rico* (Ph.D. diss., University of Wisconsin, 1962). Silva-Recio has calculated that in the process of determination of 581 wage rates by tripartite committees between 1955 and 1964 that in 44.9 percent of the hearings the decision was unanimous and labor members dissented from the majority in only 25.3 percent of the hearings. *Legislación y Procesos de Salario Mínimo en Puerto Rico* (Puerto Rico: Escuela de Administración Publica, Universidad de Puerto Rico, 1965), p. 89.

42. U.S. Congress, House, *A Bill to Provide for Amendments to the Compact Between the People of Puerto Rico and the United States, and Related Legislation*, H.R. 9234, 86th Cong., lst. Sess., Hearings before a Special Subcommittee on Interior and Insular Affairs, "Puerto Rico—1959" (Washington, D.C.: U.S. Government Printing Office, 1960, testimony of Hipólito Marcano, p. 291; see also exchange with Representative Adam Clayton Powell on p. 294 in which Marcano explained that "it is the goal of the labor movement to achieve the highest possible wages within the Federal minimum wage law. But for the time being as we struggle,

as I said before, we have to apply the exception to Puerto Rico."

43. "The Need for the Selective Application to Puerto Rico of the Provisions of the Fair Labor Standards Act," statement by Amadeo I.D. Francis, Executive Director of the Puerto Rico Manufacturers' Association before the Subcommittee on Labor, U.S. Senate Labor and Public Welfare Committee, on Fair Labor Standards Amendments of 1971, July 19, 1971. Puerto Rican Resident Commissioner Jorge L. Córdova Díaz, in testimony before the same committee the same day, stated that "there should be no substantial difference. The cost of living is substantially the same. It is a little higher if you choose to live in Puerto Rico according to stateside standards."

44. For representative statements, pro and con, of the validity of the government's policy, see H.C. Barton, Jr., "Salarios Versus Empleos, "*El Mundo*, San Juan, Puerto Rico, September 16 and 17, 1970, and Miles Galvin, "Abundancia para los de Arriba y Austeridad para los de Abajo," *El Mundo*, San Juan, Puerto Rico, August 18 and 19, 1971. For an English version, see Miles Galvin, "Poor Asked to Sacrifice More than Rich," *San Juan Star*, San Juan, Puerto Rico, June 8, 1971, p. 34.

45. An opinion survey conducted in Puerto Rico in 1971 revealed that the majority of those included in an island wide sample believed that "laziness was the principal reason for unemployment." Only twelve percent of those polled "blamed the government and what they termed its lack of effort as the reason for the island's high level of unemployment." *San Juan Star*, San Juan, Puerto Rico, December 18, 1971, p. 6.

46. Dudley Smith, *Puerto Rico's Income* (Washington, D.C.: Association of Sugar Producers of Puerto Rico, 1943), p. 10, cited by Féliz Mejías, *Condiciones de Vida de las Clases Jornaleras de Puerto Rico* (Puerto Rico: Junta Editora de la Universidad de Puerto Rico, 1946), p. 59. Family income was obtained by calculating six members per family.

47. Rafael L. Ramírez, "Pobreza en Puerto Rico: Teoría y Praxis, " *Revista de Administracion Publica* 4, no. 2 (September 1971) (Escuela de Administracion Pública, Universidad de Puerto Rico), p. 91. The estimate of $2,500 as the poverty line in Puerto Rico, compared with a much higher figure in the U.S., despite a higher cost of living in Puerto Rico, serves as a reminder of the difference between "cost" of living and "standard" of living.

48. Frank Ramos, "Study Shows the Poor are Getting Poorer," *San Juan Star*, San Juan, Puerto Rico, May 28, 1972.

49. Quintero Alfaro, "Educational Innovation," pp. 16-17.

50. "Remarks by the Hon. Luis Muñoz Marín, Governor of the Commonwealth of Puerto Rico, at Harvard University on the afternoon of Commencement Day, Thursday, June 16, 1955," mimeographed, p. 5. The Governor's pronouncement was dutifully propagated in official Commonwealth publications for some years, but otherwise fell on ears made deaf by radio and television commercialized invitations to a different sort of good life. For a synthesis of "Operation Serenity," see *The Commonwealth of Puerto Rico*, a descriptive bulletin by the Office of the Commonwealth, Washington, D.C., June, 1962, pp. 32-39.

51. Wells, pt. 2 "Cultures in Conflict," pp. 63-131. The ascription of personality and behavioral traits to an entire community is, of course a highly abstract enter-

prise. There is no doubt that different societies have different traits, but, *within* each society, which are the most representative values among those values in internal conflict? Angel G. Quintero Rivera, in his Introduction to *Lucha Obrera en Puerto Rico* (San Juan, Puerto Rico: Centro de Estudioa de la Realidad Puertorriquena, 1971), pp. 8-9, very tellingly questions the ascription of a national personality to Puerto Rican society by describing the characteristics of some very influential historical personalities, whose characteristics deviate from the ascribed norms.

52. Exactly fifty years before Reynolds and Gregory arrived at the conclusion of "managerial incompetence" in Puerto Rico, another investigator from the United States had arrived at precisely the same conclusion. Walter E. Weyl reported in 1905 that "much of the alleged inefficiency of Porto Rican labor has been due to the unintelligent manner in which it has been directed." "Labor Conditions in Porto Rico" Bulletin no. 61, Bureau of Labor, Department of Commerce and Labor, vol. 11, November 1905, p. 771.

53. Theodore W. Schultz, "Investment in Human Capital," *The American Economic Review* 51, no. 1 (March 1961), and especially, "The Economic Test in Latin America," New York State School of Industrial and Labor Relations, Cornell University, Ithaca, N.Y., Bulletin no. 35, August 1956. "Mexico and Puerto Rico have been models in improving the quality of their people as productive agents," p. 24.

54. Reynolds and Gregory, *Wages, Productivity, and Industrialization*, pp. 288 and 298-99.

CHAPTER 9

1. Everett M. Kassalow, *Trade Unions and Industrial Relations: An International Comparison* (New York: Random House, 1969), p. 309. Kassalow also singled out Mehta in "Trade Unionism and the Development Process in the New Nations: A Comparative View," chap. 3, *International Labor*, Solomon Barkin et al. (New York: Harper, 1967), p. 71, and in "Unions in the New and Developing Countries," chap. 10, in *National Labor Movements in the Postwar World*, Everett M. Kassalow, ed. (Chicago, Ill.: Northwestern University Press, 1963), p. 243.

2. Iglesias, *Luchas Emancipadoras* 1:181-84. Muñoz Rivera's editorial included an additional admonition now rarely used: that workers should be cautious about forcing wages higher precipitously because of the attraction this would have for immigrants, who would then compete for their jobs.

3. Lewis, *Puerto Rico*, p. 222, referring to an article by David F. Ross, "Gordon Lewis on Puerto Rico's Development Program" *Journal of Politics* (February 1957).

4. The professional rationale has been principally provided over the years by Hugh. C. Barton, Jr., an economist closely identified with the Popular Party. See, for example, two articles in *El Mundo*, September 16 and 17, 1970.

5. The most relentless editorialist of the official position in recent years has been A. W. Maldonado of *El Mundo*. See, for example, "El Cierre de las Fábricas," *El Mundo*, September 30, 1970.

6. Quoted in Quintero Rivera, ed., *Lucha Obrera en Puerto Rico*, pp. 164-65. See "El Progreso Técnico y los Trabajadores" (San Juan, Puerto Rico, Government of Puerto Rico, 1958), a speech by Moscoso.

7. James Tobin, et al., "Report to the Governor," The Committee to Study Puerto Rico's Finances, San Juan, Puerto Rico, December 11, 1975, pp. vi-viii, 44.

8. Reynolds and Gregory with Luz M. Torruellas, *Wages, Productivity, and Industrialization in Puerto Rico*, pp. 288, 347. The question, of course, is fundamentally unfair in that it was asked at a time when the unions had long since been deprived of a more autonomous opportunity to advance worker welfare.

9. Knowles, "Unionism and Politics in Puerto Rico," p. 10.

10. Rottenberg, "Labor Cost in the Puerto Rican Economy," p. 140 n. 49.

11. Luis Muñoz Marín, "Función del movimiento obrero en la democracia puertorriqueña," address delivered to the *Congreso de Unidad Obrera*, November 23, 1957, pp. 9-10.

12. Rottenberg, "Labor Costs in the Puerto Rican Economy," pp. 136-37 n. 47.

13. A representative sample of union leaders from throughout Puerto Rican industry was interviewed in 1949. Of the 138 union officers included, 81 had held office two years or less, and 123 (cumulatively) had held office less than six years. Rottenberg, "Labor Costs in the Puerto Rican Economy," p. 131.

14. For a personal account, see Juan Saez Corales, *25 Años de Lucha, Mi Respuesta a la Persecución*, pamphlet, n.p. April 23, 1955, pp. 29.

15. International Labor Officer, *Labour Policies in the West Indies* (Geneva: ILO, 1952), p. 165.

16. For examples of the very extensive functions of the insular Department of Labor, see *Organizaciones y Funciones del Departamento del Trabajo* (San Juan, Puerto Rico: Oficina de Relaciones Publicas, Departamento del Trabajo, Estado Libre Asociado de Puerto Rico, January 1970). The functions of the insular Department of Labor are in addition to those of the Federal Department of Labor and of the National Labor Reltions Board and its insular counterpart.

17. See *Organizaciones y Funciones del Departamento del Trabajo* (San Juan, Puerto Rico: Oficina de Relaciones Publicas, Departamento del Trabajo, Estado Libre Asociado de Puerto Rico, January 1970), p. 20.

18. See Luis F. Silva Recio, *Public Wage Fixing and its Effect on Collective Bargaining and the Labor Movement in Puerto Rico* (Ph.D. diss. University of Wisconsin, 1962).

19. Ross, *The Long Uphill Path*, p. 148 (emphasis added).

20. See Reinaldo E. Rivera, *Beneficios Marginales en Puerto Rico, Un Estudio Comparativo* (Río Piedras, Puerto Rico: Instituto de Relaciones del Trabajo and Centro de Investigaciones Comerciales, University of Puerto Rico, 1969).

21. See "La Facultad Restringida del Departamento del Trabajo en Casos de Reclamaciones Cuando Existe Convenio Colectivo (Documentos y Consideraciones)", *Revista del Trabajo* 3, no. 2 (Department of Labor, Commonwealth of Puerto Rico, San Juan, Puerto Rico) (July-August-September 1970).

22. Rottenberg, "Labor Costs in the Puerto Rican Economy," pp. 132-33.

23. For a concise summary of the factors leading to the disintegration of the labor movement during this period, see Gervasio García, review of *Notes on the Puerto Rican Revolution* by Gordon K. Lewis, in *Caribbean Studies* 16, no. 1 (April 1976), pp. 178-85.

24. Harold J. Lidin, "I.U.E. to Fight 'Stereotypes' in Bargaining," *The San Juan Star*, May 9, 1961, p. 7.

25. Juan Manuel Ocasio, "The Growth of the 'Internationals' Here," pt. 4 of a series of 5 articles, *The San Juan Star*, June 24, 1965.

26. David Ross, *The Long Uphill Path*, p. 150.

27. Fernando Sierra Berdecía, "Puerto Rico, Labor Unions and Labor Relations," *The Status of Labor in Puerto Rico, Alaska, Hawaii*, U.S. Department of Labor Bulletin no. 1191, January 1956, p. 16.

28. Guerra de Colón, *Trayectoria, Acción*, pp. 90-91.

29. "U.S. Unions in Puerto Rico," *Latin America and Empire Report* (North American Congress on Latin America) 10, no. 5 (May-June 1976), p. 12.

30. Juan Manuel Ocasio, "The Growth of the 'Internationals' Here," *The San Juan Star*, June 24, 1965, p. 42.

31. Reynolds and Gregory, *Wages, Productivity, and Industrialization*, p. 298.

32. " '*Ay bendito*' is short for 'blessed be the Lord,' but its meaning is closer to 'ah, woe is me,' and it serves as a handy lubricant for potentially abrasive situations." Wagenheim, *Puerto Rico, A Profile*, p. 214.

33. "Joint Statement Presented to the Sub-Committee on Labor and Public Welfare of the United States Senate, July 19, 1971," by Robert N. Alpert, Hotel and Restaurant Employees, Pedro Grant, Boilermakers International Union, Peter Huegel, Amalgamated Meat Cutters Union, José Caraballo, Sindicato Obreros Unidos del Sur, Osvaldino Rojas Lugo, Government of Puerto Rico Insurance Fund Workers Union (Miles Galvin, technical adviser), mimeographed version, p.2.

34. "Supplemental Statement on Behalf of the International Ladies' Garment Workers' Union with Regard to the Provisions of S. 1861 Applicable to Puerto Rico, by Walter Mankoff, Assistant Director of Research, ILGWU," before the Subcommittee on Labor and Public Welfare, U.S. Senate, July 19,1971, mimeographed version, pp. 1-2.

35. Knowles, "Unionism and Politics in Puerto Rico," p. 13.

36. For an analysis of the referred to practices, see ibid., pp. 17-26.

37. The term *colonialismo sindical* was popularized by columnist César Andreu Iglesias in a caustic series of columns in 1961 and 1965, which reportedly eventually cost him his job with *El Imparcial* newspaper. See *El Imparcial*, San Juan, Puerto Rico, October 4, 5, 6, 7, 9, and 10, 1961, and March 29, 30, and 31, 1965.

38. *Central Unica de Trabajadores de Puerto Rico, "Manifiesto a Todos los Trabajadores del Pais,"* San Juan, Puerto Rico, n. d. ca. January 1961.

CHAPTER 10

1. Rubén A. Vilches, "Union Membership in Puerto Rico in June 1970," San Juan, Puerto Rico: Bureau of Labor Statistics, Department of Labor, Commonwealth of Puerto Rico, n.d., mimeographed, pp. 6-7.

2. Harold Lidin, "Nothing Cute about CUTE," *San Juan Star*, San Juan, Puerto Rico, November 14, 1977.

3. Reglamento del Movimiento Obrero Unido de Puerto Rico, San Juan, Puerto Rico, October 16, 1972.

4. Harold J. Lidin, "Teamsters' Pagan Voted Head of Labor Political Action Unit," *San Juan Star*, San Juan, Puerto Rico, December 26, 1975.

5. "U.S. Unions in Puerto Rico," *North American Congress on Latin America's Latin America and Empire Report* 10, no. 5 (May-June 1976):16.

6. "Crown Cork Workers Fight Back," *Puerto Rico Journal of Human Rights* v. l, no. 2 (November 1, 1977): 43.

7. Manuel Maldonado Denis, *Puerto Rico, Una Interpretacion Historico-Social* (Mexico: Siglo Veintiuno Editores, 1969), p. 231, my translation.

8. The most knowledgeable expostion of the goal of radical influence in the Puerto Rican labor movement is the 1970 article by César Andreu Iglesias, "El Movimiento Sindical y la Independencia," *La Escalera* 4, nos. 6-7 (December 1970-January 1971): 11-21. See also Angel Agosto, "Objetivos del Trabajo Obrero del MPI," *Nueva Lucha*, 1 no. 2 (May 1971) (Publication of the Movimiento Pro Independencia): 21-34.

9. Tomas Stella, "Unpaid Overtime Claims Spawn Probe of Security Associates," *San Juan Star*, San Juan, Puerto Rico, December 2, 1977.

10. Jane B. Baird, "NWU Chief Jailed: Union Fined for Contempt," *San Juan Star*, San Juan, Puerto Rico, December 4, 1976; "The Case of the National Workers' Union (UNT), " *Sindicalismo Puertorriqueño* 2, no. l (February-March 1976): 1-2.

11. "El Ajusticiamiento de Allan H. Randall," *Claridad*, San Juan, Puerto Rico, November 3, 1977, pp 16-17.

12. Christopher Pala, "List of Suspects Narrows in Randall Probe," *San Juan Star*, San Juan, Puerto Rico, December 12, 1977.

13. David M. Helfeld, et al., Informe de la Comision del Gobernador para Estudiar Relaciones del Trabajo en el Servicio Público en Puerto Rico," (San Juan, Puerto Rico: Executive Press, February 1975), 1: 24.

14. Public Sector Labor Relations Information Exchange, *State Profiles: Current Status of Public Sector Labor Relations*, U.S.Department of Labor, November, 1971. Proportion of state and local employees in Puerto Rico calculated on basis of 144,589 commonwealth and municipal employees in a total population of 2,712,033 as per *1970 Census of Population, of Inhabitants of Puerto Rico* U.S. Bureau of the Census, U.S. Department of Commerce, September 1971.

15. See José Orlando Grau, "Ideas y tendencias emergentes en Puerto Rico en torno de la sindicalización de los empleados publicos," ponencia presentada al Seminario de la Escuela de Adminstración Pública, Universidad de Puerto Rico, May 9, 1969, mimeographed, p.2.

16. Frank Romero, Director of Personnel of Puerto Rico, for example, in testimony previously cited on the application of Federal minimum wages to the public sector in Puerto Rico, maintained that "the financial position of the Commonwealth Government would not permit it to pay the proposed increases without detriment to programs of high priority such as health and education." p. 4.

17. Puerto Rico Labor Relations Act, Act no. 130, approved May 8, 1945, amended by Act no. 6, approved March 7, 1946. For a discussion of the Act and its administration, see Fred Barela, *The Puerto Rico Labor Relations Act: A State Labor Policy and Its Application*, Río Piedras (Puerto Rico: Editorial Universitaria, 1965).

18. Juan R. Fernández, "La negociación colectiva en las corporaciones publicas de Puerto Rico " (Master's thesis, School of Public Administration, University of Puerto Rico, July 1963), pp. 82-85. There was also a history of collective bargaining in the case of the transportation enterprise that was transformed into a public authority, pp. 81, 104-5.

19. Demetrio Fernández, "El Ordenamiento y la Problematica de la Negociación Colectiva en el Sector Público," *Revista Jurídica de la Universidad de Puerto Rico* 42, no. 1 (1973): 8-21, esp.

20. Estado Libre Asociado de Puerto Rico, *Diario de Sesiones de la Convencion Constituyente de Puerto Rico,* 4 vols. (Orford, N.H.: Equity Publishing Corporation, 1961), 3: 1614.

21. Irma García de Serrano, *The Puerto Rico Teachers' Association and Its Relationship to Teacher Personnel Administration* (Puerto Rico: University of Puerto Rico Press, 1971), pp. 57-66, 121-392.

22. Antonio Cuevas Viret, "Problemas de derechos civiles en la administración de personal del gobierno," ponencia presentada a la Comisión de Derechos Civiles, San Juan, Puerto Rico, Escuela de Administración Pública, Universidad de Puerto Rico, mimegrafiada, sin fecha (la ponencia fue presentada el 11 de julio de 1958), pp. 33-34.

23. For a more extensive discussion of these factors, see Miles Galvin, "Collective Bargaining in the Public Sector in Puerto Rico," (Ph.D. diss. University of Wisconsin, 1972).

24. David F. Ross, *The Long Uphill Path, a Historical Study of Puerto Rico's Program of Economic Development* (San Juan, Puerto Rico: Editorial Edil, 1969), pp. 65-68.

25. Félix Morales, *Tres Maquinarias y Lucha con Fantasmas,* San Juan, Puerto Rico: Imprenta Romero, 1945), pp. 17-24.

26. Irma García de Serrano, *The Puerto Rico Teachers' Association and Its Relationship to Teacher Personnel Administration* (Puerto Rico: University of Puerto Rico Press, 1971), passim, esp. pp. 260-87.

27. Miles Galvin, "Collective Bargaining," pp. 399-402.

28. Hilda Bonilla Acosta, "Derecho a la negociación colectiva en el servicio público de Puerto Rico: caso particular, el Fondo del Seguro del Estado" (Master's thesis, School of Public Administration, University of Puerto Rico, Rio Piedras, Puerto Rico, 1972), passim.

29. The AFSCME presence in Puerto Rico had been engineered by Arnold Zander at the height of the cold war era in the late 1950s with the hope that ties with public sector unions in other Latin American countries could be developed (an activity of great interest to U.S foreign policy at the time). When Jerry Wurf defeated Zander for the presidency in the mid-1960s, AFSCME proceeded to let its Puerto Rican affiliate wither on the vine.

30. Helfeld, *Informe de la Comision,* et al., 1: 26-27.

31. Departamento del Trabajo del Estado Libre Asociado de Puerto Rico, "Secretaria del Trabajo advierte a trabajadores sobre intromisiones ajenas a los intereses obrero (sic) en Puerto Rico," communicado de prensa DT-97, 20 de marzo de 1972.

32. *El Mundo,* San Juan, Puerto Rico, December 5, 1971.

33. *San Juan Star*, San Juan, Puerto Rico, January 2, 1972.

34. *El Imparcial* San Juan, Puerto Rico, May 27, 1972.

35. See *San Juan Star*, San Juan, Puerto Rico, May 27 and 31, 1972. *El Imparcial*, San Juan, Puerto Rico, of May 29, 1972 accounts an incident in Quebradillas, Puerto Rico, where police intervention was required to prevent a clash between strikers and a group of irate citizens.

36. Helfeld, et al., *Informe de la Comision* 1:38 and 78-80.

37. *San Juan Star*, August 15, 1975.

38. *Informe Económico al Gobernador, 1975*, Planning Board, San Juan, Puerto Rico, p. A-24.

39. Harold J. Lidin, "Thrust of Island Labor Movement is Shifting," and "Island Unions on the Upswing," *San Juan Star*, March 30-31, 1975.

40. Lewis, *Puerto Rico*, pp. 224-27.

41. A Governor's Labor Advisory Council was belatedly established on September 1, 1975 (Administrative Bulletin No. 3095).

42. Rexford Guy Tugwell, *The Stricken Land* (New York: Doubleday, 1947), p. 80.

43. Arturo Morales Carrión, "The Commonwealth of Puerto Rico, Its Historical Roots and Present Significance," Paper presented at the Eighth Annual Conference of the Caribbean, University of Florida, Gainesville, Florida, December 6, 1957, mimeographed version, p. 13. (It should be noted that Morales Carrión goes on to suggest that the achievement of commonwealth status virtually elminated colonialism, a propostion that is certainly questionable in the area of labor relations).

44. Eldon Kenworthy, "Our Image of Their Problems," *The Nation*, December 2, 1968, p. 589.

Selected Bibliography

Books

Alexander, Robert J. *Organized Labor in Latin American*. New York: The Free Press, 1965.

Alonso Torres, Rafael. *Cuarenta Años De Lucha Proletaria*. San Juan, Puerto Rico: Imprenta Baldrich, 1939.

Anderson, Charles W. *Politics and Economic Change in Latin America*. Princeton, N.J.: Van Nostrand, 1967.

Anderson, Robert W. *Party Politics in Puerto Rico*. Stanford, Calif.: Stanford University Press, 1965.

Barela, Fred. *The Puerto Rico Labor Relations Act: A State Labor Policy and its Application*. Rio Piedras, Puerto Rico: Editorial Universitaria, Universidad de Puerto Rico, 1965.

Berbusse, Edward J. *The United States in Puerto Rico, 1898-1900*. Chapel Hill: University of North Carolina Press, 1966.

Brau, Salvador. *Desquisiciones Sociológicas*. Río Piedras, Puerto Rico: Ediciones del Instituto de Literatura, Universidad de Puerto Rico, 1956. (With an introduction and under the editorship of Eugenio Fernández Méndez.)

Carreras, Juan. *Santiago Iglesias Pantín*. San Juan, Puerto Rico: Club de Prensa, 1965.

Clark, Victor S. and Associates. *Porto Rico and its Problems*. Washington, D.C.: The Brookings Institution, 1930.

Diffie, Bailey W., and Diffie, Justine W. *Porto Rico: A Broken Pledge*. New York: The Vanguard Press, 1931.

Friedlander, Stanley L. *Labor Migration and Economic Growth, A Case Study of Puerto Rico*. Cambridge, Mass.: The MIT Press, 1965.

Fernández Méndez, Eugenio, ed. *Crónicas de Puerto Rico (1493-1797)*. Tomo I. San Juan, Puerto Rico: Ediciones del Gobierno del Estado Libre Asociado de Puerto Rico. 1957.

———. *Crónicas de Puerto Rico (1809-1955)*. Tomo II. San Juan, Puerto Rico: Ediciones del Gobierno del Estado Libre Asociado de Puerto Rico, 1957.

Franck, Harry A. *Roaming Through the West Indies*. New York: Century, 1921.

Fuster, Jaime B. *Los Derechos Civiles Reconocidos en el Sistema de Vida Puertorriqueno*. San Juan, Puerto Rico: Comisión de Derechos Civiles, Estado Libre Asociado de Puerto Rico, 1968.

García de Serrano, Irma. *La Selección de Personal en el Servicio Publico de Puerto Rico*. San Juan, Puerto Rico: Editorial Universitaria, Universidad de Puerto Rico, 1969.

———. *The Puerto Rico Teachers' Association and its Relationship to Teacher Personnel Administration*. San Juan, Puerto Rico: University of Puerto Rico Press, 1971.

Gayer, Arthur D.: Homan, Paul T.; and James, Earle K. *The Sugar Economy of Puerto Rico*. New York: Columbia University Press, 1938.

Gómez Acevedo, Labor. *Organización y Reglamentación del Trabajo en el Puerto Rico del Siglo XIX (Propietarios y Jornaleros)*. San Juan, Puerto Rico: Instituto de Cultura Puertorriquena, 1970.

Gompers, Samuel. *Seventy Years of Life and Labor*. 2 vols. New York: E.P. Dutton & Co., 1925.

González, Antonio J. *Economía Política de Puerto Rico*. San Juan, Puerto Rico: Editorial Cordillera, 1967.

Goodsell, Charles T. *Administration of a Revolution: The Development of Public Administration in Puerto Rico Under Governor Rexford G. Tugwell, 1941-46*. Cambridge, Mass.; Harvard University Press, 1965.

Hancock, Ralph. *Puerto Rico: A Success Story*. New York: Van Nostrand, 1960.

Hanson, Earl Parker. *Puerto Rico—Ally for Progress*. Princeton, N.J. : Van Nostrand, 1962.

Iglesias de Pagán, Igualdad. *El Obrerismo en Puerto Rico: Epoca de Santiago Iglesias (1898-1905)*. Palencia de Castilla, Spain: Industrias Gráficas Diario-Dia, Ediciones Juan Ponce de Leon, 1973.

Iglesias Pantín, Santiago. *Luchas Emancipadoras (Crónicas de*

Puerto Rico). San Juan, Puerto Rico: Imprenta Venezuela, primera edición del primer tomo, 1929, segunda edición del primer tomo, 1958, segundo tomo, 1962.

International Labour Office. *Labour Policies in the West Indies.* Geneva, Switzerland: International Labour Organization, 1952.

Kassalow, Everett M. *Trade Unions and Industrial Relations: An International Comparison.* New York: Random House. 1969.

Lastra, Carlos J. *The Impact of Minimum Wages on a Labor-Oriented Economy.* San Juan, Puerto Rico: A Social Science Research Center Study, College of Social Sciences, University of Puerto Rico, printed by the Government Development Bank for Puerto Rico, Govbank Technical Papers No. 1, 1964.

Lewis, Gordon K. *Puerto Rico, Freedom and Power in the Caribbean.* New York: Monthly Review Press, 1963.

Lewis, Oscar. *La Vida: A Puerto Rican Family in the Culture of Poverty—San Juan and New York.* New York: Random House, 1966.

Maldonado Denis, Manuel. *Puerto Rico una Interpretación Histórico-Social.* México: Siglo Veintiuno Editores 1969.

Mandel, Bernard. *Samuel Gompers.* Yellow Springs, Ohio: The Antioch Press, 1963.

Mathews, Thomas G. *Puerto Rican Politics and the New Deal.* Gainesville: University of Florida Press, 1960.

Mejías, Félix. *Condiciones de Vida de las Clases Jornaleras de Puerto Rico.* Río Piedras, Puerto Rico: Monografias de la Universidad de Puerto Rico, Series C, no. 2, 1946.

Millen, Bruce H. *The Political Role of Labor in Developing Countries.* Washington, D.C.: The Brookings Institution, 1963.

Mintz, Sidney W. *Worker in the Cane.* New Haven, Conn.: Yale University Press, 1960.

Mixer, Knowlton. *Porto Rico, History and Conditions: Social, Economic and Political.* New York: MacMillan Co., 1926.

Muñoz Amato, Pedro. *Problemas de Derechos Civiles en la Administración de Personal del Estado Libre Asociado de Puerto Rico.* San Juan, Puerto Rico: Escuela de Administractión Pública, Universidad de Puerto Rico, 1961.

Nieves Falcón, Luis. *La Opinión Pública y las Aspiraciones de los Puertorriqueños*. Río Piedras, Puerto Rico: Centro de Investigaciones Sociales, Universidad de Puerto Rico, 1970.

Pagán, Bolivar. *Historia de los Partidos Politicos Puertorriqueños*. 2 vols. San Juan, Puerto Rico: Librería Campos, 1959.

Perloff, Harvey S. *Puerto Rico's Economic Future*. Chicago: University of Chicago Press, 1950.

Quintero Rivera, Angel G., ed. *Lucha Obrera en Puerto Rico, Antología de Grandes Documentos en la Historia Obrera Puertorriqueña*. San Juan, Puerto Rico: Centro de Estudios de la Realidad Puertorriquena, n.d., ca. 1971.

Ramos de Santiago, Carmen. *El Gobierno de Puerto Rico*. 2d ed. San Juan, Puerto Rico: Editorial Universidad de Puerto Rico, 1970.

Reynolds, Lloyd G. and Gregory, Peter. with Luz M. Torruellas. *Wages, Productivity and Industrialization in Puerto Rico*. Homewood, Ill.: Richard D. Irwin, 1965.

Rodríquez Vera, Andrés. *Fantoches del Obrerismo o el Fracaso de una Institución*. San Juan, Puerto Rico: Tipografía Negrón Flores, 1915.

―――. *Federación Obrera Pan-Americana?* San Juan, Puerto Rico: Imprenta La Democracia, 1924.

―――. *Agrarismo por Dentro y Trabajo a Domicilio*. San Juan, Puerto Rico: Tipografia "La Democracia." 1929.

―――. *El Triunfo de la Apostasía*. San Juan, Puerto Rico: Tipografía "La Democracia." 1930.

Ross, Arthur M., ed. *Industrial Relations and Economic Development*. London: MacMillan, 1967.

Ross, David F. *The Long Uphill Path: A Historical Study of Puerto Rico's Program of Economic Development*. San Juan, Puerto Rico: Editorial Edil, 1969.

Rowe, Leo S. *The United States and Porto Rico*. New York: Longmans, Green and Company, 1904.

Senior, Clarence. *Santiago Iglesias: Labor Crusader*. San Juan, Puerto Rico: Interamerican University Press, 1972.

Steward, Julian H., ed. *The People of Puerto Rico*. Urbana: University of Illinois Press, 1956, 1966.

Tugwell, Rexford Guy. *The Stricken Land*. Garden City, N.Y.: Doubleday & Co., 1947.

Tumin, Melvin, with Feldman, Arnold S. *Social Class and Social Change in Puerto Rico*. Princeton, N.J.: Princeton University Press, 1961.

Van Middeldyk, R. A. *The History of Puerto Rico from the Spanish Discovery to the American Occupation*. New York: D. Appleton & Co., 1903.

Wagenheim, Kal. *Puerto Rico, A Profile*. New York: Praeger, 1970.

Wells, Henry. *The Modernization of Puerto Rico: A Political Study of Changing Values and Institutions*. Cambridge, Mass,: Harvard University Press, 1969.

Articles

Agosto, Angel. "Objetivos del trabajo obrero del MPI." *Nueva Lucha* 1, no. 2 (may 1971) (Publicación del Movimiento Pro Independencia de Puerto Rico).

Albizu, Charlie, Matlin, Norman. "The Death of Poetry: The 1968 Puerto Rico Election." *Caribbean Review* 1, no.1 (Spring 1969).

Barrett, Laurence I. "Puerto Rico: Trying to Make it Without Miracles." *Time* February 16, 1976, pp. 15-21.

Dietz, James. "The Puerto Rican Political Economy." *Latin American Perspectives* 3, no. 3 issue 10 (summer 1976): 3-16.

Fernández, Demetrio. "El Ordenamiento y la Problemática de la Negociación Colectiva en el Sector Público." *Revista Jurídica de la Universidad de Puerto Rico* 42, no. 1 (1973): 7-83.

———. "La Junta de Relaciones del Trabajo de Puerto Rico y el Sector Publico." *Revista Jurídica de la Universidad de Puerto Rico* 43, nos. 2-3 (1974): 295-420.

García, Gervasio. "Apuntes sobre una interpretacion de la realidad puertorriquena." *La Escalera* 4, no. 1 (June 1970): 23-31.

———. "Primeros Fermentos de Organización Obrera en Puerto Rico, (1873-1898)." *Cuadernos* no. 1. Centro de Estudios de la Realidad Puertorriquena (CEREP) (1974).

González, Antonio J. "Apuntes para la historia del movimiento sindical de Puerto Rico: 1896-1941." *Revista de Ciencias Sociales* 1, no. 3 (September 1957).

Grau, José Orlando. "Ideas y tendencias emergentes en Puerto Rico en torno de la sindicalización de los empleados públicos." *Seminario de la Escuela de Administración Pública* de la Universidad de Puerto Rico, May 9, 1969.

Gregory, Peter. "El Desarrollo de la Fuerza Obrera Industrial en Puerto Rico." *Revista de Ciencias Sociales* (December 1958), pp. 447-68.

———. "The Labor Market in Puerto Rico." Chap. 9 in *Labor Commitment and Social Change in Developing Areas*, Wilbert E. Moore and Arnold S. Feldman, eds. New York: Social Science Research Council, 1960, pp. 136-72.

Kenworthy, Eldon. "Argentina: The Politics of Late Industrialization." *Foreign Affairs*, April, 1967.

Knowles, William H. "The Puerto Rican Labor Movement." In *Proceedings of the 1962 Annual Spring Meeting, Industrial Relations Research Association*. Madison, Wis.: The Association, 1962, pp. 536-41.

———. "Unionism and Politics in Puerto Rico." A study done for the United States-Puerto Rico Commission on the Status of Puerto Rico, Washington, D.C., 1966.

"Labor in Puerto Rico." *American Federationist*, April 1904.

Lewis, W. Arthur. "Economic Development with Unlimited Supplies of Labour." *The Manchester School of Economic and Social Studies* 22, no. 2 (May 1954).

Marqués, René. "El Puertorriqueño dócil." *Cuadernos Americanos* 120 no. 1 (January-February 1962): 144-95.

Morales Carrión, Arturo. "The Commonwealth of Puerto Rico: Its Historical Roots and Present Significance." Paper presented at the Eighth Annual Conference on the Caribbean, University of Florida, Gainesville, Florida, December 6, 1957.

Morales Yordán, Jorge. "Desarrollo político y pobreza." *Revista de Administración Pública* (Universidad de Puerto Rico) 4, no. 2 (September 1971): 109-26.

NACLA-East and the Puerto Rican Project. "U.S. Unions in Puerto Rico." *North American Congress on Latin America's Latin America and Empire Report* 105 no. 5 (May-June 1976): 2-32.

Nazario, Alfredo. "Public Employee Bargaining in Puerto Rico." Chap. 2 in *Public Employee Organization and Bargaining*. Edited by Howard J. Anderson. Washington, D.C.: Bureau of National Affairs, Inc., 1968:

"President Gompers in Puerto Rico." *American Federationist* April 1904), pp. 293-306.

Puerto Rico Legal Project. "Crown Cork Workers Fight Back." *Puerto Rican Journal of Human Rights* 1, no. 2 (November 1, 1977), pp. 43-47.

Quintero Alfaro, Angel G. "Educational Innovation and Change in Societies with Less Advanced Technology." MS, University of Puerto Rico, 1971.

Quintero Rivera, Angel G. "El desarrollo de las clases sociales y los conflictos politicos en Puerto Rico." Ensayo inédito, Universidad de Puerto Rico, 1971.

―――. "Background to the Emergence of Imperialist Capitalism in Puerto Rico." *Caribbean Studies* 13, no. 3 (October 1973): 31-63.

Ramirez, Rafael. "Pobreza en Puerto Rico; teoria y praxis." *Revista de Administracion Publica* (Universidad de Puerto Rico) 4, no. 2 (September 1971): 89-100.

Rivera Rivera, Julio. "Origenes de la organización obrera en Puerto Rico, 1838-1898." *La Revista Historia* (Sociedad Nacional de Historia, Phi Alpha Theta) 5, no. 1 (April 1955): 91-112.

Rottenberg, Simon. "Labor Cost in the Puerto Rican Economy." *Revista Jurídica de la Universidad de Puerto Rico* 20, no. 2 (November-December 1950): 109-70.

Silva Recio, Luis F. "Cambios en los ingresos de los trabajadores de Puerto Rico en los últimos 15 años." *Revista de Trabajo* 1, no. 2 (April-May-June 1968): 1-6, 45-49. (Departmento del Trabajo de Puerto Rico.)

Vilches, Rubén A. "Empleo, subempleo y desempleo en Puerto Rico." *Revista del Trabajo* 1, no. 3 (July-August-September 1968): 1-12. (Departamento del Trabajo de Puerto Rico.)

―――. "El problema poblacional de Puerto Rico y el propósito de lograr una civilización superior." *Revista del Trabajo* 2, no. 7 (July-August-September 1969): 1-11. (Departamento del Trabajo, Estado Libre Asociado de Puerto Rico.)

———. "Comentarios sobre la situación de desempleo en Puerto Rico." *Revista del Trabajo* 3, nos. 13-14 (January-June 1971): 1-80. (Departmento del Trabajo del Estado Libre Asociado de Puerto Rico.)

Weasler, George L. "Collective Bargaining in the Public Service." *Revista del Colegio de Abogados de Puerto Rico* 32, no. 3 (August 1971): 445-93.

Whittaker, William G. "The Santiago Iglesias Case, 1901-1902: Origins of American Trade Union Involvement in Puerto Rico." *The Americas* 25, no. 4 (April 1968): 378-93.

Bulletins, Pamphlets

Andreu Iglesias, César. *Un Renegado al Desnudo; O Alberto E. Sánchez Alias Enrique Bolter y Los Salarios Minimos*. Santurce, Puerto Rico: Librería Estrella Roja, 1949.

———. *Apuntes para la Historia del Movimiento Obrero*. San Juan, Puerto Rico: Movimiento Pro-Independencia de Puerto Rico, Ediciones El Proletario, no. 1 n.d. (Publicado originalmente bajo el titulo "El movimiento obrero y la independencia de Puerto Rico," *La Escalera* 2, nos. 8-9.)

Barton, Hugh C. *Puerto Rico's Industrial Development Program: 1942-60*. Cambridge, Mass.: Center for International Affairs, Harvard University, 1959.

Bell, Patricia. *Puerto Rico, "Island of Paradise" of U.S. Imperialism*. New York: New Outlook Publishers, 1967.

Corretjer, Juan Antonio. *Albizu Campos y las Huelgas en los años 30*. San Juan, Puerto Rico: Liga Socialista Puertorriqueña (conferencia dictada en el Ateneo de Puerto Rico el 11 de septiembre de 1969).

Morales, Félix. *Tres Maquinarias y Lucha sin Fantasmas*. San Juan, Puerto Rico: Imprenta Romero, 1945, 24 pp.

Rivera, Reinaldo E. *Beneficios Marginales en Puerto Rico: Un Estudio Comparativo*. Río Piedras, Puerto Rico: Instituto de Relaciones del Trabajo y el Centro de Investigaciones Comerciales de la Universidad de Puerto Rico, 1969.

Sáez Corales, Juan. *25 años de lucha, mi respuesta a la persecución*. San Juan, Puerto Rico: Gautier Multigraph Service, 1955.

Schultz, Theodore W. *The Economic Test in Latin America.* Ithaca, N.Y.: New York State School of Industrial and Labor Relations, Cornell University, Bulletin 35, August 1956.

Sindicalismo Puertorriqueño (Puerto Rican Unionism). Bulletin of the Secretariat of Labor Affairs of the Puerto Rican Socialist Party, U.S.A. Branch. New York. Various issues. 1976.

Silva Recio, Luis F. *Legislación y Procesos de Salario Mínimo en Puerto Rico.* Rio Piedras, Puerto Rico: Escuela de Administración Pública, Universidad de Puerto Rico, 1965.

Wells, Henry, ed. *Puerto Rico Election Factbook.* Washington, D.C.: Institute for the Comparative Study of Political Systems, Operation and Policy Research, Inc., November 5, 1968.

Reports, Position Papers

Documentos sobre la Sindicalización de los Empleados Públicos. Recopilación de las opiniones del Secretario de Justicia del Estado Libre Asociado de Puerto Rico en torno al derecho de negociar colectivamente de los empleados públicos en Puerto Rico y documentos relacionados. Río Piedras, Puerto Rico: Instituto de Relaciones del Trabajo, Universidad de Puerto Rico. n.d., ca. 1968.

Establecido Sindicato de Empleados Publicos en Puerto Rico. Boletin de la Federación de Empleados Públicos de Puerto Rico. San Juan, Puerto Rico: American Federation of State, County, and Municipal Employees, AFL-CIO, n.d., ca. 1961.

Helfeld, David M., et al. *Relaciones del Trabajo en el Sector Publico Problemas y Recomendaciones.* Informe de la Comisión para estudiar relaciones del trabajo en el servicio público en Puerto Rico. San Juan, Puerto Rico: Executive Press. Vol. 1, 1975, vol. 2, 1974, vol. 3, 1974.

Informe al Honorable Gobernador del Estado Libre Asociado de Puerto Rico. San Juan, Puerto Rico: Comité del Governador para el Estudio de los Derechos Civiles en Puerto Rico, Departmento de Instrucción Pública, August 1959, reimpreso en 1969.

Lastra, Carlos J., Concepción Péréz Perez y Federico A. Cordero. *Informe sobre el Estado de las Relaciones Obrero-Patronales en Puerto Rico.* San Juan, Puerto Rico: Instituto de Estudios Administrativos y Legislativos, Inc., febrero de 1971. (Un informe al Senado del Estado Libre Asociado de Puerto Rico.)

Lo que Hizo la Federación de Empleados Públicos en Respaldo de los Empleados del Negociado de Intervenciones del Departmento de Hacienda. Boletín de la Federación de Empleados Públicos de Puerto Rico. San Juan, Puerto Rico: American Federation of State, County and Municipal Employees, AFL-CIO, n.d. ca. 1964.

Manifiesto a todos los Trabajadores del Pais. San Juan, Puerto Rico: Central Unica de Trabajadores de Puerto Rico, ca. 1961.

Morales, José Ramón. *Informe a la Junta Ejecutiva del Consejo de la Federación de Empleados Públicos de Puerto Rico.* San Juan, Puerto Rico: AFSCME, AFL-CIO, 2 September 1961.

Muñoz Amato, Pedro. *Problemas de Derechos Civiles en la Administración de Personal del Estado Libre Asociado de Puerto Rico.* Informe sometido al Comité de Derechos Civiles, October 8, 1958. San Juan, Puerto Rico: Escuela de Administración Pública, Universidad de Puerto Rico, 1961.

Tobin, James, et al. *Report to the Governor by the Committee to Study Puerto Rico's Finances.* n.p. December 11, 1975.

Valle, Rafael Angel. *Negociación Colectiva; Definición, Interpretación y Efectos; Solución a los Problemas de los Empleados por Distintos Medios; Arbitraje Compulsorio.* San Juan, Puerto Rico: Federación de Empleados Públicos de Puerto Rico, AFSCME, AFL-CIO, 7 November 1969.

Conference Proceedings

Aldarondo Galván, Etiony. *Pobreza en Puerto Rico.* Río Piedras, Puerto Rico: Ponencias presentadas en el Seminario sobre el Problema de la Pobreza en Puerto Rico, 29 and 30 April 1970. *Revista de Administración Pública* 4, no. 2, September 1971.

Puerto Rico: A Study of Democractic Development. American Academy of Political and Social Science, Philadelphia, 1953.

Addresses

Ferré, Antonio Luis. *La Relación Entre el Gobierno y el Personal PUblico y el Futuro de la Negociación Colectiva.* San Juan, Puerto Rico: Discurso a la Convención Anual de la Asociación de Personal Público, Capítulo de Puerto Rico, 11 December 1970.

Jiménez Malaret, René. *Organización Obrera*. (Discurso), San Juan, Puerto Rico: Editorial Esther, 1943.

Muñoz Marín, Luis. *Función del Movimiento Obrero en la Democracia Puertorriqueña*. Discurso Pronunciado en el Congreso de Unidad Obrera celebrado en la Escuela Superior Central de Sancturce, 23 November 1957.

Theses and Dissertations

Bonilla, Hilda. "Derecho a la Negociación Colectiva en el Servicio Público de Puerto Rico: Caso Particular, El Fondo del Seguro del Estado." Tésis inédita de maestría de la Escuela de Administracion Pública de la Universidad de Puerto Rico, 1972.

Cruz Morales, Leopoldo. "El Derecho a Organizarse que Tiene el Empleado Publico en Puerto Rico." Tésis inédita de maestria de la Escuela Graduada de Administración Publica de la Universidad de Puerto Rico, 1963.

Díaz, Manuel O. "Puerto Rican Labor Movement—A Historical Development." Master's thesis, Clark University, 1943.

Dillon, Irene M. "Problems of Labor in Puerto Rico." Master's thesis, Columbia University, 1948.

Fernández, Juan R. "La Negociación Colectiva en las Corporaciones Publicas de Puerto Rico." Tésis inédita de maestría, Escuela Graduada de Administracion Publica, Universidad de Puerto Rico, 1963.

Galvin, Miles. "Collective Bargaining in the Public Sector in Puerto Rico." Ph.D. dissertation, University of Wisconsin, 1972.

Guerra de Colón, María Luisa. "Trayectoria, Acción y Desenvolvimiento del Movimiento Obrero de Puerto Rico." Tésis de maestría, Escuela de Administración Pública, Universidad de Puerto Rico, 1963.

Monclova, Irving. Una Unión Obrera Independiente en Puerto Rico: La Unión de Trabajadores Industriales y Agricolas de Yabucoa." Tésis de maestría, Escuela Graduada de Administración Pública, Universidad de Puerto Rico, 1961.

Nogueras, Nicolás, Jr. "La Constitución de Puerto Rico y los Derechos Relativos al Trabajo." Tésis, Facultad de Derecho, Universidad de Puerto Rico. n.d.

Pou Rivera, Jesse. "Public Employee Organization in Puerto Rico." Draft of thesis for School of Public Adminstration, University of Puerto Rico, 1972.

Roca Rosselli, Carlos. "Historia de las Relaciones Obrero-Patronales en la Industria Azucarera de Puerto Rico." Tésis de maestría, Escuela Graduada de Administración Pública, Universidad de Puerto Rico, 1967.

Rosa, Vivian J. "A Historical Background for the Puerto Rican Labor Union." Master's thesis, Columbia University, 1945.

Silva, Luis Fernando. "Public Wage Fixing, and its Effect on Collective Bargaining and the Labor Movement in Puerto Rico." Ph.D. dissertation, University of Wisconsin, 1962.

Government Documents

Ames, Azel. *Labor Conditions in Porto Rico*. Washington, D.C.: Government Printing Office, U.S. Department of Labor Bulletin no. 34, vol. 6, May 1901.

Bravo, Juan S. *Apuntes sobre el Desarrollo del Movimiento Obrero en Puerto Rico*. San Juan, Puerto Rico: Departmento del Trabajo del Estado Libre Asociado de Puerto Rico, 1965.

Carroll, Henry K. *Report on the Island of Porto Rico; Its Population, Civil Government, Commerce, Industries, Production, Roads, Tariff, and Currency with Recommendations*. Washington, D.C.: Government Printing Office, U.S. Treasury Department Document 2118, 1899.

———. *Report on the Industrial and Commercial Condition of Porto Rico*. Washington, D.C.: Government Printing Office, U.S. Treasury Document no. 2091, Division of Customs, December 30, 1898, published in 1899.

Compensation of Government Executives. Report of the Governor's Advisory Council for the Development of Government Programs. San Juan, Puerto Rico: Office of the Governor, Commonwealth of Puerto Rico, March 11, 1970.

Constitution of the Commonwealth of Puerto Rico. San Juan, Puerto Rico: Office of the Secretary of the Commonwealth of Puerto Rico, 1952.

Cuevas Viret, Antonio. *Problemas de Derechos Civiles en la Administración de Personal del Gobierno*. San Juan. Puerto

Rico: Informe prsentado a la Comisión de Derechos Civiles, 11 June 1958, Oficina de Personal, Estado Libre Asociado de Puerto Rico. Version mimeografiada, Escuela de Administración Pública, Universidad de Puerto Rico, n.d.

Derechos Civiles en Puerto Rico. Informe del Comite del Gobernador para el estudio de los derechos civiles en Puerto Rico. San Juan, Puerto Rico: Comisión de Derechos Civiles de Puerto Rico, August 1959.

Diario de Sesiones de la Convención Constituyente de Puerto Rico. 4 vols. Orford, N.H.: Equity Publishing Co., 1961.

Directorio de Organizaciones del Trabajo. San Juan, Puerto Rico: Oficina de Relaciones Públicas del Trabajo e Industriales, Departamento del Trabajo del Estado Libre Asociado de Puerto Rico, annual editions.

Employment and Unemployment. San Juan, Puerto Rico: Bureau of Labor Statistics, Department of Labor, Commonwealth of Puerto Rico, various monthly reports.

Geigel Polanco, Vicente. "Apuntes acerca de la evolución histórica del obrero." *Publicaciones de Ilustración Popular del Departamento del Trabajo.* San Juan, Puerto Rico: Departamento del Trabajo, vol. 1, no. 3, 1936, pp. 1-5.

Hunter, Robert J. *Puerto Rico: A Survey of Historical, Economic, and Political Affairs.* Washington, D.C.: Government Printing Office, Committee on Interior and Insular Affairs, U.S. House of Representatives, November 25, 1959.

Informe Económico al Gobernador. San Juan, Puerto Rico: Junta de Planificación, Estado Libre Asociado de Puerto Rico, annual editions.

Machuca, Julio. *The Bureau of Conciliation and Arbitration.* San Juan, Puerto Rico: Bureau of Conciliation and Arbitration, Department of labor, Commonwealth of Puerto Rico, 1963.

Manpower Report to the Governor. San Juan, Puerto Rico: Puerto Rico Planning Board, Commonwealth of Puerto Rico, and Appendix 2, Labor Force, n.d.

Marcus, Joseph. *Labor Conditions in Porto Rico.* Washington, D.C.: Government Printing Office, Report by Special Agent of the U.S. Employment Service. U.S. Department of Labor, 1919.

Miller, Herman. *Poverty in Puerto Rico.* San Juan, Puerto Rico:

Office of the Governor, Puerto Rico Planning Board, Common-wealth of Puerto Rico, April 1964.

Monthly Economic Indicators of Puerto Rico. San Juan, Puerto Rico: Puerto Rico Planning Board, Commonwealth of Puerto Rico, various monthly reports.

Number of Inhabitants, Puerto Rico. Final Report PC(1)-A-53. U.S. Bureau of the Census. U.S. Census of Population, 1970. Washington, D.C.: Government Printing Office, 1971.

Sierra Berdecía, Fernando. *The Civil Rights of Labor and the Public Labor Policy of Puerto Rico.* San Juan, Puerto Rico: Department of Labor, Commonwealth of Puerto Rico, 1960.

Strikes in Porto Rico. San Juan, Puerto Rico: Government of Porto Rico, Department of Agriculture and Labor, June 1, 1918.

The Status of Labor in Puerto Rico, Alaska, Hawaii. Bulletin no. 1191. Washington, D.C.: Government Printing Office, Bureau of Labor Statistics, U.S. Department of Labor, Reprint from the December 1955 *Monthly Labor Review*, January 1956. (Includes articles by Samuel Weiss, A. J. Jaffe, Clarence Senior, Fernando Sierra Berdecía, Joaquín Gallart Mendía, and Frank Zorrilla.)

Vilches, Ruben A. *Union Membership in Puerto Rico in June 1970.* San Juan, Puerto Rico: Bureau of Labor Statistics, Department of labor, Commonwealth of Puerto Rico. n.d. ca. 1971.

Weyl, Walter E. *Labor Conditions in Porto Rico.* Washington, D.C.: Government Printing Office, Bulletin no. 61, vol. 11, Bureau of Labor, Department of Commerce and labor, November 1905.

Newspapers

Claridad. San Juan, Puerto Rico. Various editions.

El Imparcial. San Juan, Puerto Rico. Various editions.

El Mundo. San Juan, Puerto Rico. Various editions.'

El Nuevo Día. San Juan, Puerto Rico. Various editions.

La Hora. San Juan, Puerto Rico. Various editions.

San Juan Star. San Juan, Puerto Rico. Various editions.

New York Times. New York, N.Y. Various editions.

Index